Management for Profess

The Springer series *Management for Professionals* comprises high-level business and management books for executives. The authors are experienced business professionals and renowned professors who combine scientific background, best practice, and entrepreneurial vision to provide powerful insights into how to achieve business excellence.

Andreas Holtschulte

Digital Supply Chain and Logistics with IoT

Practical Guide, Methods, Tools and Use Cases for Industry

 Springer

Andreas Holtschulte
Walldorf, Germany

ISSN 2192-8096   ISSN 2192-810X   (electronic)
Management for Professionals
ISBN 978-3-030-89410-8   ISBN 978-3-030-89408-5   (eBook)
https://doi.org/10.1007/978-3-030-89408-5

Translation from the German language edition: "Praxisleitfaden IoT und Industry 4.0" by Andreas Holtschulte, © Carl Hanser Verlag GmbH & Co. KG 2021. Published by Hanser Fachbuch. All Rights Reserved.

This Springer imprint is published by the registered company Springer Nature Switzerland AG
The registered company address is: Gewerbestrasse 11, 6330 Cham, Switzerland

Contents

1 Connected Things: People, Machines, and Plants in the Internet of Things (IoT) 1
  1.1 Things in the Cloud: What Is IoT? 1
  1.2 How It All Began 2
    1.2.1 The First Coffee Maker on the Net 3
    1.2.2 Radio Technology as a Pioneer 4
    1.2.3 The Four Industrial Revolutions 7
  1.3 Examples of IoT Applications 11
    1.3.1 Use Cases from the Consumer Sector 12
    1.3.2 Use Cases in the Industrial Sector 16
  1.4 Potentials and Developments in the IoT Environment 18
    1.4.1 Where Does IoT Stand in Germany? 20
    1.4.2 What Do the Numbers Say? 21
  References 26

2 Blueprint for IoT Systems 27
  2.1 IoT Components and Terminology 29
    2.1.1 Sensors and Actuators 29
    2.1.2 Hot, Warm, and Cold Storage 30
    2.1.3 Digital Twin 31
    2.1.4 DevOps 33
  2.2 Features and Requirements According to ISO 30141 34
    2.2.1 Security of IoT Systems (Standard Sect. 7.2) 34
    2.2.2 Architecture Requirements of IoT Systems (Standard Sect. 7.3) 39
    2.2.3 Functions of IoT Systems (Standard Sect. 7.4) 46
  2.3 Architecture of IoT Systems According to ISO 30141 56
    2.3.1 IoT Conceptual Model 56
    2.3.2 IoT Reference Model 61
    2.3.3 IoT Reference Architecture 64

3 IoT Platforms 73
  3.1 IoT Without Internet 74
    3.1.1 Edge Computing 74

            3.1.2   Fog Computing   75
    3.2   Cloud Computing   76
            3.2.1   Software as a Service (SaaS)   76
            3.2.2   Infrastructure as a Service (IaaS)   76
            3.2.3   Platform as a Service (PaaS)   77
    3.3   The Internet of Things—A Growing Market   77
            3.3.1   IoT Providers in Competition   81
            3.3.2   IIoT as a Separate Market Segment   83
    3.4   Selection Criteria for IoT Platforms   85
            3.4.1   Fraunhofer Study as a Decision-Making Aid   86
            3.4.2   Integrated Versus Separate Sensors   89
            3.4.3   Data and IT Security   90
    3.5   Multicloud Strategies   91
    References   94

4   IoT and Enterprise Software   95
    4.1   General Tips for Software Acquisition   97
    4.2   Enterprise Resource Planning (ERP)   99
    4.3   Warehouse Management System (WMS) 108
    4.4   Transport Management System (TMS) 117
    4.5   Manufacturing Execution System (MES) 120
    References 123

5   Interaction of the IoT with Other Technologies 125
    5.1   Big Data 128
    5.2   Artificial Intelligence (AI) 132
    5.3   Augmented Reality (AR) and Virtual Reality (VR) 138
    5.4   3D Printing 142
    References 146

6   Prepare IoT Projects Successfully 149
    6.1   Design Thinking According to Rams 152
    6.2   Design Thinking: Better than Brainstorming 155
            6.2.1   Design Thinking Phases at a Glance 155
            6.2.2   Tips for Successful Implementation 162
    6.3   Reality Check for Use Cases 164
    6.4   Partners and Support for IoT Projects 165
    6.5   Buy New or Upgrade? 168

7   Use Cases for the Internet of Things 171
    7.1   Driverless Transport Vehicles in Production and Logistics 172
            7.1.1   Initial Situation 173
            7.1.2   AGV Control Station: Brand Self-Made in the Cloud 175
            7.1.3   Success Through Simplification 176
            7.1.4   Architecture and Components 180
    7.2   Container Management in Real Time 181

	7.2.1	Problem	181
	7.2.2	Solution Design with Design Thinking	182
	7.2.3	Solution	185
	7.2.4	Architecture and Components	186
7.3		Corona Warning App	187
7.4		Track and Trace in Logistics and Production	194
	7.4.1	The IoT in Intralogistics	195
	7.4.2	Theft Monitoring in the Warehouse with the IoT	200
	7.4.3	Tracking in Global Supply Chains	201
7.5		Intelligent Data Glasses in the Warehouse and in Production	205
7.6		Object Recognition with the IoT	208
7.7		Maintenance and Servicing in Production	211
7.8		The IoT Business Models in Mechanical Engineering	216
References			218

8 From Project to IoT Strategy 221
8.1		Implement Agile Projects	224
	8.1.1	Scrum	227
	8.1.2	Kanban	229
	8.1.3	Rapid Prototyping and Minimal Viable Products	232
8.2		Building a Digital Business Model	234
8.3		Strategic Partnerships for IoT	237
8.4		Innovation and Transformation	241
References			247

Connected Things: People, Machines, and Plants in the Internet of Things (IoT)

1

If we let the word "network of everything," as the Internet of Things (IoT) is also called, roll off our tongue for a moment, it sounds a lot like science fiction and not like normality—to me, at least, but maybe it's different for you. But the fact is that this "network of everything" is no longer fiction. It is reality.

This chapter shows how it came about that we are now very specifically concerned with the Internet of Things. It summarizes the historical development of the Internet of Things and explores the question of why people often talk about a revolution in the context of today's Industry 4.0 possibilities. Why is IoT so significant? And how did it all get started? We also take a look at some application examples from the private and industrial sectors. Where in our lives do we encounter the Internet of Things? How does it influence our living and leisure behavior? What role does it play in our factories, warehouses, and logistics systems? Finally, we take a look at the potentials of IoT and the developments in this field as we move on to the technical details in Chap. 2.

1.1 Things in the Cloud: What Is IoT?

The Internet of Things (IoT) is the combination of physical things and their digital images. This combination creates a so-called cyber-physical system (CPS). This CPS combines components of computer science and software with those of electronics and mechanics. In order for us to call a system cyber-physical in the context of the Internet of Things, the CPS must communicate via the Internet. Complex cyber-physical systems, for example, are linked within a production hall via wired and wireless network connections and send certain information over the Internet to the corresponding cloud, where, for example, the information from many CPSs from other production facilities is brought together. New dimensions of global production plant networks are emerging from this mesh of cyber-physical systems connecting on the Internet. On the one hand, these systems are able to react highly flexibly to new requirements from production and also to external influences. In the area of

© The Author(s), under exclusive license to Springer Nature Switzerland AG 2022
A. Holtschulte, *Digital Supply Chain and Logistics with IoT*, Management for Professionals, https://doi.org/10.1007/978-3-030-89408-5_1

logistics, this means that highly dynamic new supply chains are opened up in case delivery bottlenecks or problems arise in the course of transport in the planned manner. IoT makes it possible to network things and CPSs with each other via the Internet; thus, the things in the network can, by and large, make their own decisions.

If you picked up this book to understand what the Internet of Things is, you can now put it aside and move on to other topics. However, if you want to understand how to use the Internet of Things to build new business models, track goods and machines around the world, and fully automate entire factories and supply chains, you'll find the answers in this book. You'll also learn how other companies are taking advantage of IoT opportunities.

IoT systems represent extremely complex software and hardware architectures. No other technology combines so many disciplines. An IoT system is a complex interaction of the following technologies and disciplines:

- Network technology
- Electrical engineering
- Control and regulation technology
- Cloud technology
- On-premise software
- Integrated information systems
- Computer science

Therefore, a wide range of skills and competencies are needed to plan, build, and operate an IoT system. Fortunately, you don't have to start from scratch because the internationally active bodies International Organization for Standardization (ISO) and International Electrotechnical Commission (IEC) produced an international standard for the first time in 2017, ISO/IEC 30141, which provides a reference for IoT architectures, concepts, and models. An IoT architecture must be considered from different perspectives in order to take all aspects into account and ensure sustainable operation. The standard provides guidance on appropriate perspectives regarding functions, systems, networks, operations, and users. I will describe the technical components, features, and requirements of an IoT system in Chap. 2.

1.2   How It All Began

Getting started can be difficult, especially in the innovation sector, and can often look like tinkering and gadgetry on the part of cranky technology freaks. But it's often these very specific applications that help technology or a technology concept achieve a breakthrough, even if at first many may ask, "What's *it for*, please?" The first use cases of IoT certainly have this character. In different places around the world, some people had innovative ideas about how to make life a little easier and simplify processes. Using radio chips and relatively simple camera monitoring, for example, technology-loving scientists saved themselves a trip to the coffee machine as beverage vending machines automatically reported when they should be refilled.

When exactly did the Internet of Things begin? The obvious answer is: with the Internet. So depending on whether you refer to the early Internet as a network of a few mainframes or the resulting Internet as a mass medium, you could point to the 1970s when universities networked their computers, for example, or the 1990s when the precursors of today's browsers for everyone had their breakthrough.

Quite a few voices refer to the Internet of Things as a watershed technology that will change the world across the board and forever. If we consider IoT and Industry 4.0 as the fourth industrial revolution, we can start with the three previous revolutions to classify today's development. Then we wouldn't just be talking about 30–50 years of immediate prehistory but would trace an arc back to the emergence of the first large-scale industries in the eighteenth century. However, the term IoT is much younger. Most date the creation of the English word back to 1999. However, long before the Internet became a reality, there were thoughts of a kind of Internet of Things in the context of machine networking, systems, and communication possibilities that drew on other, contemporary words.

Whatever your opinion on the historical development is, there are two milestones at which we should pause for a moment to understand the dynamics of today's IoT world. One is RFID wireless technology, and the other is the moment when the first coffee machine went online.

1.2.1   The First Coffee Maker on the Net

Whether you use a classic device disconnected from the Internet or a modern version of an Internet-connected device, the basic functions and application options usually remain the same. Even if the smart coffee maker automatically brews coffee and takes into account your preferences outside the day and week, you still have to buy and refill coffee powder yourself and clean the filter and other parts. Well, in high-tech regions, like the South Korean capital of Seoul, you could get a little more machine assistance by going to a futuristic coffee shop, like Beat, to be served by a fifth-generation (5G)-enabled robot barista. Once you try that out for yourself, and read Marc-Uwe Kling's satire *Qualityland* to find out why robot waiters can't serve coffee without slurping, you'll get the idea that not all coffee is the same—even technologically speaking.

Trojan Room coffee machine was the name of the machine said to have been the first documented thing on the Internet. I'm sure some of you are familiar with this coffee machine. If I remember correctly, my parents also had one of these in the early 1990s. But what would this simple brewing machine from the late 1980s, sold by Krups under the brand name ProAroma, have to do with the Internet? It had neither a network connection nor a wireless local area network (LAN) adapter built in. But the ProAroma didn't need that at all.

In 1991, scientists at the University of Cambridge's Institute of Computer Science had grown tired of constantly roaming several corridors only to find—upon arriving at the Trojan Room (the institute's tea kitchen) on the second floor of the institute—that the coffee had not yet completely run through the filter into the pot. Thirsty for coffee and frustrated, the researchers had walked the arduous path back to the office again for decades without a sip of the black gold in their cup. A little walking is good for you, they say, but the annoyance of wasting time was too much after all.

So the information technology (IT) staff, led by Quentin Stafford-Fraser, thought about how they could avoid the unnecessary and frustrating trips to the Trojan Room. They wanted to receive information about the progress of the brewing process remotely so they could make their way to the hot beverage at the right moment. As with many other great inventions in human history, such as the invention of the automobile, the driver for a new technology that would change the world was simply laziness. So the researchers set up a camera that filmed the amount of black liquid in the jug and transmitted the moving images to the university's local area network. The inventors were now excitedly following the progress of the brewing process on their computer monitors—and in real time.

At about the same time as the coffee machine camera, the early Internet was taking shape, which was intended to enable not only local networking but also the greatest possible worldwide computer connections. From 1993 on, the IT specialists' Trojan Room coffee machine could be seen on the World Wide Web. The camera was the first webcam on the Internet, and the coffee machine was thus the first thing in the Internet of Things.

The intelligent coffee machine of today would not simply be filmed but would independently measure the fill level using built-in sensors and inform us directly about the completion of the brewing process or any maintenance measures, such as descaling or cleaning—for example, using push messages to the smartphone. The actual components of the machine would not even have to be changed in the process. Only a few sensors, actuators, and network connections would have to be retrofitted.

By the way, a few years older than the Trojan Room coffee machine is a Coke machine with a very similar story: at a university in Pittsburgh, Pennsylvania, some computer specialists also worked and did research, keeping themselves awake with Coke instead of coffee. Here, too, the lines were long, and often all the refrigerated cans were out of stock when the researchers finally arrived at the vending machine. What the inventors came up with is now called "the world's first IoT device" at IBM, for example [1]. They installed a board in the vending machine that relayed its light readings to the main computer via a gateway. With a bit of programming, this led to an application that allowed all computer users on the university's local network to remotely check which cans were on sale and how long they had been cooling. Since the gateway used was also connected to the Internet's precursor at the time, the Arpanet with its maximum of 300 computers, this 1980s app was also available outside the university network.

1.2.2   Radio Technology as a Pioneer

When the physical world and the things in it find a reflection in the digital world, we speak of the Internet of Things. This image emerged around 2010, when cloud platforms, architectures, and applications changed the world, merging the digital with the real. What exactly that means and how it differs from the Internet of Things are something I'll get into later in the book. Let's stay with the historical development for a moment.

In terms of technology history, the forefather of the Internet of Things was RFID technology. RFID stands for radio frequency identification. This means that objects, goods, containers, and handling units have tags that are activated by radio waves (passive tags) or send a radio signal on their own (active tags) and transmit their identity by radio. This means the objects are identified and, for example, a goods receipt can be automatically booked when passing through a gate or portal. The recipient therefore knows that the goods have now arrived in his warehouse without his warehouse staff having to scan the labels or post goods receipt slips in an inventory management system.

During research on the terms IoT and RFID, one may repeatedly come across the name Kevin Ashton. He is considered the inventor of the term "Internet of Things." The Briton is said to have chosen the phrase when he was working on a presentation in 1999. At the time, he was working as an expert on RFID topics at the then Auto-ID Center of the Massachusetts Institute of Technology (MIT). Strictly speaking, there is no need for the Internet to use RFID since the advantages of contactless and scanner-less data capture (without visual contact) already offer enormous added value, especially when the technology is directly connected to an inventory management system.

RFID technology is based on the concept that data such as the product code, serial number, batch, etc. is stored on RFID tags and attached to a given package, mesh box, container, or handling unit. Here is an example: if the material number, batch number, and date of manufacture are stored on an RFID tag, the product to which the tag is attached will carry this information on its chip throughout its entire life cycle. It can still be determined later by whom, where, and when it was manufactured. But how does this differ from a simple barcode label, which can also store the same information, which in turn can be read by a barcode scanner? At the various stations, a unit reaches carrying this tag, additional information can be stored on the RFID chip, and information can be updated, depending on the tag's storage capacity. The digital trace thus created makes it possible to track goods and merchandise across the globe, which is now known as Track and Trace or, in the case of batch tracking, Global Batch Traceability (Fig. 1.1).

In addition, this approach offers the possibility of automation, and many companies are using the technology to optimize their supply chain. Real-time bookings and high transparency in logistics lead to higher availability of goods, faster processes, inventory reduction, and thus lower process costs and less capital tied up in the warehouse.

IoT thus came about through the further development of RFID technology and its combination with wireless sensors that communicate via a network. In this intermediate stage, however, the sensors were not connected through the Internet. Therefore, the term IoT would still be somewhat inappropriate since the central ingredient—the Internet—was still missing.

Fig. 1.1 Structure of an
RFID chip (© Syrma
Technology)

In the early 1990s, this technology was called wireless sensor network (WSN). The basic concept of the Internet of Things was already realized by WSN—only without the Internet. Such wireless sensor networks were used, for example, for health monitoring in hospitals and process monitoring in factories.

While the initial focus was on tracking and automatically identifying assets in buildings, the use cases became increasingly complex. For example, the identification of items and objects triggered business management accounting processes in merchandise management, warehouse management, and production control systems. More and more, the monitoring of machines, plants, and entire factories took center stage. What we understand today under the buzzword "predictive maintenance" was already possible with WSN. For example, it was already possible to predict upcoming repairs or to initiate maintenance services by reaching defined sensor values regarding temperature, vibration, speed, or expansion.

Over time, in addition to wireless networks within factory and warehouse buildings, mobile networks also developed massively. Thus, via 3G and 4G (long-term evolution (LTE)), today's 5G mobile technology has made it possible to transmit even larger data packets in significantly shorter times. Therefore, 5G technology represents a milestone in the further development of the Internet of Things. Cars moving autonomously on public roads transmit 25,000 MB/h, which needs to be handled with the maximum mobile communications technology currently available if one wanted to upload the information to the Internet in real time and process it in the cloud. In comparison, the high-definition (HD) movie we watch in our living rooms streams about 900 MB/h from the Internet. Meanwhile, new concepts have been developed to limit the amount of data to be processed in the cloud in real time. The concepts are called edge computing and fog computing. Here, data are literally processed at the edge or in the fog of the local network, and only data that are really necessary are uploaded to the cloud and processed there. I will discuss these Industry 4.0 concepts in detail in Chap. 3.

1.2.3   The Four Industrial Revolutions

As mentioned earlier, the Internet of Things can also be placed in a broader context, especially if we look at the social and societal dimensions. Have you ever heard of the fourth industrial revolution? While "Industrie 4.0" is an original German neologism, the term "fourth industrial revolution" has now also become established internationally as a term for the holistic digitization of production and supply chains. This is because it ties in with a common and easily comprehensible narrative of progress that most of us know from school lessons. But what does the term Industry 4.0 have in common with the Internet of Things? Why fourth industrial revolution and not tenth or second? Why am I devoting an entire section to this topic?

Industry 4.0 is the industrial manifestation of IoT. Unlike other sectors of the economy, industry deals with real, physical things that are produced, transported, stored, maintained, and repaired. Thus, connecting these physical things to the Internet and equipping them with sensors and servo motors is the path to Industry 4.0. The Internet of Things field has therefore expanded the term: the Industrial Internet of Things (IIoT) is synonymous with "Industrie 4.0." Without IoT technology, what we understand today as Industrie 4.0 would be merely an empty phrase. All additional technologies, such as big data, analytics, virtual reality (VR), and augmented reality (AR) are important additional technologies in the field of industry that are always based on things and the data they generate.

1.2.3.1 Machine Age—Industry 1.0

But first, let's follow the course of history through all the industrial revolutions to the current state of technology. The first and decisive industrial revolution, industrialization at the end of the eighteenth century, was fueled by the massive extraction of hard coal and the invention and mass industrial use of steam engines. For the first time, machines, driven by water power or steam, performed mechanical work on a large scale, replacing humans in these areas of work. The machine age had dawned. You will encounter machines and devices again and again in this book. They are probably the most important "things" in the Internet of Things.

The economy and the work and life of workers changed permanently and violently. The invention of the mechanical loom and other machines in the textile sector meant that the sometimes highly skilled and well-paid textile professions of cloth shearers, weavers, and hosiery workers lost their status and were largely made redundant by machines.

Another decisive factor that shaped this phase was the cooperation between science and industry. Thus, many industrial companies cooperated with educational institutions and universities or directly established internal research and development departments.

But it was also a time when those who saw their jobs endangered by the machines used massive protest and open violence against the new machines and production processes. This group was called '"*machine wreckers*." Not only the textile industry but also the agriculture and metalworking industries were affected.

1.2.3.2 Industrialization—Industry 2.0

After the machine age relied heavily on the use of machines instead of human power, it became increasingly necessary to consistently standardize and automate processes. This led to the increased use of assembly lines in mass production in Germany from the 1870s onward. A significant and prominent name in the era of mass production, emerging assembly line production, and underlying standardization in the automotive sector was Henry Ford. With his legendary Model T, he perfected production processes using the assembly line to such an extent that the vehicle's production time was reduced from 12 h to 93 min. The massive increase in productivity in his factories brought the price of the car down from US$780 in 1911 to US$490 in 1914, making the automobile affordable to wider sections of the population and selling the Model T by the millions in America and later in the rest of the world. Another measure that massively reduced production costs was radical standardization. The Model T was offered in only one color. "You can have any color, as long as that color is just black," he told his clientele at the time. This is revolutionary from the point of view that until the end of the nineteenth century, every vehicle was still completely assembled in a kind of workshop production before the manufacturing of a new vehicle could begin. As a result, early automobiles were only affordable for the very rich.

In addition to the automotive industry, the chemical, electrical, mechanical engineering and optical industries in particular were pioneers in this development.

But what helped this revolution get off the ground and made this enormous change possible in the first place, in addition to the strong drive for optimization? At that time, it was electricity that made it possible to run generators, light bulbs, and electric motors—and to do so decentrally. The local connection between steam engine, flywheel, and machine tool was dissolved, and it was possible to work with many small electric motors that could generate their effective forces on demand at the place of consumption.

Beginning in 1880, the telegraph was replaced by the telephone, which was brought to market maturity by Alexander Graham Bell. The communications industry was born. Increasingly, research and development and their interlinking with business became more important during this period, as evidenced for the first time in history by company-owned research and development departments.

1.2.3.3 Digital Age—Industry 3.0

If we now take a leap of around 100 years, we end up in the information age, the third industrial revolution starting in the 1970s. This digital revolution was characterized by the automation of production, primarily using programmable logic controllers (PLCs) and other electronics, as well as by the emergence of information technology (IT). PLCs enabled the production as well as the use of industrial robots and modern machine tools controlled by modern control technology. How was this possible? The basis for the achievements in the digital age was the invention of microchips and integrated circuits (IC).

It was at this time that the success story of the personal computer (PC) began. This first arrived in industry and soon became the standard in the private sphere as well. The spread of the Internet and mobile communications had an additional influence on almost all the developments we associate with this revolution.

Innovations [2] in this era include the following:

- 1967: Electronic calculator.
- 1969: Internet.
- 1976: Personal computer.
- 1977: Databases.
- 1984: Analog C mobile network.
- 1992: Digital D-mobile network.
- 2001: The world's first small Universal Mobile Telecommunications System (UMTS) network goes into operation on the Isle of Man.
- 2006: The first LTE connection is made available in Hong Kong.
- 2010: LTE mobile communications technology is launched in Germany with the auctioning of frequencies.
- 2012: LTE technology is made available to more than 50% of German households (Fig. 1.2).

The development of mobile technology in the twenty-first century has a massive impact on developments in the field of IoT since we can use it to track goods, vehicles, and machines around the globe; monitor their condition; and take action.

Another important facet of this third industrial revolution is sustainable energy concepts, for example, in terms of renewable energies.

Even though today we benefit greatly from achievements such as the invention of microchips, the digital age was also marked by uprisings and protests by workers, employees, and unions that feared for jobs due to the use of new technologies, machines, and processes. The so-called "modern machine wreckers" protested against innovations in the printing industry and in mechanical engineering (e.g., computer numerical control (CNC) and numerical control (NC) machines) because they saw the modern machines as competition to their own labor and were consequently afraid of losing their jobs. They therefore took to the streets and demanded socially acceptable solutions.

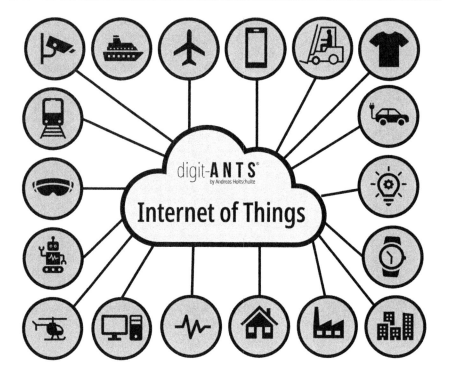

Fig. 1.2 Progression of achievements and technical innovations, which combine to form today's IoT. Source: digit-ANTS GmbH

Are Digitalization, Automation, and the Use of Machines Modern Job Destroyers?
In the long term, this statement is certainly not true. In the short term, innovations and the use of new developments in history have always meant that these innovations have taken over the work of employees and people. However, quality and productivity increased, resulting in lower unit costs. As a result, societal prosperity also increased. As for jobs, the introduction of innovations and process improvements always led to decreasing working hours and higher wages. Jobs were then often created elsewhere, with slightly higher qualifications required for the newly created positions.

1.2.3.4 Digital Transformation—Industry 4.0

We are currently entering the phase of the fourth industrial revolution. But what distinguishes the fourth from the previous industrial revolutions? The first three revolutions came about through fundamental innovations. The invention and implementation of these new enabling technologies created new products and innovations.

Today, we have several new transformative enabling technologies at our disposal, each one fueling the other. This could lead to a massive upheaval in society, work life, everyday life, and employment. Robots could soon take over many of our tasks and do them much more methodically, faster, and without careless mistakes.

Automation is driven and enabled by algorithms and artificial intelligence (AI). It is particularly easy for machines to take over tasks with a very high proportion of standardization, as well as routine tasks. The Institute for Employment Research (IAB) of the German Federal Employment Agency published a report in August 2019 noting that the share of jobs that can be taken over by machines has been rising continuously since 2013 due to innovations in technology. This means that jobs whose job profiles are highly standardized and characterized by repetition will very soon be taken over by machines. Experience shows that the proportion of employees in this standardizable environment receives training less frequently than those in areas that are much less standardizable, such as the creative or social spheres. What may be regarded as innovation, market adaptation, or "keeping up with the times" at the level of the individual company thus harbors a certain explosive potential at the level of society as a whole if an innovation becomes established and is used by everyone.

Should we be as afraid of digitization and the Internet of Things nowadays as the weavers were of the machine wreckers? Are these two factors not the job killers of tomorrow, even though they are repeatedly described as an opportunity, as the future, and as inevitable? This book is not intended to discuss ethical, moral, or philosophical issues of this kind. However, as you will see, we touch on them again and again, at least indirectly, in the context of aspects such as corporate culture and IoT projects.

Nonetheless, it is no alternative to outlaw and stop innovations related to Industry 4.0 in order to protect jobs and obsolete processes for the following reasons:

- New jobs will be created in the combination of digital and physical worlds in particular.
- Some countries could fall even further behind the rest of the world in terms of digitization, which would very quickly destroy significantly more jobs or prevent them from being created in the first place.
- From the perspective of an industrialized country with a large service sector, IoT is a topic that engineers with their deep knowledge in mechanical and plant engineering should combine with digital technology and export.

1.3 Examples of IoT Applications

What was still unthinkable for earlier generations and only imaginable as a distant, often foggy vision for pioneers is now everyday life for us: the completely networked life. Each of us carries our smartphone around day and night, uses it for almost 4 h a day [3], and unlocks it more than 50 times daily. We constantly generate IoT data with this device, data that we then send to Google, Apple, and friends. If we haven't turned Global Positioning System (GPS) off, we are constantly sending our location data. Cloud providers, such as Google and others, consolidate the individual user data sent to them by the many smartphones and use them to calculate traffic jam probabilities, road bottlenecks, or the number of visitors to hotels, stores, and restaurants.

Let's stay with smartphones and their importance to people for a moment. Why don't you try the following experiment? For 1 week, write down every function and app that you use at least once. As a rule, that's a lot more than just making phone calls. When the list is finished, think about it: What could you also do with a phone that is not connected to the Internet? The answer will be: virtually nothing.

What exactly does the phone network with for these smart functionalities? In most cases, these are location-based services, which makes them an asset in the sense of Industry 4.0 and makes the smartphone a tag. If you will, your smartphone turns you into a cyber-physical system.

Another exciting question is: What does it mean for industry that not only computers and networks but also industrial devices, machines, and plants can now be networked? I will discuss this in more detail in Sect. 1.3.2.

1.3.1   Use Cases from the Consumer Sector

In the following, I'll give you some typical examples of how IoT is used in the consumer sector. More precisely, we will look at the smart home phenomenon, that is, living in rooms and buildings that contain networked machines and devices. I would be very surprised if you still don't use any of these yourself.

You may have already taken note of the fact that, today, it is virtually impossible to buy a "dumb" TV that does what we basically expect it to do: display a moving picture, play a good sound to go with it, and provide the necessary interfaces for connecting an antenna, a satellite, and external devices. Nowadays, when you decide to buy a TV, you can't get around an intelligent TV, a smart TV. Built-in microphones, cameras, and other sensors as well as the ability to connect to the Internet make up the intelligence of these devices. This enables them to track user behavior, that is, the shows consumed, and, if necessary, to understand conversations and signal words. In principle, there is no technological obstacle in the way of sending the collected data to services such as Netflix, Amazon Prime, Google, Apple, and the like and placing targeted advertising across all of the user's channels. The mere fact that these devices can and in some cases must be connected to the Internet in order to use them is what makes them devices in the Internet of Things.

Another example from the field of smart home is the smart thermostat. It can significantly reduce your energy consumption when you're not in the house. If you integrate the heating control into your calendar, which you maintain online, the system at home switches to setback mode as soon as you are on vacation or traveling. If you grant the mobile app on your smartphone, which is usually included with the thermostat, access to your location and the distance to your home, the system switches the heating back on early so that you come home to a comfortably warm living room.

The smart refrigerator is also—well, guess what—connected to the Internet and uses your geo-information to register that you are currently in the supermarket. Did you forget to write a shopping list again? No problem. The app, which is connected to the refrigerator via the cloud, appears on the home screen and reports a red alert. The supply of soy milk is running low. Lucky. Brave new world.

Is your coffee machine still stupid or intelligent already? The intelligent brewing machine of today would only laugh out loud at the Trojan Room model mentioned earlier: "A video transmission for status and fill level monitoring? How cute!" The smart coffee maker is connected to the Internet, of course, and automatically brews coffee as needed. In doing so, it checks the owner's online calendar and alarm clock to see when he plans to get up, and it calculates when the coffee should be ready. Of course, it can also take the owner's individual and changing daily schedule into account when calculating and brewing the coffee.

Smart light switches and light bulbs connected to the Internet on the manufacturer's cloud can be controlled using a smartphone app and, of course, can regulate the brightness in the apartment based on the owner's calendar information.

When the Smart Home Seems to Go Crazy

It was cold in my apartment on Christmas Eve. My fully automatic coffee machine had not prepared my caffè crema at 6:30 a.m. as it usually does. It would have gone cold anyway since my smartphone hadn't woken me up. I woke up by myself at 9:12 a.m. on December 24, 2020, surprised, and it seemed as if the world was standing still. The lights were off, the shutters were down, and it was quiet—and cold. It was all a bit eerie. I picked up my smartphone and turned on the bedroom light. Okay, the power was on. The shutters went up after I manually controlled them in my smart home app.

I decided to take a warm shower to thaw out. But—oh no—the water was terribly cold. What was going on here? Was the heating broken? Then why hadn't my heating app warned me? Had someone hacked into my smart home environment? There had already been many cases where intruders had cracked passwords and gained access to homes by virtual means. From a safe distance, cybercriminals had disabled alarms and silently opened apartments or houses with smart door locks. They had then quietly cleaned out the dwellings while the owners were on vacation or at work. Another disturbing scenario: hackers had gained insight into the private lives of the owners through built-in Internet cameras or hijacked baby monitors and baby monitor cameras. The most common weakness here was poor or no passwords to protect the devices, each of which is connected to an IP address on the Internet. Often the

(continued)

passwords, which were set at the factory and can be found in various forums on the Internet, hadn't been changed. This made it easy for hackers.

After slowly warming up and having my coffee maker finally serve me my caffè crema, I immediately changed all the passwords on my smart devices (light switches, thermostats, coffee maker, light bulbs, speakers, security systems) and my wireless network passwords on my routers at home. In the afternoon, my calendar reminded me of a dinner date at Restaurante Vegano Bon Lloc, Carrer de Sant Feliu, 7, 07012 Palma, Illes Balears, Spain, with my old buddies Matthias and Dirk. Totally confused, I called Dirk and told him about the strange events of the morning. We remembered that last summer, we had thought about going to Spain together over the Christmas holidays.

I had booked the well-attended restaurant far in advance and soon forgot about the reservation. We had postponed the trip until next year because of the Covid 19 pandemic. A little relieved, I checked my calendar after the conversation. Indeed, I had blocked the Christmas trip to Mallorca in the calendar. Now I slowly realized what had happened: my "intelligent" household appliances assumed, based on the calendar entry, that I was not at home at that time. As a result, the heating shut down and the hot water turned off. There was no coffee for me, the apartment remained dark, and the shutters didn't go up. Unfortunately, my smart home was not smart enough to notice that I had stayed in Mannheim.

When I deleted my calendar entry, the heating went up automatically, and in the evening my apartment was warm again. After all the confusion that morning, I was very glad that I hadn't been hacked.

The story may sound a bit exaggerated here and there, but this scenario is technically possible nowadays.

We also come into contact with the Internet of Things in areas related to mobility and traffic. Self-driving cars are currently still in the development phase. However, one application is already very widespread. Who knows the situation? Before you let your smart TV, half-dead with exhaustion, decide which show to watch, you first have to pass the last test for this Saturday afternoon after an exhausting shopping marathon with your partner. The test is called search for the car in the depths of the parking garage. But luckily, you own a vehicle in the beta phase, which can park and unpark itself and find you at the touch of a button in the corresponding app.

But until now, only smart TVs have really caught on in the consumer sector. The large number of streaming providers such as Netflix, Amazon Prime, or Disney+ alone means that the devices must be able to establish an Internet connection themselves, unless you want to connect another box between the Internet and your TV. With many other use cases for IoT, the justifiable question arises: Do you really need it, and does it make everyday life easier? The reason an application catches on is that it creates an additional benefit for the user. It often seems quite fashionable to use the latest digital assistants. But does that really improve our lives, and can we possibly save time and money by using them?

A leading global manufacturer of automation and automotive technology from southern Germany chose a rather remarkable marketing strategy at the beginning of 2019 to position itself as a top manufacturer worldwide in home automation and the private use of IoT (consumer segment). Just in time for the electronics trade show in Las Vegas, the show presented its campaign, which was strongly based on the Internet movement "Like a Boss." Here, more or less gifted talents vie with their skills, stunts, and dexterity to be named boss in their discipline by the Internet community. The hero of the campaign, who was staged in various everyday situations, didn't really seem like a hero at all but rather appeared like an IoT nerd who became a hero solely through his little technical helpers.

Well, come to think of it, the difference between that and the Avengers superheroes isn't that big. For example, Iron Man only becomes a superhero because of his steel suit. So maybe there is a chance for us mere mortals to become IoT superheroes after all. By now, I've probably convinced you, and you want to know how IoT can help you become a superhero, right? Let's get back to our IoT nerd: the video sequences went viral just because of their funny presentation and definitely achieved a very large reach. But if you break the whole thing down to the actual novelty and innovation, the change doesn't look like a transformation. Even the benefits, time savings, and increase in the quality of life that result from the use of IoT in everyday life cannot really convince a rational person. He merely books IoT under the heading "nice toy." Our hero's everyday life and behavior did not change as a result of using IoT. He neither became more efficient nor faster—rather the opposite: anyone who has ever really seriously dealt with technology in everyday life will notice that it often makes things more complicated, especially since we don't like to say goodbye to old habits.

While some IoT applications can be very clearly assigned to the consumer or industrial sector, there are also applications that can be assigned to both. These include, for example, our entire power grid with its digital electricity meters (smart meters) connected to the grid, which report consumption behavior to energy suppliers at regular intervals. Equipping all households in Germany with these smart meters enables energy suppliers to analyze the exact energy requirements per household at a given time and forecast them for future times. This lets the suppliers produce electricity in line with demand and ramp up grid capacity or shut down power plants in good time. On the one hand, this makes it much easier to synchronize the energy feed-in from hydro, wind, and solar powers, which is very difficult to plan, with consumers and power plants. On the other hand, it largely prevents unneeded energy, which precisely cannot be stored well in the electrical environment, from fizzling out unused in the networks.

You have seen that the use of IoT in private environments often has limited benefits and pushes at the border of technical gimmickry. This is different in industry. Here, value-adding and beneficial IoT applications can very often be implemented. Industrial companies are able to expand their business models by using the Internet of Things and thus penetrating new markets. For example, some machine builders have realized that their machines can generate data themselves using advanced sensor technology. Engineers use these data for service, maintenance, and new billing models, depending on how the machine is used. In the industry, there are some use cases and business models that are only conceivable with the data generated by their machines at their customers' sites. Combining this with technologies such as analytics, artificial intelligence, and mass data evaluation gives the data extremely high value in the new context.

1.3.2   Use Cases in the Industrial Sector

A term that describes the Internet of Things very well, especially in the industrial environment, is the cyber-physical system (CPS). In this term, it can be seen very well that the characteristic of IoT is the digitization of physical things and thus the virtual image of reality that can be read by computers. The term "digital twin," which is based on this concept, also makes sense. Using and linking sensors, actuators, motors, microcomputers, network components, and cloud services, we create an IoT architecture that translates the physical world into the language of machines and the digital world back into reality. The result is self-regulating supply chains, driverless transport systems, autonomous trucks, and machines that report to the maintenance technician as soon as sensors indicate an imminent failure due to wear and tear.

We refer to the networking of things in an industrial context as the Industrial Internet of Things (IIoT). IIoT plays a central role, especially in the field of manufacturing and production and in global supply chains. This way, the physical movements and changes in the state and properties of the things produced and transported can be tracked seamlessly. Media disruption in this environment is the downfall for any object that wants to be tracked. Therefore, the strategy of many companies is a fully digitized, networked, intelligent, and decentralized value chain.

One example of condition monitoring of shipments is the continuous control of the cold chain. Some goods, especially medical products and foodstuffs, are no longer usable if they only briefly exceed a certain temperature during transport. So shipments, packages, or even pallets are equipped with digital temperature sensors that transmit the current temperature to a cloud at short intervals. In this way, the recipient can be informed very early on in the transport process if the cold chain breaks down and whether it's necessary to arrange for an alternative procurement of the goods. Normally, such a system also integrates the transmission of geo-information at the same time. This additionally makes it possible to calculate the shipment's time of arrival and, upon arrival, automatic collection and goods receipt posting. Even in emergencies, for example, in the event of a breakdown, accident, or traffic jam, the system can automatically calculate and arrange alternative delivery options.

An example of networked machines can be found at a company in the Swabian part of Baden-Württemberg. The manufacturer of cleaning machines and solutions developed an IIoT application for monitoring its machines at its customers. The customers work in the professional cleaning environment. At the heart of this software solution is a platform that collects and consolidates all information from the cleaning machines at the customers' sites. At the machine manufacturer's headquarters, it is possible to track whereabouts, maintenance status, fluid levels, and battery charges via a personal computer (PC) software application. For their part, if the customers have several cleaning machines, they can track them via the software and schedule their use at various locations. For tracking, the machines are equipped with a Real-Time Locating System (RTLS) and a Global Positioning System (GPS) and transmit their location information to the cloud via a wireless network or cellular data connection. An RTLS uses the information it obtains via wireless technology for orientation and positioning. GPS obtains position data as coordinates by communicating with satellites orbiting the earth. So far, so good, but what is the benefit of knowing the position of the machines? How can a cleaning company use this information to save costs or improve the service level for its customers? This question should always be at the beginning of any IoT project because no one will end up admiring you for using the latest technology at a high price without having a business case for the project that will convince all the project's sponsors.

In the case of the cleaning machine manufacturer, the matter was already clear at the beginning. The customers and the manufacturer were looking for a way to use their machines much more efficiently and to better utilize their capacities. A perimeter search, which displays machines that are currently free, makes it possible to schedule and utilize them for upcoming jobs. Furthermore, cleaning companies can reduce the number of machines since they always know when which machine is at which location and how long the assignment is expected to last. If the actual start of operation at a particular location is delayed, it is possible to reschedule immediately. The automatic recording of the operating hours per machine in combination with the load on the machine gives the manufacturer an indication that, if necessary, a more powerful model should be used from a different location or that maintenance is required before the system breaks down unplanned. If there is a defect or a scheduled maintenance appointment is due, the machine will report the incident. The technician is thus automatically informed about the incident, receives a detailed description of the defect in advance, and knows which parts to take to the customer.

At an event regarding the digitalization of the supply chain at Europe's largest software manufacturer at the end of 2019, I coined the term "smart pallet" to describe the combination of tracking pallets in real time with an IoT system and a warehouse management system (WMS). Smart pallets are equipped with a transmitter and receiver unit and report their location in real time to a higher-level IoT system. The pallet thus knows where it is and, by combining it with a warehouse management system, what its destination is. The pallet "notices" that it is being moved and then reports to the IoT gateway. Modern radio technology, which has extremely low energy requirements, keeps the batteries in these radio units running for up to 10 years, which is even longer than the lifetime of an average Euro pallet. Thanks to modern radio technology, it is possible to determine a location via GPS both inside and outside buildings—with an accuracy of a few centimeters. The cost of this technology is now in a range that makes mass deployment worthwhile. What is interesting is that the intelligent pallet forms the interface between fully automated production and logistics. Imagine the pallet inside a warehouse or on the production floor reporting that it has been removed from the storage bin. The IoT system, located between the warehouse management system and the smart pallet, "knows" that there is a transfer order for this pallet. This contains the information source, source bin, destination bin, and goods or storage unit to be transported. The system automatically acknowledges the arrival of the pallet at the destination storage bin. The new bin information in the warehouse management system is automatically updated in real time.

Now imagine this scenario in the production area: there, the movement of the pallet from machine to machine confirms one item in the respective production order. In this way, replenishments and subsequent processes can also be triggered automatically in real time.

In all these use cases in connection with intelligent pallets and automatic posting in the production planning system or WMS, the focus is on automation and the avoidance of scanning processes. In Chap. 7, you will get to know some more variants of this concept, including one in which this principle is even possible without equipping the pallets with sensors and radio technology.

1.4   Potentials and Developments in the IoT Environment

As can already be seen from the foregoing, industry has largely recognized the opportunities and possibilities in the Industrial Internet of Things and is in many cases able to develop beneficial IoT use cases. Interestingly, innovation adoption in IoT behaves differently than in other Internet technologies. For the most part, it was more the case that private users were initially familiar with the new technologies. Unlike IoT, these technologies did not find their way into the corporate world until much later.

But why has the Internet of Things only been so relevant in the Industrie 4.0 environment for a few years? The foundations were laid more than 30 years ago with the introduction of RFID, and the Internet has been available since 1990. Were today's applications and the resulting business models not relevant in the past 30 years? In my observation, the reason for the late spread is profitability calculations. Sensors, actuators, and microcomputers today cost a fraction of what they cost 10 years ago. Thus, investments in smart assets equipped with sensors and microcomputers are now possible on a large scale, whereas in the past, the budget was just enough to realize a prototype or a single digital show case. The costs of storage technology (central processing unit (CPU), random access memory (RAM)) and data transmission (broadband, mobile communications) have also fallen continuously.

In addition, there are other reasons why IoT is now so relevant and use cases are increasingly being implemented. The most important one, in my opinion, can be explained by the phenomenon of exponential developments in technology, electrical engineering, memory chips, IT, and software because digitized things in the Internet of Things, like everything in the information age, can grow exponentially in their performance and functionality due to the following influencing factors, among others:

- Computing power
- Network technology
- Algorithms

Many of you might be familiar with Moore's law in this context, which has had a massive impact on the mindset and development of the Information Age. Gordon Moore, a cofounder of the semiconductor chip manufacturer Intel, was concerned in his statement on the exponential development of microprocessors with the fact that development in this environment is not linear, as in other areas, but exponential. Moore's law states that the number of active components in a chip—and thus its computing power—doubles within 18 months. So if a lack of computing power at a given time makes a use case seemingly impossible, we can hope that Moore's law will mean that the required computing power will soon be available. This has happened time and again in the past. What is special about today's world is that not only is each enabling technology capable of completely reshaping industry and business in its own right. Due to the possibility of combining these technologies at will to create new use cases, it is difficult for us to imagine today the new business models and applications that are conceivable in the near future.

An important factor for the success of IoT in industry is the convergence of information technology (IT) and operational technology (OT). IT leaders and managers have now recognized the need for plants, machines, and corporate IT to belong together to a large extent and for IoT applications to be integrated.

For the use of IoT in the field of production, concepts were sought to avoid pushing all the data that accumulate into the cloud and, in the process, generating unnecessary data traffic where necessary. Concepts such as cloud computing, fog computing, and edge computing have therefore been developed, which divide data processing into both decentralized and centralized levels. We will explore these concepts in more detail in Chap. 2. As a result of these new concepts, new applications are already possible today, especially in the area of production, and more will follow (Fig. 1.3).

The number of Internet-connected devices is increasing every day, and the growth of devices alone, which in turn generate data and information, is fueling technologies such as artificial intelligence and analytics as these technologies rely on a lot of data. Thus, IoT is contributing to the exponential growth of other digital technologies as well (Fig. 1.4).

What does the European Central Bank's zero interest rate policy have to do with future growth in the technology sector? Well, many investors are desperately looking for ways to invest their money with a few percent interest. Also, the experience of many investors in the stock market during the corona crisis will possibly make some look for alternative investment opportunities. During the crisis, it became apparent that technology stocks alone had regained their old highs and in some cases far exceeded them, while the prices of traditional industrial companies

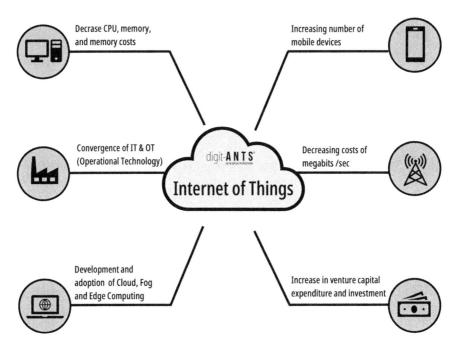

Fig. 1.3 Implications for the Internet of Things. Source: digit-ANTS GmbH

suffered greatly. This suggests that the previously already relatively high levels of venture capital investment and general investment will continue to rise and thus young, hungry, innovative companies in IoT, AI, VR, and AR could grow rapidly.

As described above, a transformation of our behavior through IoT in everyday life is rather unlikely. At the same time, we as a society and as an economy are so confronted with new technological possibilities and upheavals that new buzzwords such as digital transformation are becoming increasingly popular.

1.4.1   Where Does IoT Stand in Germany?

Germany is the land of engineers and mechanical engineering. Engineers love the possibility that the machines they create with high precision now also generate data and are able to interpret their conditions themselves. For Germany in particular, IoT offers an enormous opportunity since we can now offer both, thanks to our distinctive knowledge in mechanical engineering: machines with very high quality and the integration of these machines into the digital world. As a result, new business models can be derived from data, particularly in Germany, if we use them in a new context—provided we recognize and seize this opportunity.

But what about inventions in the field of IoT? Is Germany also the country of inventors in the field of IoT? If you take a closer look at the March 2019 study by

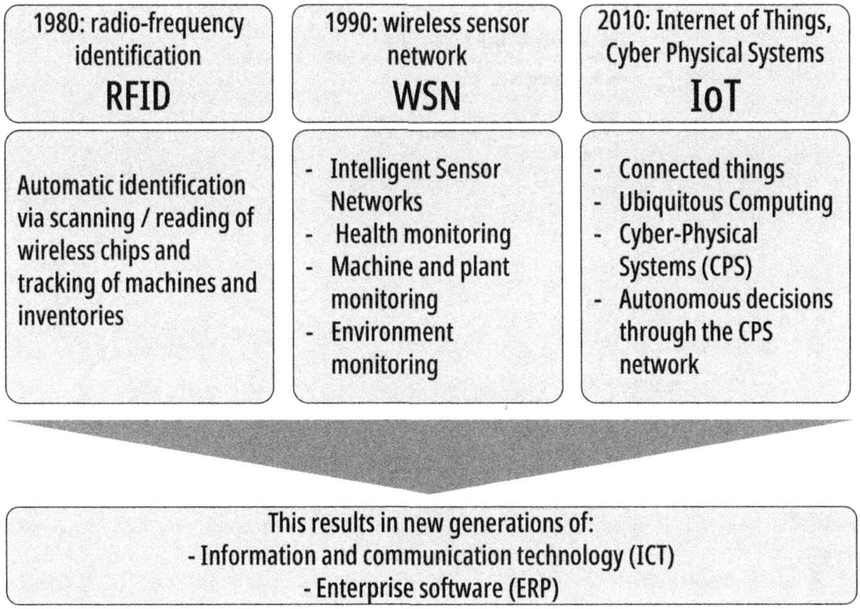

1980: radio-frequency identification **RFID**	1990: wireless sensor network **WSN**	2010: Internet of Things, Cyber Physical Systems **IoT**
Automatic identification via scanning / reading of wireless chips and tracking of machines and inventories	- Intelligent Sensor Networks - Health monitoring - Machine and plant monitoring - Environment monitoring	- Connected things - Ubiquitous Computing - Cyber-Physical Systems (CPS) - Autonomous decisions through the CPS network

This results in new generations of:
- Information and communication technology (ICT)
- Enterprise software (ERP)

Fig. 1.4 IoT technologies and their influence on information and communication technology. Source: Li Da Xu/Wu He/Shancang Li: Internet of Things in Industries. A Survey. 2014. p. 2234

IPlytics GmbH, you will see that not a single one of the 12 leading inventor companies comes from Germany. The following countries are represented here:

- South Korea (Samsung)
- China (Huawei, ZTE, Shenglu IOT Communication Technology)
- Japan (Fuji Xerox)
- Sweden (Ericsson)
- USA (Qualcomm, Intel, IBM, Cisco, Xerox Corporation, Microsoft)

Figure 1.5 shows that German companies with patents in this area do not appear at all. As of March 2019, IPlytics GmbH found out in another set of statistics that the total number of patents in Germany in the IoT field amounted to 4195. By comparison, 41,845 patents came from China and 37,595 patents from the United States of America by that time (Fig. 1.6). As far as inventiveness in modern information technology is concerned, we in Germany can still go one better.

1.4.2 What Do the Numbers Say?

To give you a sense of the potential of IoT and the developments to be expected in this field, let's take a look at a few figures below. In a 2017 study, the US consulting

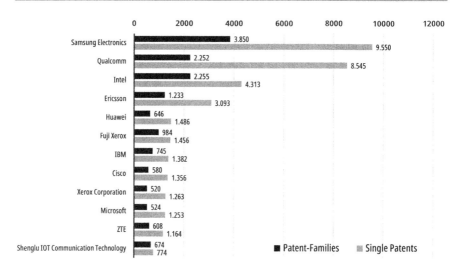

Fig. 1.5 Global IoT patents held by leading companies in 2019. Source: IPlytics GmbH, March 2019

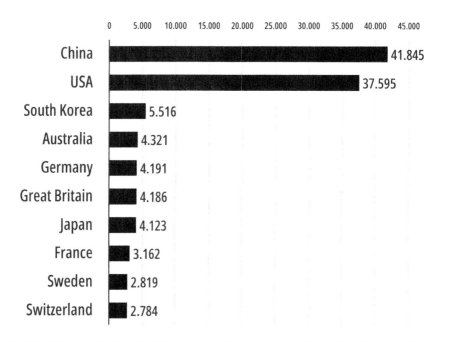

Fig. 1.6 Patent applications in IoT per country. From the report "Patent litigation trends in the Internet of Things." Source: IPlytics GmbH, 2019

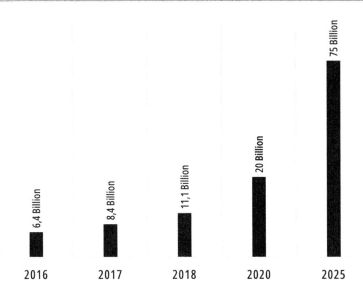

Fig. 1.7 Number of connected IoT devices worldwide from 2016 to 2025 (based on figures from Statista and others)

firm Gartner forecast the number of globally connected IoT devices by 2020 (Fig. 1.7). While there were 6.4 billion devices in 2016, this number has already doubled in 2018 and will double again to 20 billion devices by 2020. According to the Statista Research Department, we will have 75 billion devices connected to the Internet worldwide in 2025.

If you take a closer look at the factor of growth in the statistics, Moore's law can be recognized here as well. There is a specific reason for this: growth is additionally fueled by the rapid further development of sensors and microcomputers. This is leading to a drop in prices, so that even small companies are venturing into the technology alongside financially strong global corporations. As a result, more companies will use IoT to build new business models.

The experts at PricewaterhouseCoopers (PwC) forecast US$500 billion per year in revenue worldwide by 2022. At the same time, the use of IoT is expected to save US$400 billion through process optimization. Investments in IoT are expected to grow to as much as US$800 billion by 2020, according to PwC. Another consulting firm (Deloitte) published a study in 2016 in which it forecast IoT-related revenues of €50 billion in the B2B environment by 2020 (Fig. 1.8). It is interesting to note that the production sector accounts for, by far, the largest share of this.

These figures and forecasts give you an idea of the potential that IoT and the connection of machines and plants to the Internet in the field of Industry 4.0 has today and will have in the next few years.

As a country of engineers, Germany should not limit its use of IoT solely to manufacturing and the support of the production process by IoT. Rather, industry must see itself as a playing field for networked things, services, and processes since

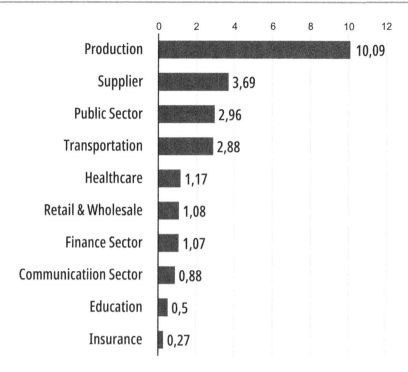

Fig. 1.8 Global revenue from IoT in industry in 2020. Revenue in billion euro. Source: Deloitte

there is very great potential in the industrial use of IoT—far greater than in the area of private use of IoT.

Every year, Germany is confirmed as the pacesetter in logistics and supply chain, winning the title of "Logistics World Champion" in the World Bank's Logistics Performance Index from among more than 160 countries worldwide. Evaluation criteria include "tracking and tracing of shipments" and "punctuality of shipments." Just imagine what would be possible if Germany, with its globally positioned companies and associated globally networked supply chains, invested further in the use of IoT since IoT is the key technology that holds such a digital supply chain together.

That is why it would be fatal to put the brakes on Industry 4.0 in Germany or to boycott it, for example, because of the threat of job losses, as we have already observed in connection with previous industrial revolutions. On the contrary, in Germany, we should promote and support developments in digitization and, in particular, in the area of IoT much more strongly than is the case today because IoT will help us achieve a new level of value creation with our products, not only for logistics but also in mechanical engineering. Particularly when thinking about the supply of jobs, one should think in the long term. After all, professional marathoners don't really step on the gas until the second half of the race.

Industrial IoT is the manifestation of Industry 4.0 in logistics, production, and supply chain. The combination of traditional industry and information technology is creating new jobs, especially at the transitions between reality and the digital world. With German capabilities in mechanical engineering and logistics and with our inventive spirit, understanding of processes, and ability to standardize, the additional IoT expertise could become our new export commodity on the world market.

If Germany, and perhaps even the EU, misses the boat in terms of IoT and digitization, more jobs are likely to be lost in the long term as a result than if we continue to rely on traditional sectors of the economy, such as the automotive industry. If we look at the statistics, we in Germany have focused on traditional technologies such as automotive and mechanical engineering for too long and have dismissed the opportunities of digitalization as a fad. It's not too late, but we should finally wake up now. In Chap. 7, I show some very good examples of how German companies can exploit the opportunities of IoT for themselves and build extremely profitable (and in some cases additional) business models.

However, easy access to technology and knowledge is also leading to a new order in the balance of power between established players and small companies. The competitive situation has seemingly been reversed. The size and financial capabilities of the traditional DAX companies no longer seem to play a role. This was completely different about 20 years ago. Today, motivated young entrepreneurs are rushing into the market, no longer satisfied with old answers and questioning the current market order. They understand their customers, use innovative technologies, and create solutions that are adapted to the specific needs of their customers. In doing so, they are extremely fast and use customer interactions to validate their products and solutions. This means that they do not try to optimize their products in their own quiet way to suit their needs but involve their customers massively in the development of the products. Take food delivery services or beverage delivery services for example. They support their customers by relieving them of activities that are annoyingly time-consuming and exhausting for them. The benefit to customers is obvious: they no longer have to wait at checkout, pack the groceries in their car, unpack them at home, and then lug them up the stairs to their apartment.

But traditional companies can also benefit from technological developments. They only have the problem that in their sometimes deadlocked structures and processes, it is difficult to change processes, project methods, and the thinking of employees and managers. Moreover, these companies have a hard time seriously developing new offerings if they threaten the traditional business model and the resulting cash flow. Kodak is a case in point. The corporation once led the world market in photographic film for analog cameras. Margins on the films were about 80%, and Kodak had a 90% market share. In 1975, Kodak engineer Steve Sasson built the first digital camera, then with 10,000 pixels, weighing almost 4 kg, and with a storage time of 23 s. The image was black and white and stored on a cassette. Kodak management initially smiled at the invention, and there was certainly little interest in attacking such a high-margin business as the film business from the internal side with the introduction of the digital camera. But in the end, the digital camera prevailed, and Kodak gave up the film business in 2013.

It doesn't have to be a completely new invention, but manufacturing companies should expand their offerings with the digital services they develop to complement their machinery and equipment. We call these digital services smart services. In this way, companies strengthen their customers' loyalty to the company and its products far beyond the actual product business. A smart service can increase value creation and help a supplier expand its business model. Through the new services and the associated subscription models, it creates new and regular income. It gains new insights from the data obtained and can make its future offerings even more suitable for its customers.

Now that we have reached the end of this chapter, I hope you will agree with me that we cannot avoid IoT—whether as consumers, social organizations, or industrial companies. In Chap. 2, I will discuss how the Internet of Things works technically and the functionalities behind central concepts of the IoT world.

References

1. Teicher, J. (2018, February 7). The little-known story of the world's first IoT device. *Blog Post.* https://www.ibm.com/blogs/industries/little-known-story-first-iot-device.   Retrieved   May 14, 2020.
2. https://www.telespiegel.de/wissen/mobilfunk-geschichte. Retrieved June 6, 2020.
3. https://www.faz.net/aktuell/wirtschaft/digitec/nutzer-verbringen-im-schnitt-3-7-stunden-am-smartphone-16582432.html

Blueprint for IoT Systems

2

Are you planning to develop an Internet of Things (IoT) system or application? Do you want to know what is necessary to build an IoT system? Are you wondering what features an IoT system should have and what requirements it should meet? Do you want to know what functions an IoT system covers and what its architecture should be? This chapter will provide you with answers to these questions.

It introduces all the important terms, concepts, and building blocks of an IoT system as well as their interaction. You will learn both the basic properties and the essential requirements of an IoT system. In this context, ISO/IEC standard 30141, "Reference Architecture on Internet of Things (IoT RA)," is also introduced, in which the aforementioned issues are considered in detail.

In principle, I have tried to present the relationships as simply as possible, but because the Internet of Things is one of the most complex disciplines in modern information technology (IT), this has not always been an easy task. So be prepared for this chapter to get very technical. If you don't need information on this level of detail at first, you can also skip the chapter (especially the part where I describe the ISO standard and the concepts behind it in more detail) and refer to it only when you realize your first use cases.

Box 2.1

The complexity of an IoT system can be attributed to the inherent combination of the following sciences and technologies that underlie it:

- Electrical engineering
- Storage technology
- Control and regulation technology
- Network technology
- Mobile technology

(continued)

© The Author(s), under exclusive license to Springer Nature Switzerland AG 2022
A. Holtschulte, *Digital Supply Chain and Logistics with IoT*, Management for Professionals, https://doi.org/10.1007/978-3-030-89408-5_2

Box 2.1 (continued)
- Cloud technology
- Software development

Only those who take all these areas into account in an IoT project will be able to develop a successful IoT solution.

In simple terms, we speak of an IoT application as soon as the following factors are combined:

1. Sensors and actuators
2. Connection and representation of a physical thing with just these sensors and actuators
3. Assignment of a unique address from the Internet Protocol (IP address) in a global network infrastructure to the physical thing

In the context of IoT, we are talking about a global, dynamic network infrastructure with the following characteristics:

- Physical and digital things are united in one network.
- Things have an identity, physical properties, and a digital individuality.
- Uniform and standardized network and communication protocols are used.
- Open and dynamic interfaces exist.

Crucial to connecting the virtual, digital world with the physical world is the uniqueness and identifiability of things. Since a physical object is unique and identifiable at a particular time in a particular place, we need to give that thing a unique identifier or key for an IoT architecture to work. Imagine if the Trojan Room coffee machine had existed in many rooms and floors in 1991. Each machine on its own would then have needed a unique identifier, for example, with the addition of floor and room numbers. Otherwise, the researchers in Cambridge would have seen a coffee machine on their computer screens but would not have known to which machine they should have run with their empty cup. Thus, they would only have exchanged the waiting time at the coffee machine for search time for the correct brewing machine.

Box 2.2

Technically, we have various options for assigning an Internet Protocol (IP) address to a thing and connecting it to the Internet:

- Local area network cable (LAN): here, the connection is established via a local network connection.
- Wireless local area network (WLAN): here, the connection is established via a wireless connection with a router that has Internet access.
- Subscriber identity module (SIM) card and mobile communications.

2.1 IoT Components and Terminology

This section introduces the main components and terminology of an IoT system.

2.1.1 Sensors and Actuators

Sensors (also called transducers) detect states of processes and convert the collected data into electrical signals. There are many different types of sensors:

- Temperature sensors
- Humidity sensors
- Vibration sensors
- Carbon dioxide (CO_2) sensors
- Smoke sensors
- Vibration sensors
- Sound sensors
- And much more

While sensors convert the real world into digital measured values, actuators convert an electrical signal into a mechanical movement or another physical quantity. Examples of actuators are as follows:

- Relays
- Heaters
- Actuators
- Engines

2.1.2   Hot, Warm, and Cold Storage

In information technology, we use an analogy to temperature for the different levels of data storage. In technical jargon, you will encounter the term "multi-temperature data management." The description of temperature as hot, warm, or cold provides information about how important certain information is and how quickly it must be retrieved during operation to ensure fluid update and processing.

> **Box 2.3**
> We distinguish between the following storage temperatures:
>
> • Hot
> • Warm
> • Cold

Hot data are usually stored close to the central processing unit (CPU). If the priority or the need for fast access decreases, the data can be stored further away from the processor core. Thus, storage media can also change according to their potential access time to data according to the storage temperature. Cold could mean that the information is stored on a datasette. This storage medium is not really known for its fast access time. However, the cost of memory is very low on this medium. In connection with memory temperatures, we often also talk about latency, the delay in processing data between input and output.

Figure 2.1 provides information about the relationship between read and write speed, data volume, and costs.

In the following, I make a detailed classification.

Hot Storage
If the read or write operations are particularly frequent in a certain time unit, then we classify the memory as hot. The way data is stored is ideally in the main memory (in-memory). The hardware you might be familiar with from your mobile devices is the solid-state disk (SSD), which enables extremely fast data access. On a PC today, you would store the operating system on an SSD to ensure a very fast boot process. In the field of Industry 4.0, hot storage is used when a certain measured value from a sensor requires an immediate response. For example, when inspecting beverage bottles before filling, measured deviations would require an immediate rejection of a defective or contaminated bottle. If the result arrives too late at the actuator or at the control of the corresponding electric motor, the bottle would not be rejected in time. So to minimize latencies, expensive storage media are used for hot storage.

Warm Storage
If the read or write operations in a given unit of time are frequent, but not at such a high frequency as in hot storage, then we classify the storage as warm. Less

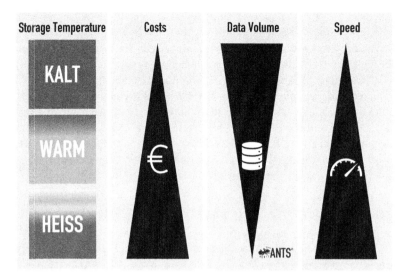

Fig. 2.1 Relationship between costs, data volume, storage speed, and storage temperatures. Source: digit-ANTS GmbH

expensive, robust storage media are used for warm storage, such as typical hard disk drives. These allow a very high number of read and write operations over a long lifetime.

Cold Storage
If the read or write operations in a certain time unit are rather infrequent, then we speak of cold memory. Hard disks or even tape storage are usually used here as well. The data in cold memory are no longer used regularly. Actually, the information is usually not used at all or for months, years, or even decades. Examples of data in cold storage are annual financial statements that have to be kept for 10 years due to financial regulations but are no longer of any use for business operations business. According to Fig. 2.1, the data volumes in this environment are often high, but the costs for storage space are very low and access times are very slow.

2.1.3   Digital Twin

To my great surprise, many of the people I talk to don't know much about the term IoT. What they have heard more often, however, is the term digital twin. After all, this is a good basis for explaining IoT and creating awareness of the topic. When I introduced the term cyber-physical system (CPS) in Chap. 1, I could have actually also introduced the digital twin right away. However, it fits better in this chapter because we need to dive a little deeper into this technology for an explanation.

Like the CPS, the digital twin is a digital image of its real counterpart (for example, a machine). But it is more than that: the digital twin is represented by sensor values. The sensor information forms the real-time link between the digital and the real twin. The digital image is capable of storing other metadata, such as technical drawings, images, instructions, and documentation. Let's imagine a thermostat in a cooling circuit in the process industry. Its digital twin would contain the actual temperature, the setpoint, the installation location, the plant in which it is installed, its own serial number, and, of course, the IP address. Just as information from the real world enters the virtual world via sensor and status data, the digital twin influences physical reality via actuators and motors in its physical twin. A complex digital twin is virtually composed of several things.

Example: Driverless Transport Vehicle in Intralogistics
This could be, for example, a driverless transport system consisting of many individual driverless transport vehicles and their individual sensors and control units. These vehicles are called automated guided vehicles (AGV). Driverless transport vehicles control the internal warehouse transport and storage processes as well as the supply of raw materials, consumables, and goods to the production team. If one wants to model a digital twin, diverse individual components and the corresponding sensor values must be represented hierarchically—for positioning, drive unit and work area. Often, an IoT application that maps the digital twin also consists of simulation software and analysis tools that use artificial intelligence to digitally run through machines, factories, or processes.

Example: Simulation of an Automated Warehouse Before Construction
Before automated high-bay warehouses are built, warehouse movements are often simulated with complex algorithms using a digital twin of the complete system. This helps detect errors at an early stage and correct expensive consequential damage to components, racks, and conveyor technology even before construction. The warehouse building with all its technology, aisles, columns, and storage locations is virtually represented by the digital twin.

In the example of the small robot shown in Fig. 2.2, the real physical twin is represented in its digital image by corresponding interfaces, images, technical drawings, a three-dimensional (3D) model, and current process and sensor data. In the area of algorithm, control, and user interface, both the software and user can influence the physical twin via a user interface (human-machine interface according to ISO 30141).

As with the automated warehouse example, among other things, digital twins help with the following:

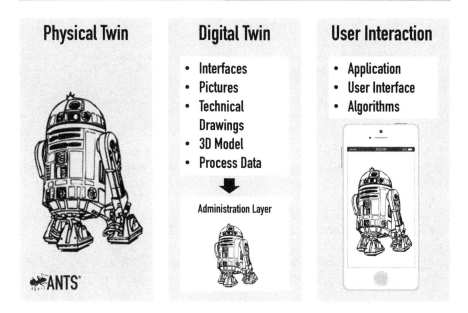

Fig. 2.2 Digital twin: physical layer, digital management layer, and user interface/application layer in Industry 4.0 applications. Source: digit-ANTS GmbH

- Manufacturing processes
- Maintenance
- The condition monitoring of machinery and equipment

The advantages are obvious. IoT devices, entire machines, plants, and production networks can be extensively tested and improved well before commissioning is even planned. The ability to test process flows and ideas at an early stage in a virtual environment reduces the error rate or disruptions later in the physical process. Using digital twins typically shortens the innovation cycle, development projects on new products or processes can be accelerated significantly, and a new path can be taken flexibly if it becomes necessary in the development process. Early testing and validation increase the quality of results and efficiency in the development process.

2.1.4   DevOps

You might look in vain for the word "DevOps" in the dictionary since it is an artificial combination of the terms development and operations in the sense of IT operations. The idea behind this artificial word is as simple as it is ingenious: it is about the convergence of software development, software and system administration, and quality assurance. The term DevOps covers a number of methods and tools for cooperation among these areas.

The goals of this integrated thinking in DevOps are to achieve the following:

- Quality improvement in software and software development
- Faster software development
- Faster software delivery
- Optimized collaboration between teams

While scrum methodically takes care of the development of the software, DevOps thinks a few phases further because it also takes into account how software is put into operation and operated. Managers, programmers, testers, administrators, and users are holistically involved in the development, roll-out, and operation process.

2.2   Features and Requirements According to ISO 30141

At this point at the latest, the chapter becomes very technical. I introduce the technical fundamentals of IoT systems that apply to each of these systems. In this context, I also introduce ISO/IEC standard 30141, "Reference Architecture on Internet of Things (IoT RA)," a joint effort by the International Organization for Standardization (ISO) and the International Electrotechnical Commission (IEC). The composition of the IoT reference architecture committee shows once again that IoT cannot be represented by one discipline alone.

The ISO 30141 standard is a generic guide that provides a fundamental basis for the basic understanding required for the design, development, and architecture of IoT systems. It explains how an IoT system is structured and the relationship between the individual components. In Sects. 2.2 and 2.3, I introduce the relevant parts of the standard and describe them in an easily understandable manner. Chapter 7 of the standard, which describes the requirements, properties, and basic functions of an IoT system, is particularly relevant.

In this section, I will first highlight the reliability, architecture, and functionality requirements of IoT systems.

2.2.1   Security of IoT Systems (Standard Sect. 7.2)

Under the section on reliability, the ISO 30141 standard summarizes, among others, the following requirements for an IoT system:

- Availability
- Confidentiality
- Integrity
- Privacy
- Reliability
- Load capacity
- Safety of people and equipment

Availability (Standard Sect. 7.2.2)
Depending on the use case, you must provide for and guarantee a necessary level of availability for your IoT system. An IoT system that is not available in a critical situation may be useless for the corresponding use case. Imagine you are developing an IoT system to detect and report incidents in a critical process in the process industry or to detect fire development or intrusion in the production hall. If your IoT system is not ready at the time the incident, emergency, or intrusion occurs, it will not be able to initiate countermeasures or report the alarm to a higher-level system. Thus, the critical situation, say a major fire or an explosion, goes unnoticed or the burglar quietly cleans out your production hall or sabotages the plant.

What can you do to increase the availability of your IoT system? Foresee situations where failures occur in your system and implement redundant power supplies or devices, sensors, actuators, gateways, and the same services in different instances so that your IoT system can continue to function in emergency situations.

You will achieve high availability if you consider the following three levels:

- **Devices:** the functionality of the devices and flawless connection to the network must be guaranteed throughout the entire life cycle.
- **Data:** the sending and receiving of the requested data must always work.
- **Services:** the service must be defined in advance in terms of its quality requirements and must also be available on a permanent basis.

Confidentiality (Standard Sect. 7.2.3)
In information technology, confidentiality refers to when information should only be accessible to a certain group of people. Certain information and data, often marked accordingly, should therefore not reach unauthorized third parties. In IoT systems, too, appropriate measures must be taken to protect confidential data from third parties that are not allowed to gain knowledge of the corresponding data.

There are different levels of confidentiality depending on the business or use case. The following metric is often used:

- **Public:** anyone can have this information, and therefore the information does not need to be specially protected.
- **Customers:** the information is only available to existing customers.
- **Internal:** the information is accessible within the company, does not need to be protected internally, but should not be shared outside the company.
- **Confidential:** the information may only be shared within a specific group of people.
- **Strictly confidential:** the information must only be accessible to certain defined persons. The group of persons must be kept extremely small.

Integrity/Originality (Standard Sect. 7.2.4)
In information security, it must be ensured that data, information, and measured values cannot be manipulated by third parties without being noticed. This would destroy trust in the IoT system. A measured value or piece of information is

considered *true* if it has its original content. If this information has been manipulated, it is *false*.

In IoT systems, automated decisions are made on the basis of the measured values transferred and other information. If the incoming data are *incorrect*, the damage can be devastating for a production plant, for example. Therefore, you must make sure that input parameters are not negatively influenced by external parameters. These parameters do not necessarily have to be malicious actors, hackers, or attackers but can also be triggered by the following things:

- Defective devices
- Unauthorized devices
- Environmental influences

Example: Control of Cooling in the Warehouse
In an IoT system controlling a refrigeration system in your cold storage warehouse, manipulation could have been made by an algorithm in an intermediate node that increases or decreases the temperature measured by the sensor. This causes the controlled cooling system to increase or decrease cooling power earlier than necessary, breaking your cold chain and forcing you to scrap the goods in the cold storage.

How do you safeguard integrity in your IoT system? You should validate the integrity of information by using digital signatures and reject information that does not pass this check.

Data Protection (Standard Sect. 7.2.5)
The General Data Protection Regulation (GDPR) went into effect in the European Union on May 25, 2018. This law has been surrounded by uncertainty, both before its enactment and until today. Thus, entrepreneurs feared a massive restriction in contacting their customers and prospects. In fact, these regulations already existed before. Now, however, companies face heavy fines if they disregard them after the law comes into force. But what is this law supposed to protect? It aims to secure privacy, personal, as well as personally identifiable data. Why are the regulations so relevant today?

International standard ISO/IEC 27018:2019 (Information technology—Security techniques—Code of practice for protection of personally identifiable information (PII) in public clouds acting as PII processors) picks up on the provisions in the law and describes what constitutes personal data under the GDPR:

> Personal data means any information relating to an identified or identifiable natural person (hereinafter 'data subject'). An identifiable natural person is one who can be identified, directly or indirectly, in particular by reference to an identifier such as a name, an identification number, location data, an online identifier or to one or more factors specific to the physical, physiological, genetic, mental, economic, cultural or social identity of that natural person (...).

In the meantime, many companies have realized that they can build trust and retain their clientele by dealing responsibly with their customers and proving that they comply with current specifications and standards by obtaining certification in accordance with ISO/IEC 27018. Examples of accredited certification bodies include the German technical inspection agency TÜV and the auditors of PricewaterhouseCoopers (PwC).

A small demarcation of terms on the side—information security and data protection are understandably often lumped together and heavily mixed. Basically, that's fine since both topics and their underlying measures are closely related. In principle, the step to the proper handling of personal data is not a big one if the company is already compliant with information security (ISO/IEC 27001) and has had itself certified accordingly. The only difference is that information security focuses on the integrity, availability, and confidentiality of information, data, and systems, whereas data protection focuses on people and their privacy as the object of protection. Legislation does not provide any regulations for compliance with information security. After all, it is in the interest of the company not to disclose any information to the outside world that is internal, confidential, or even strictly confidential. The situation is somewhat different for personal data, as we have learned from various data protection incidents in recent years. If the legislator and data protection authorities had not imposed penalties for violations, the company that caused the incident would not have suffered any damage, unlike the people affected (except possibly a loss of reputation if the incident had been made public).

Personal data can also be processed in IoT systems. Camera surveillance in a production hall or warehouse also potentially records people moving around the building. This means that personal data are processed here, which must be specially protected.

The ISO/IEC 29100 standard (Information technology—Security techniques—Privacy framework) specifies the measures for protection. For an IoT system, this would look like this:

- **Consent and freedom of choice:** the user of the IoT service must give his explicit consent before processing. In addition to processing, which may, for example, be the recording on a video from the previous example, this concerns the use and storage of his personal data. The IoT user has the freedom of choice to prohibit this at any time.

- **Legitimacy and purpose:** the use, storage, and processing of personal data in an IoT system must always take place in connection with a specific purpose and must have been expressly permitted by the IoT user.
- **Restricting data collection and minimizing data:** in an IoT system, only the data necessary for the function may be collected and only for the time period allowed by the IoT user.
- **Restriction of use, storage, and disclosure: the** personal data of IoT users may only be stored in a manner and for as long as it is needed for the purposes for which it is processed.
- **Accuracy and quality:** it is imperative that the PPDs (protection of personal data) of the IoT user are up to date and factually correct. Data that are no longer up to date must be deleted immediately.
- **Openness, transparency, and notification:** the IoT user must be able to understand the way his data are processed by simple means.

It is mandatory to comply with these specifications in IoT systems when they process PPDs. In the following functions and interactions with other IT systems and applications in particular, please ensure that the legal requirements for PPDs are also complied with here.

Sensitive areas related to legal requirements on personal data include the following:

- Interaction with other IoT and IT systems
- Identification of persons
- Data analysis
- Aggregation

If you experience a data protection incident where PPDs fall into the hands of unauthorized third parties, it is necessary to identify all compromised data and notify affected individuals and the appropriate state data protection authority.

Reliability and Resilience (Standard Sects. 7.2.6 and 7.2.7)
Malfunctions and failures of as well as changes in individual parts or components in your IoT system must not affect the overall functionality of the IoT system. The system should react flexibly in a new situation and continue to provide the previous functions with the same performance. If this is given, we speak of resilience. Thus, both the connection and performance level of the IoT devices and software applications must remain stable in error situations, and the corresponding measured values and results must be reliable.

Safety of Life and Limb and of Installations (Standard Sect. 7.2.8)
IoT system malfunction can pose hazards to people, machines, and industrial plants. This can result in the death or injury of people as well as the destruction of machines and plants. Since in Industry 4.0 IoT systems are used in particular in the environment of industry, production, and logistics, the effects, damage, losses, and injuries

can be devastating. Therefore, especially the behavior of the IoT system in case of failure or deliberate shutdown must be considered as early as in the design phase. Errors in collaboration with industrial robots or defects in the shutdown device can quickly claim a human life. System behavior and safety aspects must also be taken into account in the design phase during subsequent recommissioning. Depending on the field of application, whether production, warehouse logistics, transportation, consumer environment, or building automation, you will have to follow different applicable safety requirements and legal regulations.

2.2.2   Architecture Requirements of IoT Systems (Standard Sect. 7.3)

IoT systems, like other IT systems, have certain architectural requirements. We will highlight these in this section. These architecture features are as follows:

- Composability
- Modularity
- Heterogeneity
- Dynamics
- Dealing with existing components
- Network connectivity
- Scalability
- Reusability
- Clear identification
- Clearly defined components

In this section, we describe these requirements that apply to IoT systems before looking at the functional requirements in Sect. 2.2.3.

Composability (Standard Sect. 7.3.1) and Modularity (Standard Sect. 7.3.6)
In my opinion, composability and modularity can be excellently combined into a single point. The ISO 30141 standard has made two standard sections out of these two points. IoT systems would not be systems if they were not composed of many different IoT components. But what do we need to do to make such a "thrown together" system work? The devices must function as one system according to their composition. We must be able to combine the components. To ensure that the IoT components can be put together in accordance with ISO/IEC 30141, the components need standardized interfaces and should be interchangeable with other components of the same type via plug and play, so to speak, without any major configuration effort.

This sounds very logical when you imagine the speed with which new components are coming onto the market since Moore's law naturally is highly relevant here. The development in the field of microprocessors is directly related to the increase in the performance of new components in an IoT system—and you certainly want to enjoy the new performance capabilities of these components without having to tear down your entire system and rebuild it with new technology.

If politicians in Germany were to actually consider consumption protection laws one day, as described in the future novel *Qualityland*, the following situation would exist, and we would have to delete this section from our book: it would then be forbidden under penalty of law to expand and repair systems in order to always ensure economic growth through the consumption of new equipment and systems. Let us hope, especially for the sake of our nature, environment, and planet, that we will not experience such a thing.

It is often necessary to replace certain components from an IoT system with modern technology every few years. This way you keep the system technically up to date. Now, at first glance, more modern components are built than the existing ones. Newer components have significant improvements in terms of security, speed, and scalability.

That makes sense in terms of composability. Let's now turn to modularity: it is particularly necessary in the environment of Industrie 4.0 and IoT systems for plant operators to have a high degree of flexibility and to be able to quickly assemble components in a different context. The use cases in Industrie 4.0, like the market environment, are generally very dynamic and constantly changing. Consequently, there is a need to remove components from a system and replace them with components and modules that have the same physical and logical interfaces. If many or all components in an IoT system offer this possibility of exchange and docking with existing interfaces, the IoT system exhibits a high degree of modularity. You can guess that the be-all and end-all for modularity is the standardized interfaces and functions of the respective components because no one may want to put a lot of effort into securing the basic functionality and communication of the components. It is much more crucial that you can rely on the modularity of the components and the IoT system and take care of the design and implementation of beneficial use cases for you and your clientele.

Example: Replacement of a Thermostat on the Pipeline

Imagine the following scenario: in an IoT system, the thermostat from manufacturer A is replaced with one from manufacturer B after a defect. The component from manufacturer A is no longer available and can no longer be reordered. The thermostat of manufacturer B works like almost all modern thermostats with a microcontroller. The old thermostat from manufacturer A uses an integrated circuit for the sensor. Although the two components measure temperature in technologically completely different ways, both thermostats respond to the same inputs. Thus, they are similar in terms of interfaces and thus modularly interchangeable.

Separation of Functional and Administrative Levels (Standard Sect. 7.3.2)

Of course, you want to operate a secure IoT system. To do this, it is important to operate and separate the functional and management layers of the IoT system independently of each other. You achieve this by keeping the functional interfaces and functions of the IoT devices independent of the management interfaces. How can this division of labor be achieved? To do this, you need to provide the appropriate interfaces on different endpoints.

What belongs to the management level? The following are examples:

- Information, description, and purpose of the component
- User roles and permissions to monitor and align functions
- Classification of data types (technical and system-specific)
- System-related data

What belongs to the functional level? The following are included:

- Planned execution
- Execution and actions
- User roles and permissions for the application, data, and information
- Classification of data types (confidential, internal, public)
- Access to personal data

The risk at the functional level varies depending on the function. As a result, you must also design the security controls according to the use case. At the administration level, you should also set up different security levels, which always has an impact on the monitoring of the relevant employees. For example, an administrator has very extensive privileges. You should therefore monitor his system activities more closely than those of a normal user.

In the private environment in particular, the number of cyberattacks by hackers is increasing, either noticed or unnoticed by the user. If we consider the heterogeneous structure of an IoT system, it becomes clear that the many IoT components in the network can pose a danger under certain circumstances because a single insecure component in the chain endangers the entire IoT system. The probability of a successful attack increases. Thus, even applications and systems that actually have nothing to do with the IoT system and that are operated in well-protected data centers can be exposed to an enormous threat by a single connected IoT component.

Separating the management and functional levels helps you rule out many dangers from the outset. Authorization, authentication, and protection mechanisms are operated separately from the actual functions of the IoT system and help you determine which components and parts in the system are allowed to read which information.

Heterogeneity (Standard Sect. 7.3.3)

Heterogeneous is also commonly called diverse. At its core, this diversity refers to the functions and connectivity of the components. Nevertheless, it is true that the cooperation of the components—regardless of the dissimilarity of the components themselves—is of crucial importance if you want to build a complex IoT system because the better the components of an IoT system interact and work together, the more complex are the tasks and use cases in which they can be used. However, this does not change the fact that the components are very heterogeneous in their function and in terms of their integration into the IoT system. You must take this circumstance into account in an IoT system.

Example: Condition Monitoring of an ISO Container in Container Handling and at Sea
This use case already explains the heterogeneity in an IoT system: a smart 40-foot container transmits information on temperature, geodata, vibration, and humidity to a higher-level IoT system during its journey. At the cargo port, however, radio frequency identification (RFID) technology is used to book the container's arrival at a specific terminal. In the process, the container also transmits its identity to the gate. Consequently, the corresponding IoT system must be able to process both RFID and data from a sensor network.

Example: Expansion of Production Facilities
A factory with many production lines must be gradually expanded as sales increase, which increases the number of communication points. This increases the heterogeneity of the IoT system.

In the area of communication providers alone, which are relevant in an IoT system, there are a large number of suppliers:

- RAPIEnet: Korea's first international network standard for real-time data transmission.
- EtherCAT: network-based data transmission system for the transmission of machine data (field bus); automation technology.
- EtherNet/IP: network-based higher protocol in the USA.
- PROFINET: process automation for robotics, machinery, and plant engineering.
- POWERLINK: transmission of process data in automation technology.
- CC-Link IE: production operation from the line level to the manufacturing level.
- Modbus/TCP: client-server protocol for the secure exchange of process data.
- Fieldbus Foundation: open architecture as a basic network for plant and factory automation (FieldComm Group).
- Profibus (Process Fieldbus): universal fieldbus; manufacturing, process, and building automation from Siemens and Profibus.
- MTConnect: manufacturing technology for machine tool control.

- OPC (Open Platform Communications): open, standardized software interface for data exchange between different manufacturers.
- OPC-UA: standard for data exchange as a platform-independent, service-oriented architecture (SOA); can transport machine data and describe it in machine-readable form.
- OMG DDS: middleware for data-centric communication in dynamically distributed systems.

Dynamics (Standard Sect. 7.3.4)
An IoT system is a highly dynamic system. Consider the many changes that are incessantly recorded by the sensors and must be processed in the computing units. Changes are also constantly being made to the physical world by actuators and drive motors. Imagine an IoT system that mirrors an entire building, a city (smart city), or a global supply chain (global supply chain tracking). The devices and their objects are constantly changing their location and state.

> **Example: Real-Time Track and Trace**
> An overseas container is tracked by means of geocoordinates. A real-time locating system (RTLS) tracks the transport of this container and thus the goods it carries. Temperature, humidity, acceleration, and vibrations are recorded. When critical values are exceeded or not reached, the system must trigger an action. A container is a physical entity, many of which are tracked around the globe and whose states are always changing.

Information processing in an IoT system can take place decentrally in the local gateway or in the powerful sensor or actuator itself or in the central IoT cloud. If the processing takes place in the device, sensor, actuator, or gateway, we speak of edge computing or fog computing. I will discuss these data processing models in more detail below since they play a decisive role in Industrie 4.0.

A modern manufacturing system in Industry 4.0 is characterized by various production lines distributed and networked across continents. You may have heard of horizontal integration in this context. The assembly line can be connected to both its own and third-party factories, local suppliers, logistics service providers, sales organizations, as well as customers. It is obvious that in such a complex network, there are constant changes of state to which the integrated IoT system must react, taking into account various influencing factors.

Handling of Existing Components (Standard Sect. 7.3.5)
There may be various reasons why you want to integrate your existing components (legacy components) into your IoT architecture. Even if you want to build an IoT system that meets the latest technical requirements and possibilities, it is still necessary to maintain and integrate certain components for business reasons—for example, if the existing system has simply not yet been depreciated—or for technical reasons.

Existing components are services, protocols, systems, components, technologies, or standards, thai is, the legacy components. If you want to integrate them into a modern IoT system, it is important that these existing components do not limit the architecture of the new IoT system. The risks and vulnerabilities in an IoT system come significantly from the use of legacy components. Therefore, make sure that your standards for security, performance, and functionality are still met. But also keep in mind that today's super-modern technology will be a legacy tomorrow. And since you don't want to disassemble your entire plant every few years or even months and constantly install new components, you should already provide for the connection and management of legacy components today, even in the case of new commissioning. Imagine a complete production line as an IoT system. If you wander from machine to machine like this and look closely, each IoT system consists of diverse components in a wide variety of life cycles. So the schedules for updates and patches also vary depending on the component.

Example: Internet Protocol Changeover from IPv4 to IPv6
This topic is especially central in the area of IoT, where every single device is connected to the Internet with a unique IP address. As you saw in Chap. 1, the number of devices connected to the Internet will continue to grow exponentially over the next few years. Unlike IPv4, IPv6 offers significantly more addresses as a modern protocol. The problem is that very many of the existing standards, applications, and devices are still based on the IPv4 protocol. Therefore, due to the many different devices and the infinite combination of applications, components, and services, the changeover is extremely individual for each company. There is no standard recipe here.

Network Connectivity (Standard Sect. 7.3.7)
The sensors, actuators, and network components of an IoT system exchange information via network connections. These can be established on a wired (LAN) or wireless (WLAN) basis. IoT components that are connected to multiple IoT devices are called nodes. Only a networked IoT component can exchange information with other components. There are static and dynamic IoT networks. In a static IoT network, each node has a fixed number of neighbors. The node itself has no switching function in this case. In a dynamic IoT network, each component can be integrated in the network via what is called a mediator. An important parameter for network connectivity is the quality of service.

The quality of service (QoS) parameter is determined by latency, data packet loss rate, and data throughput. Other factors that have a significant influence on QoS are as follows:

• Resilience
• Encryption
• Authentication
• Authorization

As you know, there are IoT systems of varying complexity. While some IoT systems are connected via local networks and connect a small number of components over very short distances, there are global networks connected via the Internet, especially in the area of global supply chain networks, which connect countless components and services.

Scalability (Standard Sect. 7.3.8)
An IoT system should be able to grow in size. For example, you might equip only one machine or one warehouse area with sensors and actuators before equipping more machines or the entire warehouse complex with the technology. On the one hand, this can make sense if you only want to test and implement the functionalities in a small area according to a minimal viable product (MVP) (see Chap. 9). After the system has proven itself, further machines, warehouses, and locations are then to be equipped with the technology.

The following key figures are usually affected by an extension and expansion of the plant:

- The volume of sensor data in the system
- The number of devices to manage
- The number of services
- The number of applications

Recyclability (Standard Sect. 7.3.9)
Often, the functions and capabilities of the components in a particular location are not fully utilized in an IoT system. You should therefore check which functions of which components can be used by several systems. The systems can serve completely different use cases than the one primarily intended. In the end, this saves investment costs and leads to significantly better system utilization.

Example: Sensors for Light Control and for Reporting Burglaries
For example, you can use the sensors and motion detectors of a light control system in your warehouse additionally for the intrusion detection system and thus save sensors. You can also use a temperature sensor for your heating system in your production hall as a sensor for your fire alarm system. This sensor may then have to meet higher requirements, but you will still save the costs for redundant technology.

So with a holistic and smart design of your IoT system and recycling of components, you can significantly reduce the cost of implementation.

Unique Identification (Standard Sect. 7.3.10)
The components of your IoT system need a unique identifier to distinguish them from each other and thus secure the interaction of the components across

heterogeneous IoT systems and global use cases. A unique identifier allows you to hide the components behind the IoT gateway so that they cannot be attacked by cyberattackers.

The following identification techniques are used on the Internet:

- IPv4 address (Internet Protocol version 4)
- IPv6 address (Internet Protocol version 6)
- MAC (media access control) address: the hardware address of the network adapter
- URI (uniform resource identifier): used to identify websites, services, email recipients
- FQDN (fully qualified domain name): the complete name of a domain

For the unique identification of a physical object, we know, especially in logistics, the standard for barcode systems GS1–128 (known as EAN128 until 2009) or contactless technologies, such as radio frequency identification (RFID). People are identified using biometric information, such as fingerprint, face, or iris recognition. You're certainly familiar with the technology for unlocking your smartphone or a notebook.

Clearly Defined Components (Standard Sect. 7.3.11)
Clearly defined components in your IoT system are all the functions and features of the IoT units. These must be described. There are other definitions to uniquely address and secure the components. These are configuration, how they communicate with other components, security measures, and reliability.

2.2.3 Functions of IoT Systems (Standard Sect. 7.4)

Accuracy (Standard Sect. 7.4.1)
An IoT system is always only as good as it captures the real world and converts it into digital information. The better is the conversion of physical reality into the digital world, the better the IoT system can respond to the actual situation. Accuracy in the sense of ISO/IEC 30141:2018 is the "degree of agreement between the measured values and the actual values of these properties."

Depending on the application, the requirements for the accuracy of the IoT system can vary. For example, in the production of circuit boards with robots, tolerances of only a few fractions of a millimeter are acceptable, while picking robots that grab parts from boxes and place them in transport boxes require somewhat less accuracy.

Definition of Accuracy
Since an IoT system performs calculations based on input information from **sensors**, the accuracy of this information is critical to the accuracy of the result. A characteristic value for the accuracy of a sensor is the percentage deviation of the measurement from the real physical conditions.

Actuators influence the physical environment according to digital instructions. A characteristic value for accuracy is the ratio between the targeted action and the action actually performed. This characteristic value can be specified as a percentage or as an absolute value of the deviation from the targeted setpoint.

Example: Automatic Image Processing by Sensors
Automatic image processing uses sensors such as cameras, for example, to recognize license plates of trucks on German highways for toll calculation. Facial recognition to determine the identity of people in a crowd is also a use case. This has been discussed on and off in recent years for use at German train stations. The accuracy here is given as a percentage "hit rate." In the example of person recognition, this means: What is the percentage probability that the recognized identity of the person in the crowd actually matches the real person? In the case of facial recognition at the main train station in Berlin, percentage deviations of less than 1% are enough for several tens of thousands of people a day to be incorrectly interpreted as suspicious and for the police to be called.

Example: Precise Placement at the Storage Location by Industrial Robots
In the broadest sense, a robot arm is an actuator or a sum of actuators in interaction. It is supposed to place an object at a defined location in space, for example. The more precisely the object is placed in this space according to the digital command, the higher is the accuracy.

Auto configuration (Standard Sect. 7.4.2)
You are probably familiar with the term plug and play from your dealings with technical components. It means that the technical components insert themselves independently into existing structures, such as networks. We know that IoT devices in logistics and production applications are managed in a network. These should automatically integrate into the IoT system without manual intervention. In addition,

IoT devices need to be found on the network, reporting their respective function and role in the system. For all this to be possible at all within a network, IoT devices must of course be network-capable and it should be possible to manage them within a network. The properties that IoT devices in networks must have for this purpose are described in the ISO/IEC 30141 standard in Sect. 7.4.

An IoT system must automatically adapt to external circumstances. This requires automatic configuration. Imagine you are operating a globally networked IoT system to track your global logistics and transport processes. You want to track containers on their journey. To do this, the IoT components must be able to automatically and dynamically insert themselves into your IoT system, configure them, and also log them out again.

Features of the automatic configuration of IoT systems include the following:

- Automatic networking.
- Automatic provision of services.
- Plug and play, that is, direct usability.

The system detects the addition and removal of devices and network environments, as well as changed conditions, and reacts to them automatically. It is particularly important that only authorized components are configured automatically. This is achieved by security and authentication mechanisms, which must be designed according to use-case-specific conditions and requirements.

Compliance (Standard Sect. 7.4.3)
IoT systems in Industry 4.0 must also be designed in accordance with technical and legal regulations. You may be familiar with this in the corporate context under the term compliance. Services, components, and applications in the context of IoT must ensure conformity with rules and compliance with laws and regulations, standards, and guidelines, which is achieved through the appropriate configuration, programming, and expansion of the devices and systems.

For example, the following regulations might apply to your IoT system:

- Compatibility
- Cooperation
- Functions and capabilities
- Limitations of functions and abilities
- Balance between the common good and the interests of system operators

Depending on the use environment, this concerns other regulations. In accordance with your use case in logistics and production, you should always be aware of all laws, regulations, ordinances, standards, and guidelines before implementation. Subsequently, the necessary adaptation of the IoT system in accordance with applicable laws, regulations, etc. is usually accompanied by a loss of functionality, increased expense, or complete discontinuation of the solution. Understandably, increased safety regulations apply to IoT devices in aircraft. In households, the automotive industry, or the medical sector, different regulations are relevant. Right from the start, have a very detailed idea of the use cases to be implemented and the areas in which they will be implemented.

Regulations and laws regulate, for example, the following properties that are relevant for IoT:

- Electromagnetic radiation (frequency band, signal strength, interference signals in radio links)
- Building regulations (to be considered in connection with smart homes)
- Emissions (for example, noise emissions)

Content Awareness and Object Dependencies (Standard Sect. 7.4.4)
In IoT systems, information of different types is collected, brought together, and put into context. When this information is brought together, additional knowledge about the process can be gained. This is also referred to as object dependencies. Use cases from emergency medical care, disaster control, emergency services, and goods tracking within a global supply chain place different demands on timeliness, security, and data protection.

Information about context-specific requirements therefore provides deeper insights into and information about the captured data. This type of information is often called metadata. Based on this metadata, it is possible for devices and services to automatically update interfaces, abstract application data, increase the accuracy of information queries, and provide users with suitable interaction options.

The object dependencies of an IoT system are influenced by the following factors:

- Location
- Sensitivity of data
- Service quality requirements

The inclusion of additional features leads to the following functional enhancements in the IoT system:

- Data enrichment
- Higher data provision speed since the accuracy of data retrieval can be significantly increased
- Security through encryption

Context Sensitization (Standard Sect. 7.4.5)
Let's look at an example to start with: you are driving on the A40 autobahn at the Bochum-Hamme interchange in the direction of Dortmund. Your smartphone is constantly sending location information to services such as Google or Apple. The smartphone reports traffic congestion due to an accident between the next exit, Bochum-Riemke, and the following exits. This information is valuable to you in this specific situation since you now have the option of avoiding the traffic jam and can search for an alternative route. It will be of less interest to you in this situation

that traffic is jammed at the same time on the A5 toward Basel between the Walldorf exit and Walldorfer Kreuz.

The situation or context in which an event occurs or a measured value is announced has an essential influence on the result to be brought about. For this reason, when designing your IoT system, it is important for you to monitor and interpret the environment and events in the relevant environment.

The following aspects can influence context in an IoT system:

- Location
- Change of location
- Time
- Time
- Event
- Sequence of events

The context can vary individually or in combination with other sensor data and actuators.

Example: Hazardous Material Storage
An example of recognizing and reporting an emergency situation will help you see the value of context awareness. Imagine a hazardous material warehouse. In this warehouse, several thousand liters of chlorine bleach solution have leaked during the night. The door locks of the warehouse access points must be unlocked for the fire department without further authorization. But due to the toxic gases in the storage facility, of course no other people are allowed to enter the building. So the following combination of context situations must be given as a condition:

- The facility is in an emergency situation.
- Emergency services are on the scene.

Data Characteristics (Standard Sect. 7.4.6)
Large amounts of data are generated and processed in IoT systems. The characteristics that describe the data are as follows:

- Volume
- Speed
- Truthfulness
- Variability
- Variety

In this process, the information in the IoT system is sent and received at high speed via network connections and flows into higher-level data streams. Since errors and defective sensors can occur from time to time in a complex IoT system, the information should be checked as early as in the vicinity of the data source. The defective sensors could provide incorrect or implausible data. If a change in the velocities and characteristics of the data occurs within their service life and if this change is above a certain tolerance threshold, the IoT system must include this in the follow-up activities. The preceding data characteristics are usually only meaningful enough in combination with aggregated further processing.

> **Example: Aggregated Data Characteristics from Logistics**
> Logistics service provider Kampmann Logistik uses large amounts of data to optimize its routes and loading volumes. The system collects and processes information in real time, which the driver, the vehicles, and the shipping software generate during the tour. The IoT system uses this information for ongoing optimization.

Findability (Standard Sect. 7.4.7)

IoT devices, sensors, and actuators become discoverable in the network through the so-called endpoint in the network. We will take a closer look at the architecture, which is determined, among other things, by endpoints in Sect. 2.3. For example, you can very easily integrate a temperature sensor for building automation into the IoT system because this sensor is discoverable in the network and in the local context in the building.

Endpoints can be IoT devices, services, applications, or even a flesh-and-blood user. Discovery services report what and where the endpoint is and provide access based on specific criteria: location and service type.

Protocols such as Hypercat, AllJoyn, those from AllSeen Alliance, and Consul are used for communications that perform searches of devices, services, or systems, depending on the following characteristics:

- Geographical position
- Skills
- Interfaces
- Accessibility
- Property
- Security guidelines
- Operating configuration

Flexibility (Standard Sect. 7.4.8)

IoT systems usually have context-dependent functions; that is, they can provide a different number of functions, depending on the service, device, and component and on the environmental conditions and context. Dynamically linking IoT services to the IoT system creates this flexibility. An IoT service can be linked to diverse and different IoT systems for specific use cases.

The flexibility of IoT systems is based on the following:

* Standards
* Protocols
* Formats
* Interfaces

Example: Flexibility in the Use of a Thermostat
The "Thermostat" IoT system varies in terms of its flexibility depending on the use case. Various expansion stages are possible, from temperature control and temperature reporting to remote control via a web application or smartphone app to networking with other smart home devices or weather services.

Manageability (Standard Sect. 7.4.9)
An IoT system operates autonomously. But if individual components are defective, unstable, or incorrectly calibrated or if there is no network connection, it must be possible to maintain the system remotely. Even in global IoT systems, which have geographically complex structures, external access should be possible at all times. This ensures compliance and efficiency in operation.

Example: Managing Hard-to-Reach Components Remotely
Smoke detectors are installed in hard-to-reach places in a warehouse or production hall. This makes them difficult to maintain. The malfunction of a smoke detector means danger to life and limb. The entrepreneurial risk is enormous if they do not work.

As early as when defining the target design of an IoT system and its components, you need to design remote manageability for the entire lifecycle, from the development to the operation of the IoT system.

In addition, mutual authentication of the IoT device, server, firmware, and operating system must be ensured. Updates should contribute to authenticity and integrity and must have a digital signature. Updates must be made over a secure and encrypted connection so that no malware can be introduced.

Consider the following aspects when managing IoT systems:

* Device management
* Network management
* System management
* Interface maintenance and warnings

Network Communication (Standard Sect. 7.4.10)
Nothing works in an IoT system without network connections. Information flows over these connections to the components of an IoT system, such as sensors and actuators, and from the components back to the IoT system. The amounts of information transmitted are usually small. Even voice transmissions cause only small numbers of bytes in the networks. Just as important as network connectivity is the power supply to the components. Especially for devices that are not connected to the IoT system via cables, the question of power supply arises. Nobody wants to change all the batteries of the sensors in the IoT system on the production floor every few weeks.

Types of Network
Short-range, low-power **networks (LAN)** are used to connect IoT devices locally. They are often referred to as ambient networks. **Wide-area networks (WAN)** connect the short-range networks to the Internet. These networks can be mapped wired or wirelessly.

Devices in IoT systems often send and receive information to software services over network types, which cooperate in different ways regardless of where they are located. The software services can be local or remote.

Network Management and Operation (Standard Sect. 7.4.11)
As you have seen in the preceding sections, almost everything in an IoT system in the manufacturing and logistics environment relies on network connections. Be certain to ensure their operation and management at an early stage. Short-range networks are usually used exclusively by the IoT system. Therefore, this network must be managed as part of the IoT system.

Example: Short-Range Networks in Production
Especially in the field of factory automation in connection with Industry 4.0, sensors and controllers within the production line are usually managed by the operator of a factory via local networks. Typically, fieldbus protocols such as Profibus or Profinet are used here.

Usually, WAN is additionally used by other applications and, as a general-purpose network, is often also managed by other, external organizations. This is the case with a mobile network, for example. Via the WAN, a factory uses cloud services, for example, which can be hosted via a remote connection. The connection to the cloud services can be established via a wired or wireless network connection.

So IoT network management usually includes both types of networks and considers them as one component in the IoT system. If you use third-party networks, you should ensure that the partner provides appropriate management and operational interfaces that you can use.

Real-Time Capability (Standard Sect. 7.4.12)

For an IoT system, real-time capability means that the system can execute actions immediately and depending on recorded measured values. Information from the physical world, such as temperature, flow or pressure, and events, is permanently captured by sensors. It may be crucial that the IoT system reacts in time and acts on the physical world via actuators or calls up a corresponding service. To do this, the IoT system may also draw on previous event data, comparisons to previous event data, static data, and external data in the calculation.

> **Example: Monitoring Mechanisms in the Chemical Industry**
> An example of this is the continuous monitoring of the processing parameters of a boiler in which chemical products are produced under sensitive environmental conditions. The temperature, pressure, and inflow of a substance to the boiler must be continuously monitored. In the event of deviations from the defined target values, the IoT system intervenes in a regulating manner.

Self-Description (Standard Sect. 7.4.13)

IoT devices and systems have to send information about their own properties to the IoT system. This is particularly necessary if not only individual components are to work together in a system. This becomes even more important for each individual component when several IoT systems are to work together.

Mobile components that leave an IoT network in phases or switch to sleep mode to save power and then log back into the network must be able to describe themselves, integrating themselves ad hoc into the IoT system. This is how self-description works: components list their capabilities and inform other IoT components and IoT systems with the aim of providing composition, collaboration, and dynamic discovery information.

The following information is for self-description:

- Interface specification
- Capabilities and functions of the IoT component
- Physical type and type of device in the system
- Types of devices that can be connected to the IoT system
- Services provided by the IoT system
- State of the IoT system

When a mobile IoT device connects to the IoT system via Bluetooth or a wireless network, it provides its device name and the supported services. The IoT system on the other side broadcasts its status and supported services. The IoT device could receive this information from multiple networks and systems and decide which network to connect to based on matches.

IoT Service Subscription (Standard Sect. 7.4.14)
You may have a smartwatch or know someone who does. These IoT devices are packed with sensors and measure the wearer's (i.e., the IoT user's) vital signs and fitness levels and assess whether the wearer of this watch could perhaps use a little more exercise. They recommend standing up or taking a deep breath even when working out.

The functionality of such a smartwatch is based on an IoT service that analyzes the collected information and gives the user advice on how to improve their fitness. Whether free or paid, as an IoT user, you subscribe to an IoT service for these friendly appeals to manage your lifestyle. These subscriptions are offered by IoT service providers. The subscription process usually involves payments.

An IoT service may include the following steps:

- Installation and configuration of software components.
- IoT device installation.

Software provision and specification should be done by the IoT service provider.

When using IoT services, make sure that manufacturers of IoT systems and providers of IoT services comply with all data protection requirements, such as the German General Data Protection Regulation (DSGVO) and the German Federal Data Protection Act (BDSG). In your own interest, you should ensure compliance with these requirements because the responsibility lies with you as a user of the services. In the smartwatch example, the IoT service uses extremely sensitive personal data. Therefore, the transmission paths of the data should be stored securely and encrypted with the service provider. The operation, maintenance, and compliance with existing rules and regulations are also up to you.

Check to see if there is a market for your IoT service outside your company, if applicable. Offer your service for subscription and become an IoT service provider yourself, benefitting several times over. For example, you leverage existing structures by renting out intelligent services. As an IoT service provider, you set up your own subscription model. Your customers pay for its use. You have thus developed and implemented a digital business model and bear responsibility for the operation and maintenance of the IoT service. As a service provider, it is important for you to develop standards and simple processes for implementing and maintaining the subscription.

Rule of Thumb for Pricing IoT Services
How should you reasonably price an IoT service? I recommend a fairly simple method: if you want to offer the digital service on a subscription basis, then first think about the price for the service. Deliberately calculate the price as if your customer were buying the solution once. Now divide the purchase price of the service by the number of months from 2.2 to 2.5 years—in this case, 26.4 to 30 months. The amount that comes out of this calculation is the monthly fee that the service costs. You guessed it. If the customer uses the service for more than 3 years, then you earn really good money from the third year on. But you should also add an appropriate margin before that to make the business model work well. You can also base subscription fees on your costs and then add a margin. But always consider maintenance, support, and functional development.

2.3   Architecture of IoT Systems According to ISO 30141

In Sect. 2.2, I explained what is required of an IoT system and what technical criteria IoT systems, services, and components must fulfill. In this section, I will look at how the respective components, services, and users interact. The IoT reference architecture helps here. It describes and defines the characteristics of IoT systems, the associated terms, and the requirements for their mutual interaction. It also names the components that make up an IoT system. An IoT reference architecture is understood to be the definition and consideration of an IoT system from different perspectives and different levels of detail and abstraction.

We approach the reference architecture in three stages:

1. IoT conceptual model
2. IoT reference model
3. IoT reference architecture

The conceptual model is dedicated to the concepts of an IoT system on a generic level. The reference model looks at the holistic structure of the elements in interaction. We will trace this first at the domain level and then at the entity level. In Sect. 2.3.1, I first introduce the components and participants that describe a conceptual model and ultimately an architecture.

2.3.1   IoT Conceptual Model

What are the components of an IoT system, and how do these components interact? This describes the conceptual model of an IoT system in the ISO/IEC 30141:2018

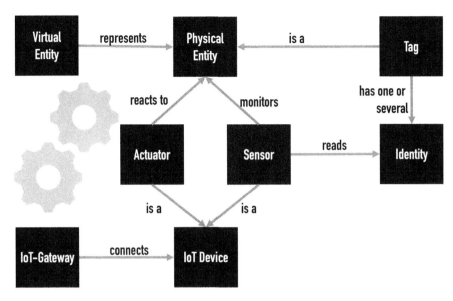

Fig. 2.3 Relationship between the components of an IoT system in logistics and production

standard on a generic and abstract level. It is first important for you to understand how the individual components of an IoT architecture relate to each other. I will explain that in this section.

The following components belong to an IoT architecture (see Fig. 2.3):

- Entities (virtual and physical)
- Endpoints
- IoT gateway services
- Software application
- Interfaces
- Data storage

The terms shown in Fig. 2.3 are defined in the following.

Entities

Whether physical, virtual, or digital—in an IoT system, every component is an entity. A distinction is made between four different types of entities:

- Physical entities ("things")
- Digital entity (the IT system)
- IoT users
- Network connecting the components to each other

Each entity has a unique identity by which it can be determined within the IoT system.

Physical Entities

Physical objects or environments, logistics chains, production lines, people, animals, and cars, as well as retail stores and individual electronic devices, are physical entities. A physical entity can contain other entities. Therefore, a production line can contain individual machines as entities. Physical entities are controlled by actuators and monitored by sensors.

Sensors and actuators are IoT devices. They connect the digital and physical worlds and are in direct or indirect contact with the real world. Let's take a closer look at these components.

Sensors

Without sensors, we would not be able to record the outside world. In technical terms and in the parlance of the ISO standard, a sensor measures and records the properties of physical entities. It transforms readings into a digital format, which it sends to the IoT system. A single IoT device can contain multiple sensors. A smartphone has an entire battery of built-in sensors that measure acceleration, Global Positioning System (GPS) position, compass direction, temperature, vibrations, and more.

Actuator

Actuators are also often called actuators in the field of control and regulation technology. They receive digital information and influence and change physical entities.

IoT Device

The conceptual IoT device model defines both physical and digital entities. This makes sense, considering that it bridges the digital and real worlds. It scans the real world, transforming real-world attributes such as acceleration, humidity, and speed into digital values. It communicates with other entities via networks, having one or more endpoints. It can perform computational operations and also provide and use its own data storage.

Tags

Physical entities usually have tags. A tag is a physical entity attached to another physical entity, for example, to mark, identify, or track it. Barcodes are passive tags because they are optically detected and read by a reader. Active tags, on the other hand, are RFID tags as well as tags used in real-time locating systems. They send information about their identity automatically. Tags can also be monitored by a sensor instead of the physical unit.

Digital Entities

Data and computing elements in an IoT system are called digital entities. We also call these virtual entities, that is, data stores, IoT devices, and IoT gateways. Digital entities can also combine other digital entities within themselves. Virtual entities are the digital representations of a physical entity and part of a service (see the following).

IoT System Users

IoT system users are entities. The IoT user is part of the IoT system, whether that user is a human or digital user.

Human Users

Human users are people who use the IoT system and interact with the software application using what is called a human-machine interface (HMI) with the IoT system over the network.

Digital Users

Digital users are digital entities that use an IoT system. They interact with the IoT system and its services via the virtual interfaces (application programming interfaces (APIs)) of the network.

Network

A network is an entity. At the same time, it connects the digital entities in the IoT system. It forms the IoT infrastructure over which the digital entities communicate with each other. It connects IoT devices and IoT gateways. Endpoints are accessed via interfaces.

Endpoints

Endpoints enable connections between entities. They are points where other entities dock because interfaces exist here. These interfaces are accessible from and invoked by other entities. Endpoints each have one or more network interfaces. Actions can be invoked by other digital entities through endpoints.

IoT Gateway

IoT gateways connect different networks and network types. They establish the connection from the downstream network, where the IoT devices are connected, to the wide-area network (WAN) and thus to the Internet. The WAN layer can connect other IoT devices. IoT gateways often have local storage. They use implemented security functions to protect the endpoints in the network from external attacks.

Services

Services are implemented as software and provide different functions via a defined interface. A service can contain further services. It requires one or more endpoints through which it is invoked. Services interoperate with other entities across different networks and can—but do not have to—interoperate with IoT devices. Services use data stores as needed. A service can work independently and alone or with other services.

Software Application
Software is the interface to humans (human interface), for example, and helps the IoT user with certain (IT) tasks. However, the IoT user can also be a digital user in addition to a human. Humans use the software via the human-machine interface and digital users via an API. Software often uses services.

Example: Identification of a Pallet at Goods Receipt (Software Application)
An example of a task that can be mapped with IoT software is the automation of a goods receipt process: if an IoT device or a tag on the pallet reports that it has been placed in the goods receipt zone of a warehouse, this can trigger a booking process in the enterprise resource planning (ERP) software. Thus, when the pallet arrives in the goods receiving zone, the goods receipt booking is triggered ad hoc and transport tasks are generated for the forklifts for putaway or cross-docking.

Ensure Software Security
Use the ISO/IEC 27034 standard (Information technology—IT security procedures—Security of applications—Part I: Overview and concept) as a guide for automating business processes. The standard provides a framework for ensuring security throughout the lifecycle of software and IT applications.

Interfaces
Nothing works in an IoT system without interfaces. They are used to request and provide actions from other digital entities (see section "Endpoints"). At the same time, they describe the behavior, capabilities, and possible operations of the entities that are addressed by the interface.

A digital IoT user uses an API to access the services of an IoT system. An API is an interface or communication protocol between different parts of one or more computer programs. APIs make it easier to implement and maintain software. Thanks to APIs, a single implementation can apply to a web-based system, an operating system, a database system, computer hardware, or a software library.

API specifications are specifications for routines, data structures, object classes, variables, and remote calls. The documentation of an API facilitates implementations. APIs are often used between project participants as a standard or contractual basis for the common interface on which the implementation partner, supplier, and customer agree. In this way, all partners ensure functionality. For example, the API documentation specifies that requests and responses must be in a particular format. The IoT platforms of major cloud providers feature generic APIs for creating, reading, modifying, and deleting any IoT device types within an IoT network.

Data Storage
IoT devices and IoT gateways can contain data stores. These are also managed by the IoT devices or the IoT gateway. Data stores hold data that relate to the IoT system. The data can be generated and stored directly by the IoT devices or originate from services and can act on the IoT devices.

2.3.2   IoT Reference Model

Now let's turn to the IoT reference model, an abstract model that explains the relationships between entities in their environment (standard Sect. 9 of ISO/IEC 30141). Normally, reference models are used for training people who usually have little to no specialized knowledge. The reference model can be used to provide a basic understanding. However, we need concrete standards, technologies, and implementation details. The IoT reference model refers to the entities and different domains, as well as the relationships between domains. These form the functional groups of an IoT system. In this context, an entity is always part of at least one domain.

Entity-Based Model
Defining the components of an IoT system according to the conceptual model forms the basis for an entity-based model. Figure 2.4 describes how the entities relate to each other. The IoT user initially accesses IoT devices via a subordinate system level using the IoT gateway with its corresponding services. This lower-level system layer is primarily a software application or service. The physical entity is monitored or influenced by the IoT device. Each entity, except for physical entities that do not have a network adapter, is connected to other entities or to other surrounding systems via networks.

In addition to the entities described above, an IoT system consists of various subsystems that together constitute the software application entity:

- Application and service subsystems
- Operating and management subsystem
- Resource access and exchange subsystem
- User devices such as smartphones, personal computers (PCs), tablets for human users, or service APIs for digital users
- Peer systems (other IoT or non-IoT systems, services)

Figure 2.5 shows that a domain in the conceptual model has different entities. Domains are described in the domain-based model.

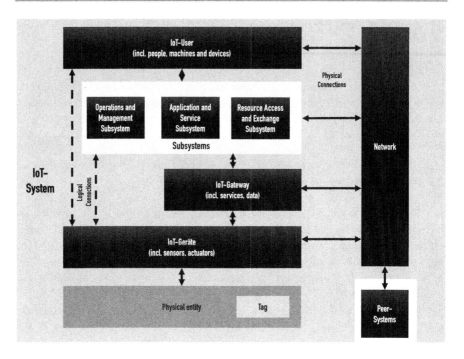

Fig. 2.4 Interaction of the entities of an IoT system in Industrie 4.0 (based on ISO 30141)

Domain-Based Model
Separating by domain lets IoT system designers divide the IoT system into different areas. This allows them to assign specific tasks to each area. Domains divide the IoT system into logical and, in some cases, physical areas. Areas of responsibility and functions are sorted by separating them according to domains.

Domains in an IoT Reference Architecture
There are different types of domains:

• The *user domain* (user area in the figure) includes human and digital users. Human users interact with the system via services, mobile applications, or desktop applications. Digital users use interfaces with services.
• The *physical entities domain* contains the physical entities. It is the area in the IoT system where the monitoring, sensing, and control of the physical world take place. People can also be entities of the physical domain.
• The *measurement and control domain* includes IoT devices, sensors, and actuators. This domain consists of values, states, and properties that sensors record on physical entities, as well as the action of actuators on the physical entities. The domain of the physical entities described above is the physical world, while the measurement and control domain is the link between the physical and virtual worlds.

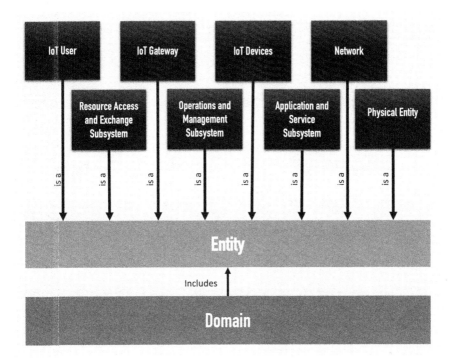

Fig. 2.5 Connection between entity and domain of an IoT system in logistics and production (based on ISO 30141)

- The *operations and management domain* is where the functions for provisioning, managing, monitoring, and optimizing the systems are located. This is also where the business process and operation support functions are provided that manage the IoT system in the business and operational domain.
- The *resource access and data exchange domain* provides mechanisms for external entities to access the functions of the IoT system. Access is mainly provided by users and peripheral systems. The IoT system provides its functions via one or more service interfaces.
- The *application and service domain* provides the applications and services consumed by users in the user domain. Applications and services can also interact with sensors and actuators to obtain measurements from them or to act in the physical entity domain. Cloud services provide these applications and services.

How these domains interact in an IoT reference architecture is shown in Fig. 2.6.

Interaction of Entity-Based and Domain-Based Reference Models
Let us now superimpose the two models of entities and domains to create a link between the two views. The relationships between the entities can be seen in the upper part of Fig. 2.7. Below that, the domains are shown. For example, the entity

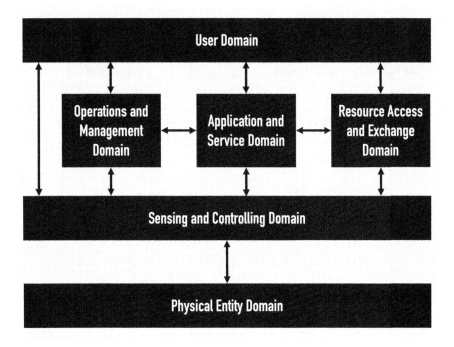

Fig. 2.6 Interaction of the domains of an IoT system in Industrie 4.0 applications (based on ISO 30141)

"IoT user" belongs to the user domain, the application and service subsystem belongs to the application and service domain, and so on.

2.3.3 IoT Reference Architecture

When designing and implementing an IoT system, the IoT reference architecture is a good template for you to use as a resource. It is a handy reference to evaluate commercial IoT applications and use cases.

Examples of Industrie 4.0 use cases where the reference architecture can help you are as follows:

- Global supply chains
- Global track and trace solutions
- Real-time locating systems (RTLS)
- Driverless transport vehicles (AGVs)
- Smart factory systems (intelligent factories)

The IoT reference architecture can be described from different views:

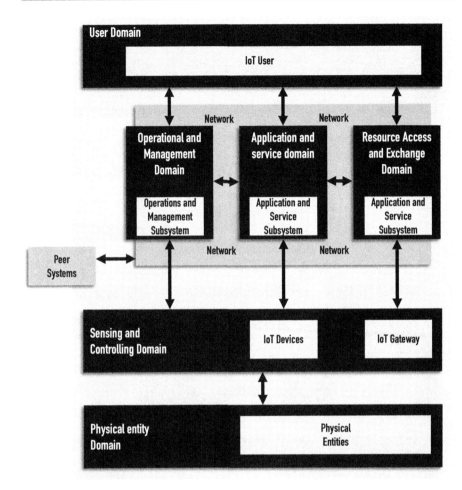

Fig. 2.7 Interaction of entities and domains of an IoT architecture in Industrie 4.0 applications (based on ISO 30141)

- Functional view
- Deployment view
- Network view
- User and role view

We will now look at these views in detail (standard Sect. 10 of ISO/IEC 30141).

Functional View (Standard Sect. 10.2)
The functional view tells us in a model-like manner which functional components are required in an IoT system. What dependencies exist between the individual components and their use? Figure 2.8 shows the functions in the individual domains.

Domain Features

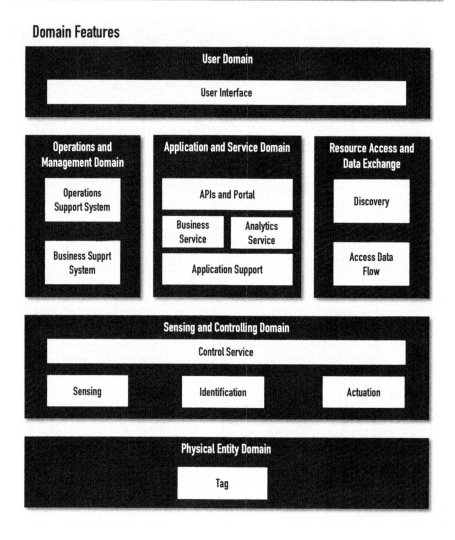

Fig. 2.8 Functions of the individual domains of an Industrie 4.0 IoT system (based on ISO 30141)

You may not need all the functions mentioned here when implementing your IoT use case. You will probably only need a fraction of them for your use case.

Let's now take a detailed look at the individual functions of each domain.

Functions in the Measurement and Control Domain
The function that reads sensor data from sensors by scanning or measuring (sensing) can be found in the measurement and control domain, where actuation means writing the control signals to an actuator. This is used to control the actuator. When

implementing the two functions, you are in the domain of hardware, firmware, device drivers, and software components. Control services provide data from sensors and other systems as input parameters. In the process, the instructions are given to actuators.

Identification functions ensure that entities can be identified in the system and that they can be found and traced. This helps the system distinguish between entities. During identification, always make sure to collect as little personal data as possible to preserve the privacy of human users and associated individuals.

Functions of the Operational and Administrative Domain
You need the functions of the operation and administration domain for the following:

- Overall management of the IoT system.
- The operation support system (service delivery, monitoring, reporting, policy management, service automation, service level management, service catalog compliance, device registration, and device management).
- The business support system (management of accounts and subscriptions, billing of accounts, and product catalog).

The operation support system and business support system are the essential functions of this domain.

Application and Service Domain Functions
Among the application and service domain functions, you will find cognitive services, streaming, process management, validation, visualization, business rules and control services, and application logic.

Application and service domain functions include the following:

- APIs and portal functions.
- Business services for orchestrating business processes.
- Analysis services for sensor data streams, system states, and context sensitization, that is, putting the collected disparate data and features into a common context.
- Application support (configuration, scaling, billing).
- Resource access and data exchange domain functions.

The resource access and data exchange domain contains all the functions required and also supports access to the resources of the IoT system and communication of resources with the IoT system. This includes services and data.

User access to the functions of the IoT system is made possible by the detection function (discovery). The access data flow function component has two tasks:

1. Control of IoT user and system access to the IoT system, as well as authentication and authorization.
2. Coverage of all processes and functions in data transmission and its preparation.

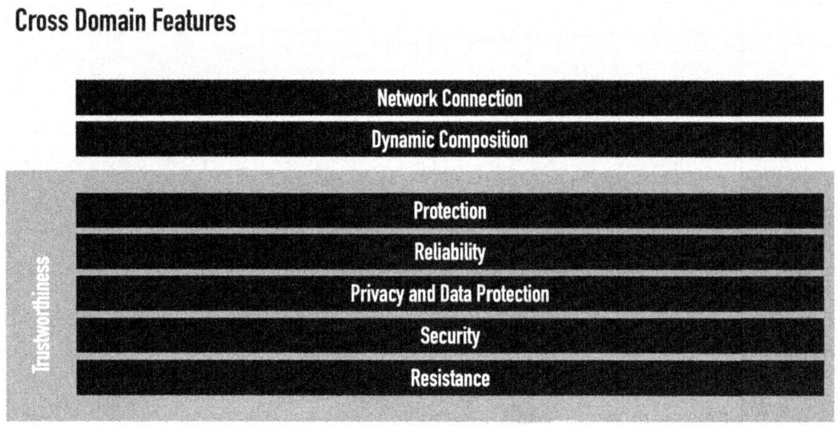

Cross Domain Features

Fig. 2.9 Functions in Industrie 4.0 IoT applications that are cross-domain (based on ISO 30141)

Functions of the Physical Entity Domain and the User Domain

In the physical entity domain and user domain functions, components such as tags, vibration sensors, and temperature sensors that can be attached to physical objects provide their services.

User domain functions let users access the capabilities of the IoT system. A user interface can be, for example, a smartphone app or a software application with graphical elements that the user can utilize via a desktop computer.

Cross-Domain Functions

Not all functions can and should be assigned to a specific domain. Cross-domain functions (see Fig. 2.9) ensure, among other things, the security and trustworthiness of the system and should already be taken into account in the design phase of the IoT system.

Deployment View (Standard Sect. 10.3)

For the deployment view, we leave the functional view of the IoT system and take the perspective of system deployment. This requires a generic description of the components. We look at the IoT system and the individual components from the perspective of the implementer.

This is what the deployment view is about in detail:

- Physical components of an IoT system (subsystems, devices, networks)
- General implementation architecture and structure of the IoT system (distribution and interconnectivity of components)
- Technical description of the components, including their behaviors and other properties

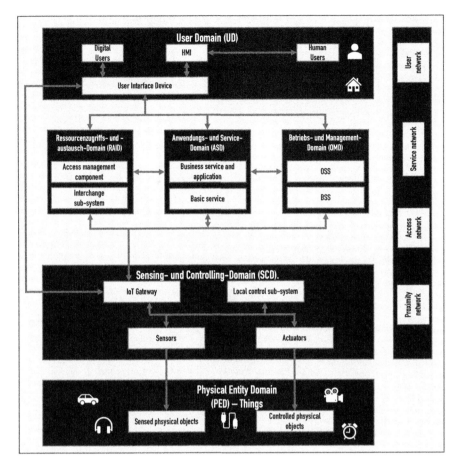

Fig. 2.10 Entities and components of the individual domains of an IoT system in Industrie 4.0 applications (based on ISO 30141)

We will now assign the points of the deployment view to the different domains (see Fig. 2.10):

- **Physical entities domain:** includes the objects controlled via sensing functions
- **Measurement and control domain:** IoT gateways, sensors, actuators, and local control systems for operations that do not have connectivity to higher-level cloud services
- **Resource access and data exchange domain:** access management and exchange subsystem components
- **Application and service domain:** hosting services and applications
- **Operation and management domain:** operation support system and business support system

- **User domain:** management of the human and technical user and human-machine interface**Network View (Standard Sect. 10.4)**

The network view looks at the communication networks that connect the components and entities into an IoT system.

The four main communication networks are as follows:

1. **Ambient network**: connects sensors and actuators to the IoT system
2. **Access network**: connects entities of the measurement and control domain with the application and service domain as well as with the sales and administration domain
3. **Service network**: connects application and service domain services with the resource access and data exchange domain and sales and administration domain
4. **User network**: connects the user with the application and service domain as well as the operation and administration domain

User and Role View (Standard Sect. 10.5)

Despite all the technical aspects, always keep the people in focus. After all, they are the ones who ultimately develop, test, operate, and use your IoT application and therefore play a central role. Standard Sect. 10.5 is dedicated to the roles involved in the development, design, and operation of the IoT system. IoT architectures always place interdisciplinary demands on the skills of your employees and partners. Here we take a close look at who should take on which roles with which profiles.

For users and roles, we differentiate between the following three levels:

1. Activities
2. Rolls and subrolls
3. Services and cross-divisional aspects

The ISO/IEC 30141 standard divides IoT system users into three major groups. IoT service providers operate and manage the IoT services and may also provide a network connection:

1. A service provider can take on the following roles:
   - IoT business manager
   - IoT service delivery manager
   - IoT system operator
   - IoT security analyst
   - IoT operations analyst
   - IoT data scientist
   - IoT chief privacy officer (CPO)/data protection officer (DPO)
   - IoT security officer
2. IoT service providers create IoT systems and applications. Employees of an IoT service provider can take on the following roles:
   - IoT solution architect
   - IoT DevOps manager

- IoT application developer
- IoT device developer
- IoT system integrator
- IoT chief privacy officer

3. You have already encountered IoT users in various previous sections. They are divided into the following:
   - Human users
   - Digital users

For the roles envisaged in the standard, there are various options for training with the certification of corresponding specialists. IIoT.institute www.iiot.institute) and digit-ANTS GmbH https://www.digit-ants.com/iot-zertifizierung) offer various formats that fit different training requirements in the logistics and production environments.

IoT Platforms

3

In the previous chapters, you learned about the history and technical basics of the Internet of Things (IoT). This is essential if you want to understand the IoT concept. But now we'll move on to the practical side of things because after all, this is a practical guide and not a proseminar. This chapter provides answers to the following questions: How do you, as a company, build an IoT platform that meets the demands of the future? What solutions are there on the market? And which of them is more and which is less relevant for your specific objective and industry?

If you're a chief executive officer (CEO) or department head who can delegate selection processes and decision-making, you may be thinking to yourself, "Why should I spend time looking for the right IoT platform (not to mention the technical principles behind it)? After all, I have my experts for that, and I trust them." And if they say, "This is the best solution for us," you believe it. I can well understand this attitude. Given this attitude, it would actually only be logical for you to skip the chapter because know-how about platforms is not on your plate and, as a busy person, you are primarily interested in results. But you might have guessed already: here comes the "but." For many companies, the decision to adopt an IoT platform is a strategic one. It entails not only detailed technical questions but also cross-company questions: How accessible and connectable are the data and processes that make up a particular department to the other divisions and departments of the company? For example, is there good networking between production, customer service, and sales? Or are there invisible hurdles and software walls that make it difficult for colleagues to collaborate and block the efficient meshing of cross-departmental operations? IoT platforms necessitate not only internal transparency and efficiency but also interaction with external entities. This ranges from government agencies and strategic partners to end customers. Speaking somewhat more generally, IoT platforms enable the use of devices, machines, and sensor data for business applications and interdependent processes. The IoT systems run in controlled, permanent interaction with the back-end systems within the company, such as the enterprise resource planning (ERP) system, the manufacturing execution

A. Holtschulte, *Digital Supply Chain and Logistics with IoT*, Management for Professionals, https://doi.org/10.1007/978-3-030-89408-5_3

system (MES), the warehouse management system (WMS), and the telematics system.

Exactly how this works and what needs to be considered will be discussed in Chap. 4. At this point, it is first important for me to show that the choice of a particular platform will influence the day-to-day operations of a company in all possible directions. Modern data management with real-time data can support, facilitate, and optimize many business processes. The IoT platform can also be significant for redesigning processes and services and for identifying weaknesses and realizing innovations.

So which IoT platform should it be? You're spoiled for choice now (and probably 2 or 3 years from now). In this chapter, we take a look at the competitive market and vendor dynamics relating to enterprise IoT platforms. I'll give you some selection criteria that will help you decide which IoT platform to choose. We'll look at selected platforms and existing studies on them. We'll also look at what are called hyperscalers as well as multicloud strategies. We will also look at security, which should not be underestimated when it comes to IoT solutions. And we look at the international context because networking with Internet-connected devices has a lot to do with EU policy, data protection, and international agreements. By the end of this chapter, you will hopefully be well equipped to select a suitable IoT platform.

3.1   IoT Without Internet

Particularly in IoT applications used in Industrie 4.0 scenarios, the question arises as to where the collected data should be processed and evaluated. Is it absolutely necessary to upload process information and data directly to the cloud, or does it make sense to perform certain computing operations on the device itself or in the local network? Particularly in the area of Industrial IoT, huge amounts of data are generated by changing physical states. At the very start of planning the IoT system, it is important to define which change may have an impact on the processes and should trigger a follow-up action and, thus, also to define the level at which data processing should take place.

In your cloud application, a temperature change of 0.01 °C at the sensor may not be relevant. The situation is quite different when it comes to the interaction of machines. On the factory floor, it might make sense to immediately initiate a reaction to the new measured value without documenting this in the cloud application, meaning that these measures are often taken and triggered not in the cloud but rather in the factory, warehouse, or laboratory. We call these layers edge or fog. I will explain their exact definitions and functions in Sects. 3.1.1 and 3.1.2.

3.1.1   Edge Computing

The respective use case determines the level at which information is processed in an IoT system. Some information needs to be processed directly at the point of origin, resulting in direct intervention in the control of a machine in terms of open-loop and closed-loop control technology. In the IoT cloud solution, in the manufacturing execution system, or even in the enterprise resource planning (ERP) system, the information is of no greater value because it does not entail any follow-up activities or even business management processes. For each IoT system, you should consider where you process or store which information: whether in the cloud, edge, or fog.

In edge computing, the information generated in your local IoT network is processed locally. Here, local means the information is first processed directly in the IoT devices before it is transmitted via network connections to the Internet and the cloud. The reason for this is obvious: sensors and actuators draw on most of the emerging data for local decisions and reactions. Beyond that, these data are irrelevant and not needed outside of the IoT gateway. Edge computing sorts the information in real time at the point of origin, deletes real-time relevant information after processing in the local system, and forwards only the resulting insights to higher-level cloud services. In this way, you derive the maximum benefit from the IoT system and avoid unnecessary latency. Furthermore, you prevent an unnecessarily high design of the Internet connection in terms of bandwidth and shield the system against attacks from the outside. So the decision for edge computing can also be made based on the security requirements of the IoT network.

3.1.2   Fog Computing

Fog computing also processes real-time data in the IoT network and only sends relevant information to higher data processing levels (cloud, ERP, manufacturing execution system (MES)). A characteristic of fog computing is that the information is processed close to the IoT device, sensor, and actuator but no longer in the actuator, sensor, or device itself. Fog computing is also called an architectural pattern for edge computing at the system level. This makes it a variant of edge computing. There are specific gateways with advanced functions that do not process data directly on the end devices as in edge computing but on the programmable automation controllers (PACs) at the edge of the network. These devices are about the size of a mini-computer, like a Raspberry Pi. They process data for one or more IoT endpoints.

When it comes to fog computing, we are poking around in the fog with regard to the IoT system. We can hardly make any statements about the availability, performance, and utilization of PACs. If you pursue this concept in your IoT architecture, you should plan for increased hardware and maintenance costs within the local network in order to provide a certain buffer. You will also need additional protection measures for the additional components.

On the other hand, without edge computing and fog computing in the Industrial Internet of Things (IIoT)—a completely networked supply chain—you will have a hard time managing all the data that accumulate in the future. What would happen if we were to send all the data that accumulate on an asset to the cloud via the Internet? Even a single aircraft turbine generates 10 TB of data on air mass, fuel quantity, fuel quality, temperatures at various positions in the engine, and much more within 30 min during a flight. It would make little sense to send all this information directly to the cloud. It is obvious that if we do not think very carefully about what data we really need in the cloud for evaluation purposes, the connections to the cloud data centers, which are already heavily used today, would collapse; clouds would fail; and latency times would increase to an unbearable level.

3.2   Cloud Computing

Cloud computing is an information technology (IT) infrastructure that is delivered over the Internet using a computer network, without requiring local installations on computers or smart devices to use it. The service provided on these infrastructures may be storage space, computing capacity, or application software. These services are provided exclusively via technical interfaces and protocols such as web browsers and mobile apps. The services cover the complete range of information technology: software, infrastructure, and platforms.

3.2.1   Software as a Service (SaaS)

Software as a Service (SaaS) is a component of cloud computing. Here, the software and IT infrastructure are operated by an external service provider and purchased by the user as a service. The service and software provided are accessed via an Internet-enabled computer, tablet personal computer (PC), or smartphone using a web browser or mobile app. Whereas with a traditional software license the user acquires the right to use the software locally and usually permanently, with cloud software, the user, as a service purchaser, generally pays a fee for temporary use.

The pricing metric can be designed on the following basis:

• Per user per month
• Depending on the scope of functions and software modules
• Depending on the number of user transactions
• Free use

SaaS models have the advantage, for the user, of no acquisition and operating costs. The service provider takes over the complete IT administration and other services, such as maintenance work and software updates.

3.2.2   Infrastructure as a Service (IaaS)

When the server is banished from the user's basement and moved to the cloud, we speak of Infrastructure as a Service (IaaS). Cloud providers offer virtualized computers, networks, and storage. The service user utilizes these resources in the cloud and installs and operates his software there. In contrast to the SaaS model, he is responsible for the functioning of the applications himself since he has only rented the infrastructure. The user enjoys the advantage that he no longer has to buy his IT infrastructure but only rents it as required and can return the resources he no longer needs at any time.

IaaS has the following advantages:

- High flexibility, since this makes one-off applications affordable.
- Interception of load and power peaks.
- Easy expansion and scaling of capacities by adding resources.
- Unneeded capacity can be released immediately.
- Simple software testing can be done by virtualizing different platforms.

3.2.3   Platform as a Service (PaaS)

The two models Platform as a Service (PaaS) and Software as a Service (SaaS) are often lumped together and then stirred vigorously. But we have to differentiate between the two approaches. Looking at the target audiences of the two service ranges helps us do that. SaaS applications focus on the end user, who then uses the software offered in the cloud. SaaS applications are based on PaaS and IaaS service ranges. The target group for PaaS service ranges is developers. If you want to set up an IoT application and system for your customers, you need a platform on which to develop the application.

PaaS comes offers the following:

- Workbench and development environments
- Containers for your applications
- Middleware services

Programmers and software developers build their applications in a PaaS environment using tools given and operated by the PaaS provider. Again, middleware services are accessed via application programming interfaces (APIs).

3.3   The Internet of Things—A Growing Market

The Internet of Things is growing and growing. Accordingly, the number of IoT services and providers has been growing steadily for years. The search for a suitable IoT platform is like a jungle expedition that is better not undertaken without a guide. It's difficult to keep track of everything and always be up to date because the IoT market, which is still relatively young, is changing so rapidly. But I will at least try. In this section, I have compiled the statements and figures from the most important reports and studies for you.

Global business and technology trends shape the new network

Fig. 3.1   Market trends affecting IoT (Source: Cisco, 2020 Global Networking Trends Report)

The papers and trend reports of the Cisco Group are a good indicator of the general development. The US telecommunications company was founded in the 1980s. From the very beginning, routers were among its most important products. The combination of hardware and software as well as the topics of Internet and networking are thus virtually part of the company's history. In the course of time, WebEx was added as a subsidiary, among other things. You may have come across WebEx in connection with video conferencing. Cisco regularly publishes reports and market studies on various IT topics, such as cybersecurity or data protection. Of particular interest for our topic is the "2020 Global Networking Trends Report," which takes into account surveys of over 500 IT experts and around 1500 network strategists from more than ten countries. The "key takeaways" of this trend analysis include the following:

> IDC estimates there will be 48.9 billion connected devices in use around the world by 2023 and the 2018 Cisco Complete VNI Forecast predicts that the average amount of data consumed across a network will be almost 60 GB per personal computer per month. [1]

So if I'm doing my math correctly, the estimate is that there will be six connected devices for every person on Earth in 2023. By 2022, there will already be significantly more IoT devices than people on our planet, if you look at the third number in the sequence in Fig. 3.1: there will be over 14 billion IoT devices in circulation by then. These IoT devices can theoretically all communicate with each other in some way.

The other forecasts are also exciting. The figures relate to developments in security, mobility, and other future technologies, such as virtual reality and big data. We look at the interactions between these and other phenomena and IoT in more detail in Chap. 5.

Regarding IoT networks in particular, the "2020 Global Networking Trends Report" states:

> In this increasingly demanding environment, there is a critical need for IT leaders to migrate to a radically new approach to networking. For an organization to flourish in the digital economy, the network needs to be able to adapt quickly to changing business requirements. The network needs to support an increasingly diverse and fast-changing set of users, devices, applications and services [...] It also needs to ensure fast and secure access to and between workloads wherever they reside. [...] And for the network to function optimally, all this needs to be achieved end-to-end between users, devices, apps and services across each network domain—campus, branch, remote/home, WAN, service provider, mobile, data center, hybrid cloud and multi-cloud. [2]

The transition from traditional corporate IT to the modern IoT platforms described here, which should be complex and powerful but also open and connectable, is in full swing. However, many companies are still at the very beginning.

Particularly in the area of integrating the existing software architecture in companies, very many companies still have major tasks ahead of them before they think about an IoT platform. After all, these weaknesses become apparent at the latest when the processes are implemented in the new IoT platform. Here, those responsible for processes quickly realize that the IoT platform cannot be connected to a patchwork of solutions. Often, the existing software architecture is then also brought up to speed at this point so that the systems can "talk" to each other.

Other publications on the Internet of Things worth reading come from Gartner, for example, a US company that bills itself as "the world's leading research and advisory company" and focuses on market research and IT consulting. You may have come across a Hype Cycle or Magic Quadrant from Gartner before. In the above quote from the "key takeaways" of the trend report, International Data Corporation (IDC) is mentioned as another address for data and background information on IoT. This is another major player in the IT analysis market, with brands and websites such as Computerworld and Macworld, for which more than 1000 analysts investigate, among other things, the Internet of Things with the claim "Analyze the future." It should be noted that the various market analyses are rarely set up in exactly the same way, for example, in terms of the selection of interviewees (sectors, minimum sales, etc.) or the market studied (with or without Asia, etc.).

If we take a step back from major international reports and narrow the market analysis a bit more to Germany as a business location, there are still a lot of relevant publications that you could take a closer look at. One of these is a study entitled "Internet of Things 2019," which was written by a team of authors led by IT trade journalist Jürgen Maurer. This study was commissioned by IDG Research Services in cooperation with Computer Bild magazine, the Telefónica group, and other partners (it was a multiclient study). It was based on more than 500 interviews from September 2018, with "top (IT) decision-makers of companies in the D-A-CH region: strategic (IT) decision-makers in the C-level area and in the business units (LoBs), IT decision-makers and IT specialists from the IT area." The sector distribution was quite broad, with the three largest fields being business services, mechanical and plant engineering, and the metal-producing and manufacturing industries (all of which had a total share of less than 15% each).

An interesting finding from the evaluated interviews with these people is as follows:

> In 55% of companies (last year: 57%), IoT platforms are considered the most important technology for the Internet of Things. Companies of all sizes agree on this. In reality, just under a third (32%) of companies are currently already using an IoT platform, but especially the large companies (38%). After all, the figure is up 10% points on the previous year [3] (translation adapted).

The data on the implementation of new IoT platforms are also revealing: on average, the companies surveyed needed about 1 and a half years to design and implement their first marketable IoT solution. In addition to defining the use cases and the technical analysis and design, the steps also included selecting the right IoT platform.

Another analysis that focuses on IoT in Germany is entitled "The Internet of Things in German SMEs: Significance, Fields of Application and Status of Implementation" and was designed as a trend study. It was prepared by a team headed by lead analyst Arnold Vogt. It was published in spring 2019 and is backed by PAC GmbH and the teknowlogy Group and commissioned by Deutsche Telekom. The methodological approach was to conduct a telephone survey of 161 experts with "decision-making authority in IoT projects or other digitization initiatives." The respondents were senior IT managers and other department heads, for example, from sales or purchasing. The target group consisted of small and medium-sized companies in Germany with ten or more employees, again from various industries and fields.

When asked, "In which of the following IoT technologies will you invest heavily, partially, or not at all in the next 12 months to implement IoT projects?" the answer turned out like this: "IoT platforms as a hub for device management and IoT data collection" was where 17% planned to invest money heavily and 42% planned to invest money at least partially. In response to the question related to upcoming IoT projects, "In which of the following areas do you plan to use external services in the next 12 months?" 55% chose the selection item "Development, implementation and operation of IoT applications and platforms."

Last but not least, the regular analyses published by Hamburg-based IoT Analytics GmbH are important for Germany as an IoT location. These are rather expensive, but they are helpful. The German company specializes in studies and market overviews on the topics of the Internet of Things, machine-to-machine (M2M) communication, and Industry 4.0. The 184-page "IoT Platforms End User Satisfaction Report 2019," for example, is part of the paid product range. The company also publishes what it calls landscapes, that is, visually quite memorable analyses of the IoT market. The most recent report of this kind, published in 2020, talks about 620 IoT platforms, which you and I can theoretically choose from.

In Sect. 3.3.1, we will take a closer look at the competition among IoT providers before turning to the selection criteria for IoT platforms in Sect. 3.4. There is a positive side to being spoiled for choice: you can distill out of many good options those that are particularly well suited to your company and its specific market situation and positioning.

3.3.1   IoT Providers in Competition

In the report "IoT Platforms Competitive Landscape & Database 2020," you will find, among other things, the chart shown in Fig. 3.2, which shows two things: first, the number of IoT platforms has grown year by year since 2015. Second, in addition to big players like Alibaba and Amazon, German giants such as Siemens and Bosch as well as unknown newer companies are also getting involved in this market.

So you'll find a lot of offers if you look around without blinkers for an IoT platform that fits your company and your requirements in logistics. Before I go into the selection criteria in Sect. 3.4, I would like to take this opportunity to present a few excerpts of how some of the providers advertise themselves and their respective solutions. This is intended to be not an advertisement or recommendation on my part but simply an insight into the arguments and also the selection criteria, which we will look at in more detail below.

We'll start with two smaller providers. The first is IOT connctd GmbH (really spelled that way), based in Berlin, which tried to convince people of its merits as follows in a special publication enclosed with the Handelsblatt in July 2020: [4]

Problem

> [...] Not only is the market for IoT platforms growing. The requirements for the use of sensors and actuators are also increasing. Despite the wide range of offerings, it is difficult to find solutions that enable a cross-technology and cross-vendor cloud representation of the properties and capabilities of devices on the Internet. Similarly, a semantic description of objects and their information is often missing. Interfaces such as REST API and Graph API are also often not available.

Fig. 3.2 Growth of IoT platforms in 2015–2019 (Source: IoT Analytics GmbH, IoT Platforms Competitive Landscape & Database 2020)

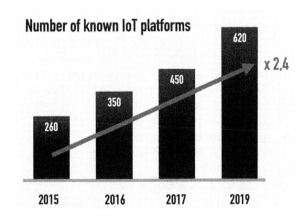

Number of known IoT platforms

620

x 2,4

450

350

260

2015   2016   2017   2019

Proposed Solution

> The platform from Berlin-based provider IoT connctd stands out from the crowd by meeting
> these challenges with an innovative approach. In comparison, one point in particular sets IoT
> connctd's platform apart from other solutions: device and data interoperability. To achieve
> this, the provider operates an open and scalable semantic IoT platform that undergoes
> constant development. Technical boundaries between protocols and infrastructures are
> eliminated. The platform offers service developers the ability to read (sensors) and control
> (actuators) devices. For this purpose, the platform allows modular device descriptions
> (Thing Service) that are compatible with the emerging standard of the W3C data model.
> Likewise, a context description (Unit Model) becomes possible. This is important in order to
> be able to understand and classify the data from the devices at all. Thanks to this approach,
> devices will be machine-readable on the one hand, and on the other hand they will be
> prepared in a way that can be understood by humans. Incidentally, this includes not only
> machine data, but also meta-data and context information describing operating environments
> and similar aspects. As one of the few providers from the IoT sector, IoT connctd also relies
> on innovative graph technologies, which, compared to REST APIs, offer developers the
> possibility of designing extensive and nested queries much more easily [. . .] Overall, it is
> clear from the IoT platform comparison that IoT connctd's solution is convincing in several
> respects. In particular, openness, security, stability, scalability and efficiency are worth
> mentioning.

The second smaller provider is the company "IN-Integrierte Informationssysteme GmbH," which is headquartered in Constance and, according to its own information, has specialized in integrated business processes since it was founded in 1989. Its solutions include the IoT platform sphinx open online, advertised among other things in the advertising block section of the partners involved in the multiclient study "Internet of Things 2019." There, warm words are found for this product: "sphinx open online is a powerful IoT platform which has been in use and continuously expanded since 2011. In conjunction with machine learning methods, complex systems are optimized through active interventions. Whether in the smart factory, on the store floor, in smart devices or as a smart service: Complexity becomes manageable, decisions are optimally supported and processes are optimized and automated. The platform is used worldwide in production control technology, energy management, electromobility, safety, logistics, etc.[5]".

Let's add two big fish that are fueling the competition for IoT platforms to the two small ones: SAP and Oracle. If you want to shortlist SAP for your platform, I would like to recommend the book *IoT mit SAP* (ISBN 978–3–8362-7472-2), which I wrote together with Martina Mohr and Michael Stollberg. In it, we present the various SAP platforms and products in detail. The Group is, of course, a flagship in terms of software and IT, with premium customers such as BASF, Volkswagen, BMW, Daimler, and the Swiss Federal Railways. In addition, experience is definitely a criterion that can be put forward when it comes to dynamic markets and disruptive technologies. In the foreword to the book, which was published by Rheinwerk Verlag (SAP PRESS), CEO Christian Klein puts it this way: "Since SAP was founded in 1972, we have been automating business processes there [. . .] From the very beginning, our unique selling proposition has been the ability to map business processes seamlessly across the entire value chain." The present book, on the other hand, is not a SAP book but a platform-independent IoT practical guide for logistics and production. Let me put it this way: for some, SAP will have the most compelling tools and IT instruments. But the competition never sleeps and may be a better fit for you.

You might decide to go with Oracle, my fourth and final vendor example. In an online text [5] published by the company in collaboration with Intel, big data strategist Paul Sonderegger writes:

> Not even service providers easily escape the competitive issues raised by the IoT. Banks are worried because watches, rings and even jacket lapels with corresponding electronic equipment are getting involved in payment transactions. Health insurers are grappling with the implications of wearable health sensors. They're all wondering how to deal with it. The first answer is cloud technologies. Oracle's Internet of Things cloud service, for example, can establish secure two-way connections to such devices (directly or through a portal), analyze data from those devices in real time and link it to enterprise apps, then do something with it. But it doesn't have to stop there. Oracle IoT Cloud Service also uses Oracle Database Exadata Cloud Service to link said device data to operational warehousing. Another great connection is with Oracle Big Data Discovery Cloud Service: this facilitates the exploration of device data in parallel with the analysis of data about customers, customer service or specific business operations—where new correlations and patterns may emerge.

Let me briefly summarize a few keywords that we have encountered in the advertising offerings in particular: there are the virtues of openness, security, stability, performance, scalability, and efficiency. We find the goal of being able to map business processes seamlessly across the entire value chain. It's about device and data interoperability, about the possibility of reading devices with the help of sensors and controlling them via actuators. The special features of device descriptions, interactions with machine learning processes, and cloud technologies will also be addressed. Do you need all this? Is anything particularly important? Hopefully, we can approach the answers to these in the following sections. As I said, no one has a monopoly on the perfect IoT platform. Competition is fierce, and the market remains in flux. Logistics 4.0 and Industry 4.0 are driving forces here.

3.3.2 IIoT as a Separate Market Segment

The term Industrial Internet of Things (IIoT) was already introduced in Sect. 1.2.3. In the following, I would like to elaborate on the specifics of the Industrial Internet of Things in a bit more detail. The Industrial Internet of Things differs from the general IoT in that IIoT technologies are designed for use in asset-intensive industries with many assets and special environments. The deployment requirements in IIoT are complex and often regulated. An IIoT solution must also take into account operational systems (OTs) such as industrial control systems (ICS), process control systems, or supervisory control and data acquisition (SCADA) systems. IIoT platforms should be compatible with both these OT and enterprise IT applications.

Reliability and resilience are central to most IIoT solutions, especially because there may also be regulated security factors. The data generated by IIoT sensors are often critical to the operation of end devices. They can also affect the security outside of enterprises. Monitoring and managing critical devices and services essentially require constant availability. Compared to commercial and consumer-facing IoT solutions, some of which can reach millions of endpoints, IIoT solutions have significantly fewer endpoints. However, the volume of data generated by the endpoints, as well as the frequency and velocity of the data, is typically very high. Sensors often transmit data at millisecond intervals. IIoT solutions are therefore considered device-light but data-intensive.

Parallel to the growth of the general IoT market, the IIoT market is also growing larger as an important subsegment. Of the companies surveyed for the aforementioned "Internet of Things" study, one in four were already using IIoT, and more than one in three classified IIoT as an "essential technology." If we believe the "Magic Quadrant for Industrial IoT Platforms" published by Gartner in summer 2019, the use of IoT platforms in industry will double between 2019 and 2023:

> By 2023, 30% of industrial enterprises will have full, on-premises deployments of IIoT platforms, up from 15% in 2019. [6]

The German market for the Industrial Internet of Things and Industrie 4.0 is considered one of the largest in the world. The study "The German Industrial IoT Market 2017–2022: Facts and Figures," backed by eco-Verband der Internetwirtschaft e.V. and market research firm Arthur D. Little, has predicted that the German IIoT market is expected to grow to around 16.8 billion euros in annual revenue by 2022. That would be more than double the 2017 figure. The reasoning was plausible in itself, considering that Germany has a fairly high robot density for Europe, a strong automotive industry, and a globally important role in mechanical and plant engineering. However, the following applies to these reports— and of course all the other forecasts and trend reports cited here: no one could have anticipated the corona pandemic that hit us, our economy, and our lives so suddenly in 2020. We will have to validate and reassess everything again at our leisure, which is why all the figures quoted here should be treated with due caution.

Analyst Knud Lasse Lueth from IoT Analytics GmbH (see Fig. 3.2) recently classified the market development for IoT platforms as a further fragmentation rather than market consolidation. However, there is a concentration: the top ten providers have a combined market share of almost 60%. According to Knud Lasse Lueth, half of the IoT platform providers surveyed focus on manufacturing and the use of IoT in industrial environments, that is, IIoT. Energy and mobility are also large market segments. The typical use cases cover fields such as condition monitoring, energy management, and quality control. Predictive maintenance is also important, which I will discuss in more detail in connection with artificial intelligence.

If you ask me personally, my opinion is as follows: Germany continues to play a leading role in mechanical engineering. All we have to do now is be open to the new business models and opportunities that arise from the linking of different technologies that IIoT makes possible.

3.4   Selection Criteria for IoT Platforms

As you have seen, a wide range of IoT platforms is available on the market. This includes an IIoT solution tailored to Logistics 4.0 and Industry 4.0, which is growing continuously. The solutions differ in price, of course, which is almost always a decisive criterion at the end of the day, if you ask me. But as I have already indicated, the decision in favor of a particular platform is in many cases a strategic choice. Those who see it that way are unlikely to take the decision lightly or be skimpy on budget, whatever the constraints may be at the time. Platform functionality can be tailored to specific industries or can be more generalist. One platform is particularly secure and the other particularly flexible and customizable. On the provider side, as you have seen, there are not only established software providers such as IBM, SAP, Microsoft, Amazon Web Services, or Cisco but also start-ups with special IoT offerings. In addition, transforming traditional companies such as Bosch and Siemens are shaping the competition.

In my book *IoT with SAP* (ISBN 978–3–8362-7472-2), you will find a small criteria catalog on page 134 with the following three guiding aspects: scenario, hardware, and processes and IT systems. With regard to the scenario, you could ask yourself, for example, in which area of application IoT should be used (primarily in production or rather in plant management). Should the data analyses be linked to the process-controlling IT systems, or would it be sufficient to present the insights from the IoT data separately? One hardware question is about integrated sensor systems vs. separate IoT hardware, which I discuss in Sect. 3.4.2. Another might be: Do we need edge computing for our purposes (see Chaps. 1 and 2)? The third guiding aspect means criteria such as: Which business processes does the IoT scenario include, and which IT systems are relevant for these processes?

In an online article at the [7] end of 2018, author Jan Rodig, who is also familiar with the subject, summarized ten topics (slightly abbreviated here) that could be used for comparison:

1. **Embedded software development kit (SDK)**: Which device and gateway implementations does the SDK support?
2. **Cloud connectivity**: How are certificates and firmware on devices to be updated in the field?
3. **Scaling**: Does the solution scale automatically, and to what extent does it do so?
4. **Server-side interaction with IoT devices**: Are online and offline events actively signaled by the IoT devices?
5. **IT security and data protection**: Can user and operational data be stored separately?
6. **Vendor lock-in**: What changes are necessary when switching providers, and how much effort is required?

7. **IoT device production**: How are device identifiers generated?
8. **Administration**: How can certain administration functions be efficiently integrated into existing enterprise applications such as ERP or CRM?
9. **Hosting**: Does the IoT provider support geographically distributed rollouts?
10. **Support and SLAs**: Do the response and recovery times of the IoT service provider's support services match?

In Sect. 3.4.1, I would like to present a Fraunhofer study in more detail, which is a good starting point for clarifying for yourself which functions and criteria you want to look at when comparing different IoT platforms. As is the case with trends and dynamic markets, there are occasionally a few competitors mixed in with the many great providers that don't quite offer what you would imagine an IoT platform would offer in 2021. So even if you don't work with the criteria catalog or the study, be a little careful that someone doesn't label M2M connectivity or Infrastructure as a Service (IaaS) solutions with the IoT platform label when in fact they are still missing the functionality necessary for that.

In addition to the overview study and its comparison criteria, we will look at the difference between integrated and discrete sensors in Sect. 3.4.2 because, after all, not all IoT devices are the same. In Sect. 3.4.3, I will say a few words about data and IT security in the context of IoT platforms since this topic is becoming increasingly important. In Sect. 3.5, you will find a small digression on the subject of multicloud strategies, which also has something to do with the previously mentioned aspects of hosting and vendor lock-in.

3.4.1 Fraunhofer Study as a Decision-Making Aid

In summer 2017, the Fraunhofer Institute for Industrial Engineering IAO in Stuttgart published "IT Platforms for the Internet of Things (IoT). Basis of Intelligent Products and Services." Six authors joined forces for this: Tobias Krause, Oliver Strauß, Gabriele Scheffler, Holger Kett, Kristian Lehmann, and Thomas Renner. The aim of this study was to give companies "as objective an overview as possible of the most important IoT platforms on the German-speaking market and to make them comparable on the basis of concrete functionalities." The study is intended to serve as a "selection tool in the search for a suitable IoT platform for the development of individual, intelligent products and services."

Probably the biggest disadvantage of this study is that it is from 2017 and therefore already partially out of date. Accordingly, some providers are missing, for example, the 2017 foundation IOTech and Adamos, an Open Manufacturing Platform with a network of more than 20 machine and plant manufacturers and ten supporting software companies. Alibaba is also not mentioned. This Chinese online giant also recently engaged in the market of IoT and cloud platforms. On the other hand, there is no more recent follow-up study by the aforementioned institute (as of fall 2020), and the analysis has advantages that may well offset these disadvantages. With Fraunhofer as the source, it is comparatively objective and to a certain extent vendor-neutral, at least more neutral than Cisco, SAP, or IBM could be in comparable publications. One selection criterion for the vendors studied was that they have significant sales and support for Germany. The methodology used by the authors for their comparison is based on an easily comprehensible pattern that you could adopt for your own assessment or modify and supplement. The publication costs just under €100 from Fraunhofer. It can be ordered online at https://shop.iao.fraunhofer.de/publikationen/it-plattformen-fr-das-internet-der-dinge-iot.html. However, you can also find the study free of charge on the web by going to IT sites like Funkschau.de.

If we look at the names of the platforms and platform providers analyzed, the whole thing still seems topical in 2021, especially since most of the solutions—at least in their first version—came onto the market before 2015, with manufacturers such as SAP, Oracle, Microsoft, Bosch et al. making a marketing overhaul every few years and adapting their names to what the market supposedly understands better and what supports their positioning. In addition to OpenIoTFog from the Fraunhofer Institute for Open Communication Systems (FOKUS), the following platforms were evaluated in detail:

- IoT Cloud Service (ORACLE)
- ThingWorx (Parametric Technology PTC)
- edbic, edpem (eurodata tec GmbH)
- S/4HANA (SAP SE)
- Bosch IoT Suite (Bosch Software Innovations)
- FIWARE – Open Source Future Internet Ware (Smart Labs)
- M2M and IoT communication solutions for mobile communications, satellite communications, and low-power radio networks (Arkessa GmbH)
- IBM Watson IoT Platform (IBM)
- HPE Universal IoT Platform (Hewlett Packard Enterprise Germany)
- elastic.io Integration Platform (elastic.io GmbH)
- Pivotal Cloud Foundry as a Service (Virtustream Deutschland GmbH)
- MES HYDRA (MPDV Mikrolab GmbH)
- MindSphere (Siemens AG)
- CENTERSIGHT IoT platform (Device Insight GmbH)
- PULSE (Agheera)
- BEDM Industry 4.0 Framework (BEDM GmbH)
- BEDM Energy Monitoring (BEDM GmbH)
- iTAC.MES.Suite (iTAC Software AG)
- AXPERIENCE (Axiros GmbH)
- People System Things (PST) (M2MGO)
- Cloud of Things (Deutsche Telekom AG)
- Software AG IoT Platform Services & Edge Services (Software AG)

These vendors and solutions are characterized and compared using a reference model—a similar approach to the one you learned about in Chap. 2, only in this case for platforms rather than an overall IoT architecture—that looks at eight core areas

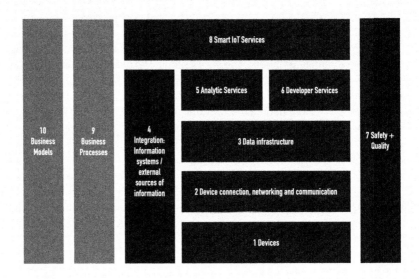

Fig. 3.3 Reference model of the study for the classification of platforms based on "IT Platforms for the Internet of Things (IoT). Basis of intelligent products and services," the Fraunhofer Institute for Industrial Engineering in Stuttgart, IAO (2017)

and also at business processes and business models as cross-cutting areas (see Fig. 3.3).

In the main section, the products are evaluated with overview tables that show what is and what is not included in the solution in each case. Such comparative inventories are somewhat reminiscent of the German consumer advocate magazine Stiftung Warentest, even if the striking scores are missing. They are available for the aspects of industry coverage, infrastructure, and hosting and services for analysis, development, and security, among others.

The analyses also look at whether the services included are part of the in-house service or whether functions and interfaces from third-party providers are added. This is interesting, for example, with regard to data centers and the international data agreements discussed in Sect. 3.3. While the tables help with quick comparisons, product profiles can provide more detailed information about the favored offerings.

As I said, if you are most interested in precisely those providers that are not represented in the study, the methodology alone is unlikely to be of interest to you, in which case the whole shebang will probably not be worth the time invested for you. But this Fraunhofer study is definitely useful as an introduction to market research and also as an expert opinion on specific solutions.

3.4.2   Integrated Versus Separate Sensors

An important difference in the context of IoT networks and IIoT platforms concerns the interaction of physical things, sensors, and data. In general, we can distinguish two groups of IoT hardware: integrated sensor systems are already built in; they are already present in machines or industrial plants. Separate sensor systems are only attached subsequently, either to the devices and machines or to special equipment.

Most industrial plants and machines today have control systems and software that not only control processes but can also pass on data. Common systems for this are programmable logic controllers (PLCs) and supervisory control and data acquisition (SCADA). If data flow from such systems into the IoT network, the IoT applications connected to the platform can also tap into the information of interest for their purposes. In most cases, only part of the acquired status and control data is relevant for the application, which is why selection and data filtering are continuously being developed. One approach is services that rely on edge computing (see Chap. 1): gateways can thin out data before passing on, for example, only temperature or position data. After all, systems should not be clogged with data garbage when it is sufficient to report only anomalies and boundary violations or certain triggers for follow-up actions. Telematics systems in cars and trucks, which record things like position, acceleration, and fuel consumption, also typically belong to the group of integrated sensor systems. Such data, which are of interest to logistics experts and traffic managers alike, can be recorded via adapters to the vehicle's internal networks. The on-board diagnostics standard (OBD) is commonly used for this purpose.

Separate sensor systems are, on the one hand, typical for retrofitting older plants, devices, and machines. For economic and practical reasons, such retrofitting often makes more sense for companies than completely replacing old models with new series and generations. On the other hand, separate systems also exist to make rather "hard" hardware such as Euro pallets or containers smarter on their own. Basically, any technology that is retrofitted to machines or equipment in order to capture real-time information and make it usable for business processes falls into this category. This ranges from small Global Positioning System (GPS) trackers on pallets in warehouses to complex sensor systems for seamless monitoring of containers in global logistics processes. Data are transmitted via a wireless local area network (WLAN), Bluetooth, radio, GPS, or the mobile network. In order for the sensors and algorithms in the IoT platform to understand each other, they must speak the same language. The protocols already briefly mentioned, such as http or OPC, are particularly important for this. Since many hardware manufacturers include some form of software solution that separate sensors can interface with, it is important that an IoT platform be able to integrate third-party solutions appropriately so that no data is lost. In the digital world, it has to be possible to associate IoT devices on containers with the relevant logistics or transportation process. This is most often referred to as pairing. This comes into play, for example, when a good has arrived at the end of a supply chain and it is therefore appropriate to unpair product X and IoT thing Y again. In addition, the separate systems must also function in the physical world.

Perhaps they need to withstand water, wind, pollution, or temperature fluctuations. In addition, battery and rechargeable battery life should meet requirements. These points concern logistics and often additionally the use behavior of end customers.

3.4.3   Data and IT Security

Competition among IT companies and software houses is one side. The other side is that when it comes to computer technology, there is still an arms race between hackers and cybercriminals and the providers of IT security, data security, computer security, mobile phone security, etc. While it can already have unpleasant consequences for private computer and Internet users if someone with criminal energy exploits security gaps, the risk for companies is of course incomparably greater—even more so if they are involved in critical infrastructure (CRITIS) (in the physical or digital world). The 2018 Cyber Security Study, in which the German-government-initiated Alliance for Cyber Security, of which I am also a member, surveyed IT security leaders at more than 1000 companies (and organizations), states the following: programs were injected into corporate IT to perform malicious operations in 53% of the IT attacks on record. More than 80% of those affected experienced operational disruptions and outages as a result.

For the "Internet of Things" study mentioned above, the market researchers also asked companies about their fears and security concerns. The result is as follows: "As in the previous year, companies are most afraid of hacker attacks and DDoS attacks [...]." In case you're just wondering what DDoS means: it stands for distributed denial of service, that is, server outages and overloads that are triggered intentionally (by criminal or politically motivated hackers) or unintentionally (by excessive demand). In any case, the result is that the website is down—and that can cause quite a few problems these days, especially since consumers are becoming more impatient with than tolerant of online accidents.

Just as consumers pay attention to security when they visit websites, join networks, and use apps, IT and data security is also increasingly becoming a decisive criterion when companies opt for IoT platforms and related services. This is not just about protection against disruptions and failures, in the sense that IT runs reliably over the long term. Data security is also part of the equation: internal business data should be protected from unauthorized access. End-customer data should be collected and processed in such a way that they benefit the company without harming customers. It is precisely for such aspects of data protection, which touch on legal issues as well as technical details, that the security of cloud solutions plays an important role.

On the one hand, we can increase security with flanking measures: additional software components, virtual private network (VPN) services, antivirus programs, and firewalls. We can also set up and monitor rules that take into account the human risk factor in order to control access to cloud components by our own workforce. In addition, as a company, when choosing suppliers and partners, you can make sure that the other companies and individual contractors take the concepts of security and privacy by design/default seriously. This can be demonstrated by appropriate certificates and successful lighthouse projects. In addition, cloud-specific security standards help us. The Cloud Security Alliance (CSA) has developed the Security, Trust, Assurance, and Registry (STAR) certificate for cloud providers. An IoT cloud provider receives this certificate after passing a specially designed examination. This examination is based on the requirements of the International Organization for Standardization (ISO) standard for information security (ISO/IEC 27001). The CSA has developed a cloud control matrix that analyzes several processes and matches them with proven solutions. Other security standards for cloud solutions and IoT networking include the Open Information Security Management Maturity Model (O-ISM3), the Information Security Forum (ISF) standard, and the COBIT (Control Objectives for Information and Related Technology) standard.

Bundesdruckerei, a limited liability company owned by the Federal Republic of Germany, is also in the running for the most secure cloud solutions. As such, it is allowed to advertise like its competition, which it does, for example, in trade magazines such as IT Mittelstand. The warning "No server is unhackable" is followed in the advertisement there [8] by the caption "Why data is safest in the cloud, of all places" by advertising for the bDrive solution, a particularly secure cloud offering. According to its own information, Bundesdruckerei works exclusively with ISO-certified cloud service providers from Germany. The quality seal "Made in Germany" has become "Hosted in Germany" here. This local brand is likely to be quite important in the future. Bear in mind that data protection is not quite as important in the USA and China as it is in the European Union (EU). I will come back to the current legal situation in Sect. 3.5. A second trick used by Bundesdruckerei is a special encryption technology called CloudRaid, which not only encrypts files but also splits them into several parts that are stored decentrally instead of centrally. The idea behind this is this: a hacker could thus steal fragments of a file at most, but only authorized users have all the metadata and decryption elements needed to access the entire file. The end-to-end encryption algorithm, combined with the decentralized clouds and identity management, should ensure maximum security in the cloud. The government-oriented "Hosted in Germany" competes with the Nextcloud offering, which has already won over government agencies in several EU countries. Both cloud services, in turn, are of course in global competition with near-worldwide solutions from Microsoft, Dropbox Inc., Google, etc.

3.5 Multicloud Strategies

Surely you don't want to be dependent on a single provider for all your applications, platforms, and services in the Internet of Things. The multicloud concept is primarily aimed at this need not to be locked into the cloud by one provider and to minimize dependencies. In contrast, of course, is the desire of corporate IT to have to manage as few contacts and providers as possible.

Multicloud architectures use multiple cloud computing and storage services for applications, software, and services in a heterogeneous architecture. The services used come from different cloud hosting providers. Multicloud architectures can consist of two or more public clouds and several private clouds.

Public clouds provide cloud services to a large number of users over the public Internet. Private clouds provide services exclusively and privately for specific organizations. In contrast to a hybrid cloud (a mixed form of public and private clouds), the different deployment modes (public, private, legacy) are not important for the multicloud.

Typical of a multicloud strategy is to use multiple cloud providers for IaaS, PaaS, and SaaS services simultaneously.

Arguments in favor of a multicloud strategy include the following:

- Cost reduction in cloud services
- High flexibility due to more choice
- Facilitating local compliance (within a region or country)
- Geographical distribution of processing requirements to physically tighter cloud units
- Minimization of latencies
- Disaster defense

You've probably already guessed it: anyone who deals more intensively with (I) IoT platforms cannot avoid the topics of cloud computing and cloud security. Cloud-based applications are increasingly replacing the costly IT in-house operation of the past, especially since service-oriented reference models are an important part of the digital transformation, for both business-to-business (B2B) and business-to-consumer (B2C) markets. You only have to run through in your mind how often you have to deal with Amazon Web Services, Google Drive and Google One, Microsoft Teams and Azure, or Apple's cloud services, both privately and in your day-to-day work. In this context, the terms hyperscaling and hyperscaler come up again and again. What is meant by this is that large Internet companies need the largest server farms, the most powerful data centers, and the most computing power for their own business models and have thus created a market position for themselves that allows them to offer end customers particularly cost-effective and efficient solutions. Scale and economies of scale meet the computing and online business, if you will.

The term multicloud stands for the idea of avoiding dependence on a single cloud provider. There can be different reasons for this. Technically, the question of where and how nodes and platform components are distributed geographically may be relevant. A combination of cloud providers may reduce latencies. In terms of security, data concentration may also not be desirable because that would give hackers and viruses too much power. And then there are the political requirements for IT and data security, which, for example, strongly affect data traffic with the US companies that are central to the cloud market.

A new data protection regulation has been in force in the European Union for a good 5 years, updating initial laws in 2016 after several years of preparation, and has been fully applicable throughout the EU since May 2018. The General Data Protection Regulation (GDPR) has created new challenges for businesses, including medium, small, and one-person businesses. Even nonprofit associations, which have no budget at all for IT infrastructure and information security, must now comply with the law, which led in some cases to very sensitive measures. For example, contact data in sports clubs were only released to club colleagues in a very restrictive manner, which sometimes greatly complicated club life.

The fact that the legislation is intended to take into account professional and commercial activities; that some passages concern data traffic via apps, software, and websites; and that it also contains requirements for data protection officers, evidence, and penalties worth millions of euros has increased the pressure to systematically address the issues of data protection and data security. Since the General Data Protection Regulation (GDPR) also affects software use, there is a debate on every solution on the market, as it were. In times of corona, this mainly affected Zoom's video conferencing service. But even corporate bestsellers such as Microsoft 365 or Google Analytics are considered problematic in terms of the requirements of the EU-wide data protection regulation when interpreted strictly.

The US Clarifying Lawful Overseas Use of Data Act, in turn, was enacted a few weeks before the 2018 GDPR took full effect. This law, which is intended to regulate US authorities' access to stored data on the Internet and also affects companies from other countries, obliges Internet companies and IT service providers in the USA to grant the authorities there access to stored data, regardless of whether these data are stored inside or outside the USA. Authority sounds very innocuous here, but please think of the Central Intelligence Agency (CIA), the National Security Agency (NSA), and Edward Snowden, then we've reached the appropriate level of excitement. If a provider of cloud or communication solutions has to disclose its customer data, this may also include companies from Germany that are not actually allowed to share their data if they, in turn, take the GDPR seriously. Status: it's complicated. Since July 2020, it has become even more complicated. After the failed Safe Harbour agreement, the EU has now had to scrap the successor agreement with the USA, known as the Privacy Shield, because the European Court of Justice sees the data of EU citizens on the American side as not being sufficiently protected. More and more often, I see that cautious companies are looking for alternatives to Google, Microsoft, and the like that are developed and offered in the EU. This applies to individual software areas, such as calendar tools, and also to large software packages, ranging from office software to IoT platforms. Therefore, fueled by the data protection discussion, I see a new opportunity for European software and cloud providers because the American and Chinese services are likely to be used with very high concerns and precautions in the medium term for certain issues due to the previously mentioned circumstances in certain areas. Thus, the GDPR could act as a meaningful protection for the European software market, provided that we in the EU manage to offer scalable solutions before American and Chinese companies set up their server farms in the EU to comply with European data protection requirements.

A multicloud architecture should be heterogeneous, meaning you should use different cloud computing services and storage services for applications, not just software and services from a single source. One strategy may be to use multiple cloud providers for IaaS, PaaS, and SaaS services simultaneously. As a reminder, the concepts of Software as a Service (SaaS), Infrastructure as a Service (IaaS), and Platform as a Service (PaaS) were already introduced in Sect. 3.2. A multicloud architecture could also be composed of several public clouds and private clouds. Once again for a quick recap—public clouds provide cloud services over the public Internet so that as many users as possible can access them openly. Private clouds limit access, for example, to protect exclusive or security-relevant data and information. SAP, for example, has solved this problem for itself and its multicloud strategy in the age of hyperscaling by entering into partnerships with the American giants Amazon Web Services, Microsoft Azure, and Google Cloud Platform, plus Alibaba Cloud. Similar collaborations can be found with other groups. The way the market is currently developing and moving, there will probably also be a lot more happening in terms of partnerships and collaboration in the coming years.

Let me conclude this chapter by referring once again to the "Internet of Things 2019" study, in which companies were also asked about the role of cloud applications and about multicloud strategies. Almost every second company surveyed (48.1%) was already using cloud applications. Cloud services were at the top of the list of planned investments (38.8%). In response to the question "Which functions of cloud platforms are essential for you?" a quarter of company employees named the criterion "multi-cloud capability (networking of infrastructures)." Only security and data storage functions received more mentions. The networking of infrastructures will be the subject of Chap. 4 when we look at how IoT platforms and typical forms of enterprise software interact and (hopefully) harmonize with each other. I hope you are at least a little smarter about your IoT platform decision after this chapter.

References

1. Cisco. (2020). *Global networking trends report*, 5.
2. Cisco. (2020). *Global networking trends report*, 16.
3. Mauerer, J., et al. (2019). Internet of Things. *Study*, 19.
4. Handelsblatt. (2020). *IoT platform comparison: Berlin provider scores with interoperability.* 01.07.2020. https://unternehmen.handelsblatt.com/iot-plattformen-vergleich.html
5. Sonderegger, P. (n.d.). *Big Data and IoT. How IoT and Big Data together open up immense opportunities.* https://www.oracle.com/de/big-data/features/bigdata-and-iot.
6. Gartner. (2019). *Magic quadrant for industrial IoT platforms.*
7. Rodig, J. (2018). *Welche IoT platform ist die Richtige? Kriterien für die Auswahl (Which IoT platform is the right one? Criteria for selection).* Dec 18, 2018. https://www.channelpartner.de/a/welche-iot-plattform-ist-die-richtige,3332900
8. Advertorial. (2019). Why data is safest in the cloud, of all places. *IT Mittelstand*, 9.

IoT and Enterprise Software

4

Enterprise information technology (IT), enterprise software, and IT infrastructure are increasingly contributing to competitive advantage—and for some, disadvantage. In addition to high-tech technologies, cloud applications, and mobile apps, this particularly affects the enterprise core with its classic enterprise software components. For some years now, the System Analysis and Program Development (SAP) has been using the term digital core, which I find very appropriate for the entire on-premise software world. The image of the core makes sense insofar as the company as a business organism has certain core processes, and these have not changed significantly despite the digital transformation. Companies have to prepare balance sheets, write invoices, make purchases, process sales, make offers, and much more. These processes affect the core of the company.

Interacting with service providers, partners, suppliers, customers, machines, and things, companies are outward looking and need ways to integrate their core processes with the outside world. If you want to network in the Internet of Things (IoT) in the 5G (fifth-generation technology standard for broadband cellular networks) era, taking connectivity and speed, as well as security standards for hardware and software, into account, you need both IoT systems and classic enterprise software. The IoT systems and the networked devices and machines interact with the backend systems within the enterprise, such as enterprise resource planning (ERP), manufacturing execution systems (MES), warehouse management systems (WMS), and transport management systems (TMS). This requires new generations of enterprise software that can handle modern, up-to-date protocols and interfaces while also ensuring up-to-date security standards.

> At this point, I would like to clear up a misunderstanding regarding enterprise resource planning (ERP) and business intelligence (BI) software. An ERP system integrates the central functions in the company. In doing so, its

(continued)

A. Holtschulte, *Digital Supply Chain and Logistics with IoT*, Management for Professionals, https://doi.org/10.1007/978-3-030-89408-5_4

architecture and centralized data structures alone help break down silos. ERP software collects, stores, and manages data on business activities. It can cut process costs and make processes transparent. BI software and ERP are very closely interwoven in terms of processes and data and are therefore often lumped together. However, BI and ERP are completely different applications. While ERP collects and calculates data on business incidents, BI software analyzes that data, presents the results in dashboards, and shares the results with other systems using certain interfaces. BI software aims to present data in an understandable and easily accessible way. With a certain and concise presentation of the results, business executives get the information, analysis, trends, and forecasts they need to make strategic decisions.

Today, IT managers dealing with the renewal or initial acquisition of software in the company are quickly faced with fundamental questions and strategic challenges. This often involves more than simply adopting a single service to the existing software landscape. More and more often, the art is to bring everything together sustainably and create an agile working environment in which workloads and processes can change and move flexibly. For example, if you want to migrate your ERP system from its predecessor SAP ERP ECC to the current product version SAP S/4HANA, it would be smart to also consider compatible offerings from infrastructure providers, platform providers, and software providers as part of a multicloud strategy (see also Chap. 3). Or let's take the area of customer relationship management (CRM) as an example: CRM software supports you in managing customer relationships and enables the structured, and in some cases automated, collection of customer contact data. Such software allows us to plan customer campaigns such as mailings and campaigns. It automatically reminds us of events related to customers. As a rule, these offerings can be obtained as Software-as-a-Service (SaaS) solutions that are available in the cloud. But there are also various on-premise solutions or even free versions. You can book specific packages—from quoting and sales pipeline to landing page management and automatic newsletter series. New CRM software should integrate with the existing ERP system in a way that makes sense, including keeping master data all in one clean place.

In the following, we take a closer look at the enterprise resource planning (ERP), manufacturing execution system (MES), warehouse management system (WMS), and transport management system (TMS) software areas since these solutions interest us in the context of IoT. Indeed, they generally manage things that are actually physically moved in the real world and that have an impact on business management processes. On the one hand, I'll explain the role of each software element and show you how to find the most suitable solution for your business; on the other hand, I'll go into the interaction between the Internet of Things and these software systems.

4.1   General Tips for Software Acquisition

After countless software tenders in the logistics environment and many years with one of the largest software manufacturers in the world, I can give you some advice and assistance for purchasing and implementing enterprise software. These basically apply to all software solutions that you could purchase and implement for a lot of money: enterprise resource planning (ERP), warehouse management systems (WMS), transport management systems (TMS), manufacturing execution systems (MES), and telematics systems or even customer relation management (CRM).

The following aspects must be taken into account:

- **Requirements**: analyze, describe, and document your requirements. This helps you internally, and you show the software manufacturers that you have concrete ideas and don't want just any old solution. I myself stick to a standardized procedure when analyzing and recording processes so that I can scan and evaluate the software offers on the market very quickly. Experience shows that the work invested here is saved later: in the creation of requirement specifications, blueprints, solution concepts, solution designs, and specifications. These are still all the traditional terms that come from the waterfall model. But believe me—if you do your homework when describing the requirements, you will also get through an agile software implementation much more relaxed, if that's what you are planning.
- **Codesign**: involve your employees in the selection, decision-making, and imple-mentation whenever possible. After all, they will be working with the software later—and if they don't like it, satisfaction will drop, which will have a negative impact on team spirit and productivity. Regular meetings, demos, and mailings can help keep them informed about the project and selection process.
- **Heads**: find the perfect project manager for your software project. Whether internal or external, you should trust this person 100%. In the project team, the most important representatives from the involved areas work together. If you are following through with your project in an agile manner, find a product owner and scrum master who will pull colleagues along and communicate the method well.
- **Budget**: plan a suitable project budget with an appropriate buffer. If necessary, get help with a rough project cost evaluation. Once you have the budget and buffer, add another 20% on top.
- **Independence**: opting for a complete package from a single source for software implementation, support, and purchase can be convenient, but it could also result in a strong dependence on this one partner (keywords: lock-in effect, vendor lock-in). This applies to prices, for example: if the vendor, which offers consulting and support at the same time, decides to increase its daily rates for support and consultants by 20%, you have little room for maneuver. Some software vendors offer a good network of partners that maintain the software and do the consulting on site. This would be a slightly more flexible way of working together.

On the manufacturer's side, you should take a close look at the following points:

- **Vendor profile**: When selecting vendors, take a good look at how they have evolved over the past few years. What does the roadmap of the companies look like? Can you identify a release strategy? By this, we mean the following: Does the software vendor plan innovation in the next few years that will be a benefit to your business? Has the vendor actually implemented topics on its roadmap in the past, or were they mostly just visions that burst like a soap bubble as soon as they were supposed to be incorporated into the product?
- **Support**: Pay attention to what the software vendor's support structure is like. Is there a global network of people to take care of your problems with the software, and should it matter? No one wants the warehouse management system to fail and not be able to get a shipment in or out of the warehouse. A production control software failure should not be underestimated either because then you wouldn't be able to produce anything.
- **Cloud solutions**: It is also interesting to see how the vendor relates to cloud solutions. For example, does it offer cloud alternatives for traditional programs that it originally launched and sold as on-premise solutions? Are there certain hybrid models that might fit your requirements better?
- **Base technology**: Is the base technology used by the software vendor still future-capable? Some solutions that you could use to control your business were developed on a technological base that is no longer supported or maintained. If, for example, the interfaces and application programming interfaces (APIs) are outdated, then leave them alone.
- **Usability**: Does the software vendor provide apps for mobile devices? Can employees log in to the enterprise software system via a browser? What do the user interfaces, the screen masks, that your employees would work with on a daily basis look like? Should app- and computer-savvy employees get nostalgic every workday because the user interface design and user processes remind them of the early 2000s? Not a good idea. A more modern, intuitive user experience looks more professional, shortens training time, and increases the fun factor when working with the software.
- **Customizing**: Check the extent to which the system can be adapted to your specific company requirements. The more you can customize the system settings to your processes, the less you will have to spend later on individual programming, which always involves risk and is significantly more expensive than using standard functionalities.

I have experienced projects in which the implementation of enterprise software was rushed. In retrospect, these projects can unfortunately only be summarized as follows: poorly done and expensively paid for. On one occasion, for example, very complex business processes were implemented in the ERP software in a very short time. Sensible standard functionalities, for example, for the separation of sales channels, were not used. The result was that, after the fact, extensive programming was done in the interface to support this functionality. It's better to take enough time for implementation and employee training. I wouldn't rush into anything when it comes to purchasing, either. Don't buy until you are 100% convinced. Why do I mention this? Isn't it a matter of course? I have often seen my clients buy several software solutions from one vendor at once in order to get a higher discount. However, by doing so, they bought software that they didn't need afterward, or they bought too many software licenses that weren't needed in the end. Surplus licenses and unneeded software/package components can usually only be returned under poor conditions, which is why they often gather dust on the shelf as so-called shelfware but still incur costs for maintenance or subscription. Therefore, it's better to be a little hesitant about buying them. As long as you haven't signed the contract yet, in my experience you usually get relatively good support from the software vendor. Remember, the potential new customer is king. But if the vendor already has the signed contract in his pocket, things can quickly look different.

4.2   Enterprise Resource Planning (ERP)

The word resources can stand for many things: it can be about money that you have or don't have, about raw materials and energy production, and even about the skills that different people bring to the table. If I were to ask my children, for example, what comes to mind when they think of this term, they would probably come up with Fridays for Future rather than economic models or the ERP software that their sometimes rather strange father deals with from time to time. Enterprise resource planning (ERP) is an established term for the entrepreneurial task of planning, controlling, and managing resources such as capital, personnel, operating resources, materials, and technology in a timely manner and in line with the company's objectives. Since computers can calculate faster and more reliably than humans, professional companies have been using software for calculating for a while now. It's clear that business management has a lot to do with numbers: on the one hand, personnel and material costs, rent, taxes, and other expenses and, on the other, the booked and projected revenues, sales, profits; then the number of pieces, quantities, and hourly, daily, and weekly planning; the delivery intervals—Who calculates all this voluntarily without resorting to aids? Do you? Are you that in love with mathematics?

Guess which programs Claus Wellenreuther, Hans-Werner Hector, Klaus Tschira, Dietmar Hopp, and Hasso Plattner developed first when they founded the company SAP (System Analysis and Program Development) in 1972. The first programs handled payroll and accounting. Today, you can find these functions in any ERP system, wrapped up with other resource management functions. The business processes you organize and perform in your ERP system are essential: finance, controlling, purchasing, inventory management, distribution, sales, personnel management, and taxes. You map all these areas digitally in ERP software. Closely linked to ERP is the material resource planning (MRP) module. In order to purchase next months' material for production according to customer orders or demand, I have to take into account what sales are like. I have to think about factors that are relevant to my products and services, such as the weather. Maybe it's snow shovels or umbrellas. MRP is also an important area in the apparel industry. To estimate material quantities correctly and plan purchasing, I need an overview of customer orders.

ERP software is more than pure accounting software, also more than pure enterprise resource planning. The functionality is more holistic, focused on all figures and processes in the company. That's why the ability to interact internally and externally is so important: with the central IoT platform, with devices, and with other software in your own company and in other companies. Of course, you want to have a good and reliable system for this digital enterprise core around resource planning. For companies, it can be a milestone to introduce such a system for the first time after they have been in their market segment for a while and have grown. Modernizing an aging ERP software system in a sustainable way is also a challenge. Some time ago, I read the following in the trade journal IT-Mittelstand: "The introduction of a new ERP system is usually on the agenda of every IT manager of a medium-sized company only once in his professional life. Because if it is successfully introduced, the useful life is 15, 20 or more years [1]." On the other hand, many a business leader such as the chief information officer (CIO), chief finance officer (CFO), or even many chief executive officers (CEOs) have ended their careers in the chaos of an ERP, WMS, or TMS implementation.

I consider 15–20 years to be a steep proposition in view of the rapid IT developments and the dynamic software market, but the core of the statement is correct. In Sect. 4.2, I go into ERP systems in more detail. Among other things, this includes an interview in IT-Mittelstand [2] with two specialists, from which I have selected an interesting passage below about the right time for ERP modernization. The editors interviewed Ralf Bachthaler, then CEO of Asseco Solutions AG, which has a +++coffee count on its website and calls itself an ERP pioneer, and Karl Tröger, business development manager of PSI Automotive & Industry GmbH, which has a +++walnut in its logo and ERP and MES systems in its product range. The question was: When should a proven ERP system be modernized with a view to transforming digitally? When is it mandatory to replace aging software? The two experts had the following to say about this:

> The ERP system still represents the central information hub in the company. In the course of Industry 4.0 and digitization, networked production data is now being added. [...] Accordingly, the architecture of the solution must be structured in such a way that external data sources such as machines or third-party applications can be easily integrated. If this is not the case or can only be realized at high cost, there are few alternatives to replacing the legacy system with a modern, future-proof ERP solution in my view.
> – Ralf Bachthaler.
>
> One [...] top requirement for every player in a production system is integration capability. This applies equally to machines and software. Today's modern ERP

(continued)

systems usually—not always—have the necessary connectivity and offer the described APIs for accessing the objects and methods of the ERP system. However, the full range of functions may not be available. It is then important to determine whether a) the given functionality is sufficient and/or b) can be extended. If [. . .] success-critical factors cannot be sufficiently taken into account, a company probably cannot avoid a reorientation [. . .].
– Karl Tröger.

Tröger also added that "cherished systems" can certainly be contemporary but that one should not cling to them so much that one closes one's eyes to meaningful innovations from newer competing products.

I think an elementary question when setting up and renewing ERP software, to be used as sensibly as possible in the IoT age, is: Which information and data are of permanent enterprise-wide interest, and which are not? For a better understanding, here's a practical example: sensors are in use in a production plant. These sensors record temperature curves for electric motors. They also record what current the motor is accessing. Increased demand could indicate that the motor is running at full load, perhaps even defective, or that the conveyor belt it is driving may have a defect. Experience shows that the motor will not sustain this load for very long since it was not designed for this. Now, does this information need to be taken into account in an ERP system or not? You could argue in favor of this: maintenance costs money. Prevention can prevent expensive repairs. That is resource planning. Shouldn't the software therefore use such sensor data to include them in model calculations and evaluate them from a business point of view so that we have a basis for decision-making and can plan the deployment of a maintenance technician and immediately order spare parts that are replaced on a regular basis during such maintenance?

As you will see in Chap. 5, regular maintenance according to the calendar will face competition in the future from predictive analytics and maintenance, that is, from the use of IoT in combination with artificial intelligence and algorithms for automated condition control and device monitoring. So it would be good if a modern ERP system would somehow integrate such sensor data. Let us now take the opposite position, which is incidentally already a mini-exercise for all those who have never had anything to do with design thinking (more on this in Chap. 6). So the skeptics counter: these data would overload the software instead of help. After all, the data would be pouring into the global planning software every millisecond, with no direct business information value. The whole software infrastructure would reach its limits. To take such a risk just so that you might have usable scenarios for maintenance issues wouldn't make sense. Hopefully, this fictitious discussion has not reminded you too much of real-life disputes and conflicts. It was simply meant to illustrate: it is not so easy to clarify at what point information becomes relevant to enterprise software. Not all information is useful at every point in the enterprise, and this is truer than ever in the age of big data (see Chap. 5).

Today, the Internet of Things can provide an industrial company with sensor data on the order of millions of data items. But merely collecting and analyzing this information is not enough. To truly benefit from these oceans of data, the insights must also lead to actions that improve business processes, whether maintenance schedules, logistics, or the actual products. The IoT data from Industry 4.0 environments should be operationalized in a meaningful way using the ERP system. Here, we're at the interaction of ERP software and the IoT platforms presented in Chap. 3: if the ERP tool is integrated into an IT architecture that allows sensor data and other IoT information to be collected, stored, and filtered, the huge amounts of data can be meaningfully compressed and passed on to the ERP system. If the software is running "on-site," that is, directly in the plant or production facility, it is probably enough for a small computer to absorb and process the information. Should any anomalies occur, targeted countermeasures can be taken in the right place. If the motor were to exceed a relevant value and run hot, maintenance would of course be required as quickly as possible. However, the product development and financial accounting departments and probably also management would not have to deal with this maintenance directly. That is why the ERP tool is better left free of such technical details. After all, in order to be able to manage, plan, and administer efficiently, you only want to find data there that are relevant to the overall operation.

If you are already a little deeper into ERP or regularly deal with process automation, you've probably come across the topic of robotic process automation (RPA) as an alternative to ERP software. I'd like to briefly address that discussion here by summarizing the pros and cons of RPA applications, which, simply put, are a play on bots. If you're in an industry where it's very important to automate and digitize processes but your company has a somewhat dusty ERP system in place, adding new functionality could be difficult while switching to modern software may be out of budget. "RPA offers a way out of this dilemma. That's because the technology mimics a human's interactions with user interfaces of software systems, replacing the programming interface." At least, this is how Dirk Bingler, CEO at Gus Deutschland GmbH, argued in an interview [3] on the interaction of RAP and ERP. He went on to explain that RPA technology can be used to accelerate and automate processes without having to intervene in existing ERP systems. As examples of applications, he mentioned master data maintenance, material management, processing of notices of termination, accounting processes, and searches for price comparisons. One could also add vacation requests or job applicant preselection. As Bingler puts it, "In principle, RPA makes sense wherever it's a matter of completing simply structured activities that follow recurring rules faster and more accurately than a human." This is because according to him, RPA applications are fast, available around the clock, do not make any careless mistakes, and document all work steps without gaps. With a view to the development of artificial intelligence (see Chap. 5), Bingler assumes that the so-called cognitive RPA "will also become a must-have in SMEs in the future—whether as an integrated component of ERP systems or as a stand-alone solution." That he is not entirely alone in this opinion is demonstrated, among other things, by the fact that SAP recently purchased the French RPA provider Contextor (more on SAP's role in the ERP market in Sect. 4.2).

But there are also voices that warn: RPA is only a glitch in historically evolved system landscapes; it cannot be a permanent solution. You can find some of them, for example, in a technical article [4] on RPA solutions entitled "Via the provisional solution to the goal." In it, several experts are rather critical of robotic process automation. If the RPA users do not coordinate well and transparently, this can lead to untraceable chaos on the front end. In addition, the quality of the data sometimes leaves much to be desired because RPA bots have problems with data duplicates and inconsistent master data. Value-added processes with compliance guidelines and processes with multiple approvals and decision-making levels are also not recommended as RPA playgrounds, according to the critics. One final thing—some vendors are touting the use of artificial intelligence in this environment. Be sure to take a closer look under the hood here before you get blinded by modern buzzwords. In almost all cases, you won't find artificial intelligence in these solutions. It's all about process automation, workflows, and the use of more or less complex algorithms for processing. In the end, it doesn't matter what the provider calls the technology. Make sure that the solution does what you expect it to do and have it demonstrated to you in a proof of concept (POC), that is, a small/mini-project, before you make an investment decision. We support such POCs at digit-ANTS and IN3-Group usually under the name Sprint 0.

So much for RPA. Let's get back to the ERP systems. Another challenge in resource planning with ERP software is to get the data flow technically clean. At the latest, when two platforms talk to each other—let's say a purchased IoT platform, as you learned about in Chap. 3, and the company's own ERP solution—we need a foolproof procedure to exchange and store the data. For example, if a workpiece leaves a certain area, geographical boundary, or defined production area, a signal is sent to the ERP system to prompt, "Please mark or post a new order for the workpiece." The software recognizes where the materials come from and where they go to. Based on this, the system draws its logical conclusions and acts accordingly following programmed rules—if everything works, anyway.

The deletion concepts and routines, as well as archiving, also play an important role in ERP. Storage space itself hardly costs any money, depending on the database technology, but at some point, it becomes expensive when a lot of data are generated. After all, it has to be sifted through and evaluated, backed up, and utilized. This takes time and capacity. Even if storage itself no longer costs much money, the more data that have to be evaluated, the longer are the evaluation times. And if you invest in a database solution such as SAP HANA, which combs through the data no longer on a row-by-row basis but rather on a column-by-column basis and keeps them in the main memory, then this contributes a lot to fast availability but is again an investment because less sophisticated database solutions also cost less.

Data collection mania can be an indicator of disorientation in companies. IT and software consultants therefore often conjure up offers for data inventories from their vendor's tray. Getting rid of superfluous data can be a very cleansing process for a company. You're now welcome to imagine cleanup champion Marie Kondō, if you know her, health-minimizing a US household that has gone off the rails. However, streamlining the digital lumber rooms and computer messes should be a matter for the boss.

As I have already mentioned in the general tips, even apart from such one-off maneuvers, it is advisable to clarify who is in charge of the company when it comes to ERP. Looking after the system and deciding what is to be evaluated in the software is an ongoing process that usually involves more than one competence. Usually, we need interdisciplinary teams with at least two people for this. At least one person should be well versed in the IT landscape and know how data are generated and stored. In most cases, the controlling department is also required so that we know what information is needed in the ERP in order to draw meaningful business conclusions.

Because it is business-relevant, sometimes sensitive, data that converge on your ERP system, it is important to regulate access authorizations wisely. Which employees have a legitimate interest to work with the systems and which do not? An example is this: a pragmatic employee wants to create a data record for a new supplier, post the goods' receipt, and confirm the invoice at the same time because this seems to him to be an efficient, sensible combination of individual steps. Seen in this light, it is understandable. But such seemingly innocuous processes can become a security risk: if the supplier's account data are stored, someone with the requisite criminal energy could feel invited to redirect the flow of funds. Unauthorized siphoning of cents quickly turns into millions when big data and a savvy hacker collide. All you have to do is read the annual IT security status report published by the German Federal Office for Information Security. The most recent such situation report available to me while writing this book is the one from 2019. It says some disturbing things: over 300,000 new malware variants enter circulation every day, and up to 110,000 bot infections of German systems a day enable dark schemes across the networked data world. In any case, the German Federal Office for Information Security (Bundesamt für Sicherheit in der Informationstechnik BSI) attests to the cybercriminals' "high level of expertise and innovation" [5]. As I mentioned in Sect. 3.2.3, malware is regularly infiltrated into corporate IT to perform malicious operations, leading to operational disruptions and outages time and again. I'm sure you'll agree when I say that in these times of big data and IoT, data protection has an important role to play. Widespread networking in the IoT era leads to new challenges for companies' protective measures. Theoretically, any part connected to the Internet can be hacked and taken over. In the industrial sector, when we talk about the Industrial Internet of Things (IIoT), you have to additionally consider that not only new but also retrofitted devices and machines are in use and send data to the ERP. The Internet of Things has reached a point where downstream security is no longer reliable enough. Better is the "Nip things in the bud" approach, which you have probably already encountered in the form of the labels "Security by Design" or "Security by Default" or "Privacy by Design/Default" explicitly for data security.

As far as the role of ERP solutions in the cloud is concerned, many experts share the following assessment by employees of ERP provider IFS Deutschland GmbH & Co. KG:

In terms of a holistic IT landscape, the ERP system itself will increasingly move to the cloud in the medium term; however, the private cloud model will primarily prevail in this country. In Germany, but also in Austria and Switzerland, companies are very reluctant—in contrast to the USA, for example—to outsource business-critical data to the public cloud. [6]

ERP Provider

The ERP market has a similar dynamic to that of the market for IoT platforms presented in Chap. 3: the market leaders SAP, Microsoft, and Oracle are competing with young, innovative companies and established IT companies that are making a positive splash with their own ERP offerings. The aforementioned ERP focus of IT-Mittelstand magazine [7] puts it this way: "ERP platforms now exist even for highly specialized industrial companies that 20 years ago could find absolutely no suitable offering on the ERP market and therefore had to create their own solutions by necessity." Today, on the other hand, there is a wide range of ERP platforms. Between complete packages and individual solutions, a number of solutions from specialized providers are available. According to Martin Hinrichs of ams. Solution AG, another expert interviewed, these industry-specific, evolved programs now achieve process coverage rates of over 90%. So we are again spoiled for choice. But have no fear: I have once again committed myself to the idea of service and have picked out a reasonable source for you to inform yourself and compare. Eric Kimberling, the CEO of Third Stage Consulting Group, posted a video on YouTube in the fall of 2019, in which he outlines what his team of specialists believe are the ten best ERP systems for 2020. While there are also specified recommendations from Third Stage for smaller companies, specific regions, or industries, this top ten list is the most general ranking and therefore quite suitable as a global overview. Here's what the ranking looks like:

1. Oracle NetSuite.
2. Microsoft Dynamics 365.
3. Oracle ERP Cloud.
4. IFS.
5. Sage.
6. SAP S/4HANA.
7. Salesforce.
8. Infor.
9. Workday.
10. Service Now.

People in the know can already see from the names on the list that classic ERP systems with a basis in finance and controlling are represented here, as well as more personnel-centric or service-centric solutions. Oracle NetSuite and Microsoft Dynamics 365 were also in the silver and gold positions of this consulting firm the year before, and in parallel, a few new names have appeared on the current list. People who are not yet so well versed probably notice nonetheless that the rankings do not reflect the market shares 1:1; otherwise, Salesforce and especially SAP would have to be higher up. No, this is about defined criteria, such as flexibility, interoperability, complexity versus user-friendliness, the degree of maturity, and successful implementations to date. This ranking and the similarly good performance of Oracle NetSuite elsewhere once again illustrate the importance of cloud solutions in the IoT age. Eric Kimberling puts it this way in his analysis video:

> If you look back at its history [...] it has been a cloud SAAS solution since way before cloud and SAAS were cool to do. And so, for that reason, their product is much more mature than some of the other, newer entrants into the cloud and SAAS space. Even more established ERP vendors like SAP and Microsoft have not caught up quite to Netsuite, simply because Netsuite has such a big head start on this. [8]

Feel free to have a look at this video and the market analyses linked in it. It's worth it. Alternatively, there is the free German-language comparison website erpkompass.de on the Internet, which, according to its own statements, is vendor-neutral.

As far as the top dogs are concerned, SAP and Microsoft are somewhat stronger in Europe and Germany than Oracle. IFS is one of the hidden champions in our region. In the German-speaking countries (D-A-CH region), the company has branches in Erlangen, Dortmund, Mannheim, and Neuss, as well as in Zurich. Although the provider and its name are not particularly well known, IFS is, according to its own information, represented in about 50 countries by local branches, joint ventures, and a constantly growing partner network. Product development takes place mainly in research and development centers in Sri Lanka and Sweden. Support operates in the three major regions of North and South America, EMEA (Europe, Middle East, and Africa), and APJ (Asia, Pacific, and Japan). In addition, there are numerous smaller providers, about which I can unfortunately not give you the last detail here. As an example, I would just like to mention the company TH Data, which is located in Berlin's Potsdamer Platz. Their solution INPAC is an ERP software for medium-sized production companies. The process-oriented workflow enables a high level of functionality and simple operation. Versions are available for the metal and sheet metal processing, electronics manufacturing, and food production sectors.

In the previous sections, I have already quoted from an article [6] written by employees of the ERP provider IFS. In it, the authors recommend, among other things, the following functionalities for an ERP system for use in Industry 4.0:

- It can be flexibly adapted to changing conditions by configuration instead of modification.
- It can process a wide variety of data types generated by sensors and devices.

- To communicate with resources on the shop floor, it can connect to different production control systems via open plug and play interfaces.
- Powerful multisite and intersite functionalities ensure the control of the extended information flow across all sites, including international ones.
- To quickly connect new partners, it offers open and easily configurable electronic data interchange (EDI) interfaces as well as special business-to-business (B2B) portals.

I would like to briefly show you here what corporate IT and larger companies look to for inspiration when selecting software and service providers. The American software consultancy Gartner is very often quoted in connection with the Hype Cycle and Magic Quadrant. The Hype Cycle is intended to map the maturity of technologies and innovations on an annual basis. The Magic Quadrant shows where certain software vendors or consulting firms stand in comparison to others in Gartner's opinion. Gartner distinguishes here between niche vendors, challengers, visionaries, and leaders. I would like to point out here that Gartner is certainly a good address as a first orientation. However, please note the following points:

1. Gartner can certainly not represent your personal requirements in your company in a general quadrant. Therefore, you should always conduct an individual search and tender for your software and, if necessary, seek professional help here.
2. Depending on the analyst and focus, the rankings look very different. Therefore, always look at several opinions and ratings and only decide which players to invite after a detailed market and requirement analysis.

Just for the sake of completeness, I will once again list the names of the vendors as Gartner sees them in the May 2019 analysis for the ERP market in general (cloud and on-premise).

Leaders:
- Oracle ERP Cloud (USA).
- Workday (USA).
- Oracle NetSuite (USA).

Visionaries:
- Sage Intacct (USA).
- SAP (DE).
- Microsoft (USA).
- Acumatica (USA).

Niche Providers:
- FinancialForce (USA).
- Unit4 (NL).
- Ramco Systems (IN).

You can see that the US consulting firm Gartner from Stamford increasingly lists software companies from the USA in the ranking. In any case, it is important that you consider how you set up your support structures. If you choose a niche provider for your ERP in India or the USA with headquarters in Europe, you should carefully check whether the provider has good service and support structures in your region; otherwise, the ERP implementation may be a nightmare for you.

4.3   Warehouse Management System (WMS)

A warehouse management system (WMS) helps map the complete internal material flow and thus all physical goods movements within your company. With regard to Sect. 4.2, you could also put it this way: while the ERP system is more concerned with value flows in the company, we see the physical flows of goods via WMS. First, a word about the terminology—I use the terms warehouse management systems and warehouse management software here. But you will also find the terms warehouse logistics software and warehouse management system (WMS). Basically, it's all the same thing. What is important at the end of the day is the functionality. While simple systems are limited to administration, more elaborate tools also deal with the independent control and optimization of fully automated warehouse processes up to the control of complete automated warehouses and driverless transport vehicles.

If you're not up to date on the processes surrounding warehouse management, I have the following reading suggestion for you: a standard for setting up a warehouse management system, namely VDI Guideline 3601 (Warehouse Management Systems). I like to recommend this text to stressed managers when they can't fall asleep from worry: one page and you'll be slumbering like a baby. But now, without irony, this guideline can provide guidance as to what is required of warehouse management software. The guideline increases the understanding of the core concepts in warehouse management. It helps us understand how a WMS supports the relevant areas as far as automation and process optimization are concerned. Anyone planning a tender should definitely look at this standard, or they can ask me for help. I have developed a standardized lean process to maneuver my clients through the request for proposal (RFP) and implementation of warehouse management software. At this point, hopefully the following overview will suffice. Otherwise, you know where to find me.

What does a WMS do? Basically, it manages quantities and storage bins, conveyor control, and scheduling. In addition, it provides control mechanisms and methods, such as a warehouse management monitor, which determines status, condition, progress, as well as key figures and presents this information. As a rule, a modern warehouse management system supports you with various operating and optimization strategies.

That may not sound too spectacular now. But think about how a package is dumped from a truck onto a conveyor belt in a sorting center and distributed within the distribution and sorting center with its several 100,000 peers to the vehicles that then bring the package to your doorstep. Meanwhile, such a parcel travels several kilometers within the fully automated sorting center on conveyor belts, and it is repeatedly guided into the right lane by light barriers and scanners.

The system that triggers the activities in the warehouse and thus also in the warehouse management software is usually the ERP system, when there is one. For example, a sales document may have been processed in the ERP system, and now the goods are to be picked up in the warehouse. To do this, the ERP software sends the given warehouse and delivery-relevant information to the warehouse management system. In many cases, a material flow control system (MFCS) is integrated into this system. This communicates directly with the programmable logic controllers (PLCs), which in turn control the conveyor belts, gates, doors, and rack vehicles. However, warehouse automation can also be performed by another system subordinate to the warehouse management system (WMS).

In warehouses that have a medium level of complexity and where the industrial trucks are still controlled by people, it is now largely normal for the forklift drivers to no longer make their own decisions. They simply execute what they are instructed to do on the forklift terminal or the mobile scanner with a graphical user interface. The fact that intelligent machines can access parts and objects in the warehouse, control them, and obtain information from them has advantages; higher efficiency, for example; or, the bottom line, higher availability. But it also brings new challenges involving different levels of security and the smart use of data and software. The drivers' job is to make sure that no people, racks, or industrial trucks come to harm. I think we've all experienced situations where we've overruled or ignored technology because there was an obvious error or malfunction. But in a corporate context, there's another question that's not quite as acute in private: How is the warehouse worker supposed to prevent cybercriminals from hacking into the company's network from his workplace? If theoretically anyone can access machines and equipment from any corner of the globe, as long as he knows how to misuse automated warehouse technology, then modern software must include protection and security measures that automatically ward off attacks or at least warn and support staff in some way.

Twice a year, the logistics company Hermes, a subsidiary of the Otto Group, publishes its "Hermes Barometer," in which the results of telephone surveys of around 200 logistics professionals are presented on the respective key topic. The seventh of 12 barometers currently published dealt with IT and data security in the supply chain. Of those surveyed at that time, three quarters considered themselves well enough positioned to "limit threats to IT systems to a tolerable level." At the same time, there was a sense of respect for new security risks posed by networking in the Internet of Things. When supply chains increasingly have cross-enterprise information architecture—with supply chain management systems, warehouse management software, or ERP clouds—some security issues arise anew. More than half of the logistics professionals surveyed expected to be more affected by information security incidents involving their customers, partners, or suppliers in the future. In larger companies, whose networking is in many cases already more advanced, as many as three quarters of respondents thought so. Here's an interesting aspect of this: this assessment is also fueled by the fact that only a good third of the

Will companies have to invest significantly more in the future to ensure IT and data security within the supply chain?

Companies up to 200 employees:

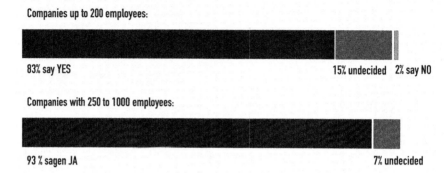

83% say YES   15% undecided   2% say NO

Companies with 250 to 1000 employees:

93 % sagen JA   7% undecided

Fig. 4.1 Survey results on IT and data security in logistics (source: Hermes Barometer No. 7, Fall 2017)

companies have comprehensive information on their partners' IT security systems. As Fig. 4.1 shows, there was widespread agreement that companies need to spend more money to ensure the security of their supply chains in the long term.

A second challenge that people today can hardly master alone is this: How do I separate the data garbage from the important information? Let's take my favorite example—the intelligent pallet. I'll construct for you a relatively typical situation in intralogistics: for a tracking solution, all pallets and forklifts in the warehouse were equipped with tags. These are small transmitters with a unique identification number that are located in the warehouse via radio antennas. They show the responsible employee exactly where pallet X or forklift 11b is in the warehouse, down to a few centimeters. The tags on the pallets report where they are around the clock. Since the material is constantly in motion, these movements generate a tremendous amount of data. How are these data relevant for your business management software or for the programs that control logistics and production, for example? What should be permanently incorporated into warehouse management software, and what should not? Let's say machine Alpha is to process a certain material. When the corresponding storage unit of this material arrives at this machine, it is logically missing from the warehouse stock. So it would be good if the movement or location would be posted so that the company can keep track of the stock in the warehouse and reorder needed resources. The corresponding transfer order, triggered in the warehouse management system, can be posted in real time as soon as the storage unit reaches the area of the machine defined as the production supply area and located in the system. This would confirm and acknowledge the transfer order. This would then also be reflected in the ERP or WMS system.

Different machines are used in the production processes. These require different materials to be processed, which in turn must be delivered through a transfer or warehouse order. The process is repeated when the material has been completely processed in the production process by machine Alpha and is sent on its way to machine Beta. The next order is generated as soon as the upstream machine has completed its work. A new transfer order is generated and confirmed as soon as the material has reached the defined boundary of the new production supply area: the geofence, that is, the virtual target line. Whenever the workpiece leaves a defined area and reaches a new one, it sends signals and triggers various automated processes and booking procedures. The smart pallet described here thus sends its location data to the company's IoT system every second, whether that is a cloud solution or another platform (see Chap. 3). This information is certainly of great use for visualization. In the ERP or WMS, however, this real-time information has no added value because it does not trigger a booking until the objects have reached the zone that is defined as relevant for a booking in the ERP or WMS. It would therefore be completely superfluous to map all movement flows completely in the ERP or WMS anyway. It would be sufficient to restrict oneself to the relevant signals, the triggers, which are exchanged between the IoT cloud and the ERP or WMS in order to specifically carry out a business-relevant process or a booking.

The Internet of Things is a valuable source of data for logistics and transport processes, if you get it right. IoT data can flow into an intelligent, networked supply chain from a variety of sources:

- Directly from the actual product.
- From the containers and vessels used for transportation.
- From the cars, ships, trains, or planes transporting the goods.
- From buildings in which goods are (temporarily) stored.
- From barcode scanners or other devices that interact with the goods.

In spring 2018, the eighth Hermes Barometer looked at trends in supply chain management and the status of digitalization in companies. One of the questions posed to decision-makers and managers concerned technological developments. Figure 4.2 shows how the experts responded to this.

So in spring 2018, at least of those surveyed here, only one in three ranked IoT and only one in four ranked cloud services as particularly important technologies. In the Barometer text itself, this is classified as follows: "Digitization and the associated use of new technologies have not yet arrived across the board in practice. Companies are aware of the need to digitize their supply chain processes and the majority attaches great importance to it. What is missing are empirical values and best-practice examples that companies can use for orientation. Therefore, uncertainty prevails and promising technologies such as cloud services and IoT still play a subordinate role."

As I said, this survey dates back to the first few months of 2018. Of course, companies have not been idle since then, especially with only 200 people surveyed at the time. As an example of the many attempts to intelligently bring IoT and

Which technological developments in supply chain management do you attach the greatest importance to your company?

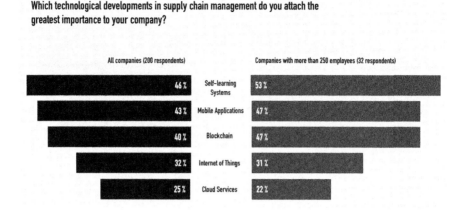

Fig. 4.2 Survey results on the importance of IoT in logistics (source: Hermes Barometer No. 8, Spring 2018)

warehouse management together, I would like to tell you at this point about the drone project of Körber AG; you can find more detailed information on the project in the company's 2019 annual report, among other things. A French underwear manufacturer wanted a drone that could detect individual garments in the warehouse, even if the parts were still packed in boxes. To make it happen, Körber Supply Chain experts teamed up with the start-up doks. Innovation GmbH, founded in 2017 in the environment of the Fraunhofer Institute for Material Flow and Logistics (more on partnerships with start-ups for IoT projects in Chap. 8). The doks developers created the drone solution Inventory, which can also read radio frequency identification (RFID) tags using electromagnetic waves. This allows individual products to be tracked throughout the supply chain. Test flights in the warehouse showed that if 100 undershirts are stacked in a box, the drone can have problems with overlapping signals. But the 96% hit rate took the wind out of the skeptics' sails. Anyone who knows how much time employees in such large warehouses spend looking for things can immediately see the potential of such innovations. In terms of software, however, the project has its challenges: after all, the data from the drone should flow automatically into the warehouse management system so that the customer has an overview at all times. Another IoT aspect—the drones, which don't have enough battery life to fly around the warehouse all day, are supported from the ground. Self-driving charging stations (see Fig. 4.3) will refuel them as needed without a human having to mediate.

Warehouse management software should on the one hand be compatible with ERP solutions and provide standard interfaces, and on the other hand it should be able to control the automated processes efficiently and securely. You will learn how and where to find such software in the following section. Further use cases can be found in Chap. 7.

Fig. 4.3 Self-propelled charging station with intermediately landed drone (source: doks. Innovation GmbH)

WMS Provider

Let's say you were looking for a new software solution for your warehouse management and support for its implementation. If I were to manage this tender, I would not only ask you about your current requirements but also work out with you where you want to head with your company in the next 10 years. After all, the warehouse management system has to work in the future setup of your company. I know myself that it is convenient to buy a common and halfway affordable solution, after all: what fits for so many others will also fit for us. But assuming that after a few years it doesn't fit anymore, the changeover and implementation of the new solution will probably cost significantly more than a few additional workshop days, including professional consulting would have cost back at the fork in the road.

You probably don't want to blindly rely on consultants and recommendations but rather find out for yourself about the WMS solutions on the market. What's the best way to go about it? Of course, Aunt Google and Uncle Bing will help. For online research, you could consult the German-language website trusted.de, for example. The company responsible for this, trusted GmbH, calls this online presence Germany's leading comparison and evaluation portal for business tools and software: "Originally launched in 2010 as a comparison for cloud storage, we now test and compare everything to do with business—from project management to HR and from accounting to customer support." Accordingly, the testers have already looked at software for warehouse management. The website distinguishes among three types of software [9].

Type	Characteristics	Price per month
Single warehousing software	Central management of small and medium-sized warehouses, little automation	From 10 €
Warehouse software in software suite	Partially functionally limited but supplemented by additional software for specific industries	From 15 €
Complex and individualized WMS	Extensive automation for large warehouses and logistics hubs	Negotiation

The variety of providers is not quite as large as for ERP software, but it is not exactly poor either. According to their own information, the trusted testers compared the providers shown in Fig. 4.4.

The editors determined the following top nine:

1. LogControl.
2. Megaventory.
3. E + P LFS.
4. Odoo Warehouse Management.
5. orgaMAX,
6. AJE Consulting.
7. Storelogix.
8. JDA.
9. CIN7 Warehouse management.

Don't ask me why it didn't become a top ten list. Unfortunately, I have not found an explanation for that. You can read the profiles for places one to nine online.

Now I would like to add a ranking from the English-speaking world. The website https://theecommmanager.com published a comparative article in September 2020 and created its own top ten list for the best warehouse management software of the year. As I said, the terms are unfortunately not used by everyone in a really distinctive way, which is why I would recommend that you search for a suitable software solution using all the terms (WMS, WMS, warehouse logistics software, and what seems to make sense to you beyond that). At The Ecomm Manager, the ranking looks like [10] this:

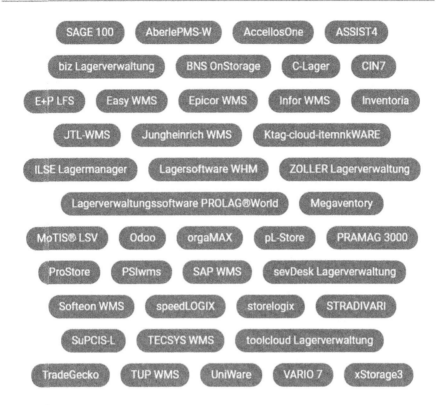

Fig. 4.4 Providers compared by the trusted testers (source: https://trusted.de/lagerverwaltung)

1. mobe3 WMS
2. SphereWMS
3. Infoplus
4. Odoo
5. SkuVault
6. IRMS360
7. HighJump
8. Bluelink
9. Manhattan
10. Infor.

Specialized providers with a certain tradition in Germany, such as ProLogistik or Jungheinrich, apparently did not convince the evaluators mentioned here. For the top ten ranking from the English-speaking cosmos, there is at least an extended provider list in which the following 11 systems are advertised in addition to the WMS version of Oracle NetSuite: Fishbowl Warehouse, 3PL Warehouse Manager, Shipedge, Iptor, Zoho Inventory, Agiliron, Clear Spider, TradeGecko, Channel Advisor, Tecsys, and SnapFulfil.

You've probably noticed: SAP is missing from both lists. Why? Well, as you have already seen in Sect. 4.2, what you see in the evaluation always depends on who prepared this evaluation. Therefore, I will round out the picture with another market analysis from the consulting firm Gartner and reproduce the assessment as a Magic Quadrant here. Be aware once again that Gartner focuses very strongly on the integration or embedding of ERP in large companies and corporations. Thus, the evaluation by the Americans looks significantly different. Among the leaders in the area of warehouse management systems, we find SAP with its WMS solutions alongside the following competitors:

- Manhattan Associates.
- Blue Yonder (formerly JDA).
- Körber (formerly HighJump).
- Oracle.
- Infor.

Now you're a bit smarter about the avalanche beacon market. But with these three rankings in mind, I think it's unlikely that you'll make a purchase. The Fraunhofer Institute for Material Flow and Logistics (IML), which I mentioned earlier, founded a "warehouse logistics team" 20 years ago. One task it has is to bring together customers and suppliers of WMS systems "according to requirements and to support the process of selection and introduction of WMS in an advisory capacity." As of October 2020, this team's database, which you can find at https://www.warehouse-logistics.com/de/wms-online-auswahl.html, listed 89 companies and the software each of them uses. This probably helps give you a bit better overview of your own industry. Incidentally, SAP appears relatively frequently here.

If you want to learn more about SAP Extended Warehouse Management (SAP EWM), SAP Stock Room Management, SAP Warehouse Management, SAP Industry Features in Warehouse Management, SAP WMS Decision Support, SAP Transportation Management (SAP TM), and SAP Yard Logistics, I recommend specialized literature. I am currently working on such a book.

Another plus point of the Fraunhofer portal is the publications, which include a few helpful guides and papers. The [11] white paper "WMS and ERP—Functional Differentiation," for example, deals with the not always easy assignment of functionalities to the WMS or ERP systems.

As helpful as the databases, white papers, and books are, you need to move from theory to practice in your actual day-to-day business. I would therefore strongly advise you to have the potential software demonstrated to you in live tests. Reputable, professional providers should be able to make this possible for you. In specific cases, it may also make sense to run through certain warehouse processes live in a demo system together with the software provider.

4.4 Transport Management System (TMS)

The "Digitalization of Logistics" innovation radar, published by the German Freight Forwarding and Logistics Association (Bundesverband Spedition und Logistik e. V.) (DSLV) in spring 2019, states:

> The optimization of internal processes, online booking of forwarding orders and the use of digital transport management systems are already standard today [...] The ongoing linking of shippers from industry and trade, logistics and transport companies creates the prerequisite for additional network effects that can multiply the economic benefits of the technologies used. Thus, the digitalization of logistics forms an elementary connecting element within the entire value chain of industry and trade. [12]

On the one hand, existing companies in the freight forwarding and logistics industry have an advantage over new digital competitors because they have mastered processes such as transport, picking, storage, handling, and customs clearance from the ground up—processes that do not undergo any structural change. It is possible to add "a digital backbone" to logistics processes, but software cannot completely replace the skills that have been important up to now. On the other hand, according to critical assessment, many companies still lack the right awareness for digital transformation and rethinking on a larger scale. Cost reductions are often the main argument for digitization. Improving one's own business model with the help of IoT is apparently not quite as important a driver, although it is precisely in the area of the business model that the future survival of a company can be secured.

What can and should a transport management system (TMS) do today? TMS helps your dispatchers and carriers optimize transports. It shows you the condition and location of vehicles, and it clarifies the utilization of your fleet by providing an overview of completed, current, and upcoming transports. The software helps reduce the number of empty runs, carry out consolidated transports, and make optimal use of vehicles as well as rail or air capacities (keyword: real-time route planning). Transport management systems are designed to find and schedule the right vehicles for specific requirements. This, of course, also brings us to personnel planning, which can also be designed using TMS.

The history of the Internet of Things, which was recapitulated in Chap. 1, has many points of contact with transportation logistics over the past 30 years. As early as the 1980s, goods tracking using RFID and barcodes played a role. Over time, various applications based on Bluetooth, near-field communication (NFC), or RFID became established along supply chains. In the 1990s, the first telematics systems appeared. Today, we actually hardly find any transport management software that does not implement the combination of a telematics system and mobile devices on the vehicles. A truck telematics system locates the vehicle in real time and sends the information to the TMS with all the other vehicles in the fleet. It is able to read the driver's card, the tachograph, and the vehicle's data, allowing it to evaluate the driver as well. Telematics systems are equipped with a GPS receiver and a SIM card to send the vehicle's information to fleet management, and thus the vehicles are integrated into the Internet of Things.

Today's Internet of Things, with its sensor technology and networking at so many points in the supply chain, adds new possibilities, such as continuously monitoring the condition of goods and taking external factors such as the weather into account. There are also new challenges: just ask your favorite logistics expert if the totally transparent and absolutely secure supply chain is actually on his Christmas wish list.

The IoT devices on the roads (and waterways and airways), like the drones and self-driving vehicles in warehouses, are autonomous data sources that we cannot ignore for sustainable logistics. They continuously generate data that we want to use in such a way that we can derive control commands and logistical actions from them. For fleet and transport management, it is of course very valuable to be able to supervise assets via IoT without humans having to measure or read anything. Telematics systems in cars and trucks, which record such things as position, acceleration, and fuel consumption, also typically belong to the group of integrated sensor systems. Data of this kind, which are of interest to logistics experts and traffic managers alike, can be recorded via adapters to the vehicle's internal networks. The on-board diagnostics standard (OBD) is commonly used for this purpose. Via the IT units in vehicles, the data reach the Internet, the servers, and the software in the shipping company. Conversely, information can also flow from the planners to the vehicle via TMS, so that the driver, for example, has changes to the plan of his forwarding company automatically on the tablet or dashboard.

Common functionalities for a TMS include the following:

- Transport control and route monitoring with the help of telematics.
- Route planning and scheduling.
- Management of transport orders.
- Cost calculation.
- Tracking.

It has to be said, however, that TMS solutions sometimes differ significantly from one another, which is due not least to the fact that transporters have different requirements than, for example, shipping companies. Stefan Anschütz, a founder of initions AG from the University of Hamburg, summarized this well in an online article:

> For the transporter, the execution of transports represents the core of the value creation of his company. Almost all processes revolve around this core. With regard to the support provided by software, the transporter therefore has the requirement of being able to map all company processes in as single a monolithic system as possible. To satisfy this requirement, 'forwarding software systems' have been developed since the end of the 1980s. Initially, however, they focused on the sales and commercial requirements of the transport companies. Later, simple functions for dispatching and route planning as well as execution monitoring were often added to the systems. With the advent of the TMS term, these freight forwarding software systems were then also sold under the Transport Management System label. [13]

He therefore finds the view that today's transport management systems represent a further development of conventional forwarding software that's understandable and also a bit too one-dimensional. After all, the shipper's transport management, customer administration, quotation preparation, or invoicing—or in more general terms, administrative, commercial, and sales tasks—would normally be mapped by ERP systems and not via a TMS. For the shipper's transport management software, the planning, optimization, and monitoring of transports as well as functions for the selection and data connection of transport companies are much more important.

In the following section, I provide guidance on searching and finding software for transportation management.

TMS Provider
As I mentioned earlier, the software label TMS can stand for different functions and use cases today. Therefore, always check out the solutions that have a "TMS" in the title or are advertised accordingly as best as you can.

A German-language online address for software searches is the website https://www.speditionssoftware-vergleich.de. You probably won't find a 100% objective and vendor-neutral evaluation here because behind it are the Munich-based SCC Center (Supply Chain Competence Center Groß & Partner) and Trovarit AG, that is, two private-sector players. Their joint platform has been on the market since 2019. The whole thing works like this: you register and pay with your data instead of money. Then you can use a research tool, where you can prioritize criteria and services, to automatically search for suitable software. At the end, you have a report with the top 20 providers for your requirements in your hand—at least that's the promise of the website makers.

I would recommend additional research in the English-speaking world, as is actually always the case when it comes to software. In doing so, you will come across, for example, a comparative blog post [14] by Rick LaGore, founder and CEO of the US company InTek Freight and Logistics. His top 13 current TMS solutions (as of February 2020) look like this:

- 3Gtms.
- BluJay.
- Cloud Logistics.
- Descartes.
- JDA.
- Kuebix.
- Manhattan.
- MercuryGate.
- Oracle.
- SAP.
- TMC.
- TMW.
- Transplace.

The software is sorted alphabetically here, not according to price or technical criteria. So at least you already have a preselection from the expert, which you can compare in more detail.

The same applies to the list on [15] the website CompareCamp, which presents itself as the leading comparison site for SaaS software. Their top ten of current TMS solutions (as of May 2020) looks like this:

- Cloud Logistics.
- Kuebix
- 3Gtms
- SAP Transportation Management
- FreightDATA
- Cario TMS
- Transport Pro
- MyRouteOnline
- LogistaaS
- WEBFLEET

For the sake of completeness, I would also like to mention here how Gartner assesses the market for TMS. So we end up back at the Magic Quadrant and learn that the American consulting house makes the following classifications: in its February 2020 evaluation, Gartner sees SAP, Oracle, Blue Yonder, and Manhattan Associates as leaders for transportation management solutions. According to Gartner, there are no visionaries in this environment.

4.5   Manufacturing Execution System (MES)

Let us now turn to manufacturing execution systems (MES). Manufacturing execution system is the common term, but the terms production control system and manufacturing software, as well as the not-so-clear production data acquisition, are also common.

Industry 4.0 in manufacturing means that production is transforming from a dull vicarious agent into a modern, flexible service center. Of course, to achieve this, we need to be able to control and execute our manufacturing steps more flexibly. This is done on the basis of data, preferably real-time data, which allows us to intervene immediately in the processes to achieve optimal results. If you are somewhat familiar with ERP software and now object that the production modules of an ERP system already cover this well, you're basically right. But an ERP system is geared more toward medium- to long-term optimization. With it, we look at the processes in the factory in a much coarser way. In the ERP solution, for example, we have order data and information about material availability. ERP, which is upstream of MES in terms of process flow, could assign orders to shifts but would tend not to operate with exact times. It might assign machine groups, but it would not link individual resources to individual machines in detail. While we use the ERP system to report back the start and completion of component production, here we lack data on processing, machine start time, and machine operating time. Such information and the resulting plant and process controls can be found in a manufacturing management system. Some ERP systems even support detailed planning to the extent that orders can be split into operations and we can assign machines and personnel on a small scale for production intervals. But real-time monitoring is still a matter for the MES solutions because if an employee spontaneously goes down, a machine gives up the ghost, or tools break, this is not reflected in the ERP solution.

> At this point, I would like to make a literature recommendation for company managers, production managers, supply chain managers, and programmers. The guideline VDI 5600 gives very good hints and recommendations on how to design an MES and for which areas it should be used.

According to the guideline VDI 5600 from the Association of German Engineers, an MES has the following functions:

- Planning and control of manufacturing processes.
- Establishment of process transparency.
- Mapping of material and information flow.

I think it's important to note that MES systems, which focus on production and production-related IT, are basically designed to ensure production reliability first. On the one hand, this is imperative because you don't want to have uncontrolled processes, which lead to malfunctions, failures, or even accidents. On the other hand, it has the consequence that the interaction between the physical world and the software is more immediate. An ERP system would still forgive some downtime in certain cases. But if the MES fails, work in the warehouse and factory is interrupted. Imagine that the software that handles the production processes (or even the warehouse processes) and machine control fails. At that moment, your production comes to a standstill. You can no longer deliver goods from the warehouse to the customer or your partners.

If we were to take a tour of Germany's small and medium-sized enterprises (SMEs), it would naturally become apparent that not all companies are using modern MES solutions, whose developers were already able to think along with IIoT and smart factory the way everyone is talking about today. Often, these tasks are taken over by in-house developments, which have been expanded over the years to meet the new requirements. This can lead to problems if software from other companies and even the in-house ERP system cannot properly connect to this architecture and interfaces. I remember a client who was faced with the decision of whether to roll out the MES solution to new plants abroad. We advised against it at the time for two reasons:

1. The solution originated from a development environment that was getting on in years in a way that is best avoided with software: it had not been further developed by the software and operating system manufacturer for years, and maintenance had already expired. Software without support and up-to-date interfaces and APIs is no basis for a future-oriented company.
2. The MES provider behind the solution was well positioned in Germany. In principle, it also had sufficient consultants and support staff. But abroad, he did not have a resource that was familiar with the software. This was another knockout criterion.

If you also feel that you need to do something about production control and manufacturing software, see the next section for some vendor search tips.

MES Provider for Production Control Systems
Basically, before selecting, tendering, expanding, and implementing an MES, you should ask yourself exactly and very critically what you need. In which geographical environment are you operating? What does the target architecture look like, and how does the solution integrate with other solutions in your inventory and into the world you want to map in your company in the future? As with all other enterprise software solutions, keep in mind and heed the points made in Sect. 4.1 because they always apply.

Here's a good example of a niche provider: Böhme und Weihs Systemtechnik GmbH & Co. KG specializes in software solutions for quality and manufacturing management. The company, which got its start in Wuppertal in 1985 and now also has offices in France and Russia, took a look at what makes good manufacturing execution software in early 2020. The full blog post, which of course promotes the company's own solution MESQ-it and also includes useful general assessments, can be found at https://www.boehme-weihs.de/q-blog/mes-wissen/mes-manufacturing-execution-system.

In general, it is advisable to pay attention to the following criteria:

• **Standardized**: compliance with standards, such as VDI guideline 5600 and the VDMA standard sheet, ensures that the MES can meet the requirements as a production management system. This also includes the use of standardized technologies, such as OPC-UA for standardized machine communication.
• **Web based**: access via a web browser allows the MES to be operated flexibly from different end devices and locations.
• **Cloud based**: a cloud-enabled system offers the option to network with any of your machines in any plant worldwide, an important step toward Industry 4.0.
• **Highly transparent**: data acquisition and processing should be done in a few seconds so you have a real real-time record of your production steps.
• **Intuitive**: intuitive and simple operation ensures short training times, acceptance by your employees, and rapid information gain in everyday production.

In terms of usability, you might ask yourself whether you and your workforce need an English user interface. The blog post also emphasizes that good interaction between the MES and computer-aided quality assurance (CAQ) is beneficial. If they harmonize well, one would have a holistic view of process and production quality. In addition, money could be saved by purchasing CAQ and MES from a single source because the additional effort required to network the systems via an individual interface or the like would then be eliminated. Often, smaller niche providers are just the right choice for companies, but always consider where you want to go and whether a software product limits you in your growth plans.

What else is there besides MESQ-it? Of course, SAP is also involved in the market for production control systems. SAP ME (SAP Manufacturing Execution), for example, is a fully configurable MES system for discrete manufacturing. SAP MII (SAP Manufacturing Integration and Intelligence) is designed as a solution for the process industry. More tailored to the requirements of Industry 4.0 are the Jumpstart Package and the Accelerator Package, which can be used to plan and monitor networked systems and production processes, with relatively extensive analysis and maintenance functions also included in the functionality. SAP Distributed Manufacturing also includes services for additive manufacturing (three-dimensional (3D) printing). With the introduction of the new Advanced Package, companies are expected to benefit from additional key advantages in the future. These also include functions for machine learning and analysis applications for quality assurance and maintenance.

Now I have presented a rather unknown software product and the portfolio of SAP. What other software is there to choose from? For a current market overview, you could, for example, refer to Gartner Peer Insights [16], which generally provides a good orientation to software experiences and are much more reliable than customer reviews on Amazon. In October 2020, I clicked through reviews there for more than 40 MES options. These included products from SAP, Oracle, Samsung, Aveva, and Siemens. The "customers' choice" label indicates at a glance what was particularly popular with peers. These included Honeywell Connected Plant and TrakSYS from Parsec, as well as Shopfloor-Online from Lighthouse Systems.

I have developed a standardized procedure for MES systems that accompany clients during need assessment, tendering, selection, and implementation of MES systems. In addition, I have been offering seminars for my clients for several years. Here, in addition to the selection and negotiation criteria with vendors, participants learn to move from reactive ERP-supported action to a strategic leading position in production by using MES and IoT in a targeted manner.

References

1. *IT-Mittelstand*, issue 12/2019, p. 28.
2. Wesseler, B. (2019). Intelligent ERP systems for the next step. From the column "Three questions to …". *IT-Mittelstand*, issue 12. https://www.it-zoom.de/it-mittelstand/e/intelligente-erp-systeme-fuer-den-naechsten-schritt-24986

3. *IT-Mittelstand*, 11/2019, p. 40.
4. Hoffmann, D. (2019). Via the provisional to the goal. *IT Director*, issue 11, p. 42ff. https://www.it-zoom.de/it-director/e/ueber-das-provisorium-zum-ziel-24513
5. Federal Office for Information Security (BSI). The state of IT Security in Germany 2019, p. 27.
6. Issing, S., & Schulz, P. Integrating ERP systems into IoT platforms from the cloud. https://line-of.biz/industrie-4-0-und-iot/erp-systeme-in-iot-plattformen-aus-der-cloud-integrieren
7. *IT-Mittelstand*, issue 12/2019, p. 31.
8. Top ERP systems for 2021. Best ERP software, ranking of ERP systems, top ERP vendors. https://youtu.be/saqmQhVALnM
9. https://trusted.de/lagerverwaltung
10. https://theecommmanager.com/warehouse-management-systems-software
11. Fraunhofer Institute for Material Flow and Logistics (IML): WMS and ERP—functional differentiation. Whitepaper. http://www.warehouse-logistics.com/152/1/veroeffentlichungen.html
12. German Freight Forwarding and Logistics Association (DSLV). (2019, April). *(DSLV): Innovation radar "digitalization of logistics"* (p. 4). https://www.dslv.org/dslv/web.nsf/id/li_fdihbctkgj.html
13. Anschütz, S. What is a transport management system and how does it differ from freight forwarding software? Online article. https://www.initions.com/transport-digital/was-ist-eigentlich-ein-transport-management-system-tms
14. https://blog.intekfreight-logistics.com/best-transportation-management-software-tms
15. https://comparecamp.com/tms-software/#2
16. https://www.gartner.com/reviews/market/manufacturing-execution-systems

Interaction of the IoT with Other Technologies

5

When we say the Internet of Things can help us protect the planet and make life more livable for humanity as a whole, we're not really talking about a future technology at all. Instead, we are talking about the parallel coexistence of several future technologies, which can be combined and complement each other. If we look at them in isolation from one another, it doesn't quite do justice to reality: Where does all the data for big data strategies come from? What good are VR goggles if they don't have a network connection? How smart can an AI system get if it can't access the data sets of devices that can share analyzable camera images or computable sensor data with the world in a language that algorithms can understand? Or take augmented reality as an example: visualizations using this technology can help engineers plan or workers on a company's shop floor assemble components, but it requires an adequate IT infrastructure with digitized and interconnected devices. To truly realize the full potential of a 3D printer, you can't look at the physical world and the virtual world as two parallel worlds that have nothing to do with each other. Rather, you have to bring them together. That is a central aspect of the IoT.

Remember the idea of cyber-physical systems from Sect. 1.1. For the concepts of the IoT platforms, which were the subject of Chaps. 3 and 4, future technologies such as artificial intelligence are now being considered. In the following, I will show you three diagrams to illustrate well what I mean (Figs. 5.1, 5.2, and 5.3). Figure 5.1 shows a model of the intelligent enterprise strategy that SAP unveiled in 2018. Figures 5.2 and 5.3 are taken from Cisco's latest trend report for IT networks, the "2020 Global Networking Trend Report."

As you can see from Fig. 5.1, "smart" technologies play an important role here. Artificial intelligence (AI), machine learning (ML), the IoT, augmented reality (AR), and virtual reality (VR) are mentioned by name. The term "analytics" implicitly resonates with big data and evaluation methods such as data mining. Blockchain methods for decentralized data management are also implied.

Even though Cisco's "2020 Global Networking Trend Report" is structured somewhat differently because it deals with new IT networks instead of a product

A. Holtschulte, *Digital Supply Chain and Logistics with IoT*, Management for Professionals, https://doi.org/10.1007/978-3-030-89408-5_5

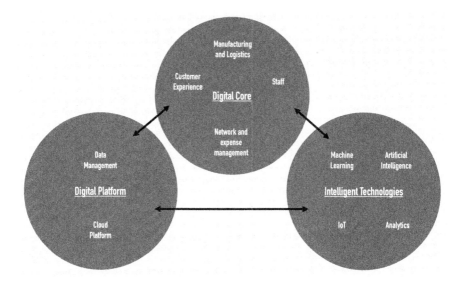

Fig. 5.1 The IoT and smart technologies in a SAP model (source: Holtschulte, Andreas; Mohr, Martina; Stollberg, Michael: IoT mit SAP. Rheinwerk Verlag 2020, p. 102)

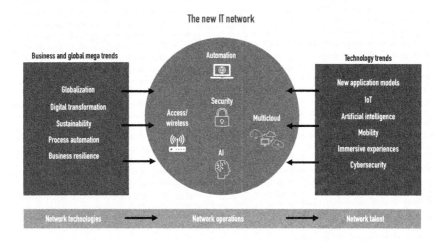

Fig. 5.2 Model for IT networks and trends (source: *Cisco:* 2020 Global Networking Trend Report, p. 8)

family like SAP's, the weighting is similar. In Fig. 5.2, the technology trends on the right-hand side take up just as much space as the "other" trends from the world of work and society on the left-hand side. In Fig. 5.3, AR/VR and artificial intelligence are mentioned in addition to the IoT and cloud, with the heading indicating the technologies as driving or determining.

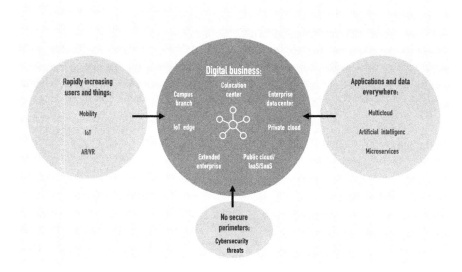

Fig. 5.3 Technologies as drivers (source: *Cisco:* 2020 Global Networking Trend Report, p. 15)

Without the IoT, many doors would remain closed to us in the future. At the same time, problems such as climate change and feeding a future world population of ten billion people obviously call for new ways and innovative solutions. Digitization and, in particular, digital transformation, which we have heard and read so much about in recent years, are processes that cannot be thought of without the Internet—and therefore also without the Internet of Things. This applies to such big questions of humanity as those I have just alluded to, as well as to concrete use cases in logistics and industry.

If, for example, a logistics service provider who until recently printed out his picking lists in the central warehouse on paper and crossed off the picked items from the list by hand digitizes these work steps and switches to mobile data capture, this information will henceforth be recorded digitally. As a result of the modernization, warehouse management can now see the status of warehouse tasks in real time. The company could also make this information available to partners and customers so they can see when the delivery is expected to arrive. The digital data on activities in the warehouse can be integrated with other processes such as transportation and distribution. It can also feed into customers' software and individual applications. Consider the typical shipment tracking system we use to check if and when our packages arrive at their intended destination. This kind of object detection—and, more generally, tracking and tracing in the mobile world—needs big data and the IoT in equal measure. Even if the scanner is no longer the technological invention of the twenty-first century, it could well be another technology in the sense of the IoT that records and processes the location and change in state of a package, a pallet, a storage unit, or a handling unit.

No matter how much data is collected, it is of no use if the package constantly produces location data on its journey that the customer's technology cannot translate into comprehensible information. The information must not be too inaccurate or arrive too late, nor must the data exchange overtax the customer's technology, for example, by overloading his smartphone processor or causing the app to crash.

The following sections will focus on the interplay between the Internet of Things and the future technologies such as big data, artificial intelligence, augmented reality (AR), virtual reality (VR), and 3D printing: How do these technologies work? To what extent do we already use them? How will they change our lives and economies in the future? And what about the interactions with the IoT technology?

5.1   Big Data

We live in an age in which data flows second by second almost everywhere in the world. The volume of data flows into a gigantic sea of data or, to describe it more aptly, into a huge lake landscape, whereby the lakes are still connected to each other by rivers and smaller streams. You have probably already heard the term "data lake." It refers to a collection point of all the information you collect, both internally and externally. Some also speak of a data mountain.

However, the term "big data" does not allow for an overly narrow definition—it's all over the place, even though the term is gradually entering adolescence, judging by the number of years it has been in circulation. Moreover, the English "big" just means big for now, while some experts argue that what characterizes our data streams circulating today is not just the size of the data volume but also its complexity, level of detail, and the speed of data transmission, as well as the relationship between the data streams. After all, intelligence only emerges when we relate information to each other. You've probably come across the word "data highway" a few times, too. Some use big data only for the data assets themselves, whereas others also use it to describe the methods and tools for data management when they use the term. A big data strategist, for example, who exists with this or similar designations in various companies, does not have the task of producing as many data sets as possible. Rather, this person is there to make the data available in the company, to combine it, and to enrich it with external data from competitors or market studies so that the company can learn something about itself and the future of its products and services.

Even if a clear definition is not quite easy, the following is beyond question: in the global Internet world, people with all their Internet-enabled devices are producing more data today than ever before. In some cases, the data also flows automatically without a human being having to take action, which leads us to the question of what happens to all this data. Powerful, high-speed computers are no longer the privilege of the elite. Of course, NASA, the CIA, the NSA, the BND, military institutions, or even the teams working at particle accelerators have more computing power and better hardware at their disposal than you and I do. It would be strange if that were different. But even an average smartphone can manage large amounts of data in real time and compute reasonably complex simulations. Let's realize that the operating systems, the software, and all the apps we use on our Internet-enabled phones are not static collections of information, as used to be the case with the old hard copy encyclopedia, for example. Rather, the flow of data is something dynamic. New data is constantly being collected and forwarded, received, and processed. Let's return to the image with the data lakes: cold and warm water layers are in permanent exchange. Chemical processes are taking place. The saying that you can never step into the same river twice is also applicable to the continuous movement of data in the Internet of Things.

The individual, device-specific data movements alone ensure constant input and continuous traffic on the data highways. Since almost everyone now uses a smartphone, gigantic streams of data quickly accumulate and flow through the everything network. The fact that we live and work in a data-driven age is also easy to see in retrospect, namely, on the basis of the history of our data carriers and storage media. People have always been interested in data and information, but for most of that time mankind had to get by without libraries shrunk to the size of USB sticks, let alone completely virtual cloud storage. Even just before the moon landing in the 1960s, punched cards were still in circulation that, from today's perspective, could hold a paltry 80 bytes of data. When I was born in 1983, audio and video cassettes were the standard, while in the computer sector we mainly used floppy disks and—if we needed a bit more memory—magnetic tapes. I still remember my Commodore 16, yes, not the Commodore 64, which many teenagers later used for gaming, but the predecessor, which loaded in every program and game via a cassette. During the loading process, you could make yourself a cup of tea or do your complete morning washing before the digital adventure could finally begin.

Today, the average teenager can easily buy a USB stick with 64 GB storage capacity, if they even want to bother. It's actually comparatively inconvenient to carry data from A to B in the physical world when you can fall back on mailing and transfer services, on sharing, and on cloud platforms that conveniently do it for you digitally: sharing photos with the world via Instagram or Facebook; giving away music and audio books at the click of a button; working together in the cloud on group work for school or university, all simultaneously in one document; and experiencing in real time what your colleague is currently spouting off on page 16—all this is quite normal these days. What applies to everyday life and leisure time also applies to the world of work and daily interaction in companies.

In addition to the ubiquitous smartphones, other devices are increasing data traffic with every breath we take: Internet-enabled televisions and stereos in homes, drones and fitness trackers in parks, and sensors in factories, industrial plants, refrigeration systems, and shipping trucks. It's no coincidence that the number of terms with "smart" in their names is growing alongside the size of what they refer to: from smartphones to smart homes, from smart homes to smart cities. And what's next? The smart planet or the smart galaxy? We're not just talking about simple signals along the lines of 0 for off and 1 for on. In the age of YouTube and Instagram, image transmission for photos and videos accounts for a large share of data streams. Added to this is the audio track. Technically speaking, every voice chat or every online conference could be recorded and analyzed, even though we naturally don't do this with a view to costs, benefits, and efficiency, not to mention data protection. In the area of remote maintenance, which you will learn a bit more about in Sect. 5.2 on artificial intelligence, audio diagnostics are already a reality.

Just as you can't read all the books ever written, you can't make sense of all this data circulating through the everything network. No matter how you look at it, much of it is and remains data garbage. But on the other hand, there is also a huge treasure trove of data waiting for us, which we just have to retrieve. Data collection and analysis are now possible on a grand scale: as I said, storage space has become a commodity. We still have to worry about the power supply, for which we still have to put real buildings and lines into the physical world. But the advantages of a well-managed digital library with intelligently searchable and linkable files and documents over an analog library should be obvious to everyone. You don't have to be a librarian or a data scientist to see this. If it is an open data source in the sense of open source for citizens or scientists, for example, thanks to the Internet, LTE, and 5G, more people than ever before will be able to access the available knowledge and work with the data simultaneously. Often, of course, access will be limited if the data comes from market-oriented companies in competition, or even security-relevant players in the so-called critical infrastructure have to protect their data stock from manipulation and hacker attacks.

Companies like Google, Facebook, Instagram, and Netflix show that you can earn a lot of money, reach a lot of people, and achieve a lot with data-based business models. Social media and streaming have become an integral part of our society. When I use my cell phone to browse the offerings of IKEA or Amazon to order a few products of my choice via One Click, this is also based in part on the mechanisms of big data and device networking.

The interaction between technological developments is particularly intense in the area of traffic planning. Think of the first and today's navigation devices, of route planning 10 years ago and mapping services such as Google Maps, of sensors in the roadway, of digital traffic signs and display boards, and of visions of self-driving cars or even air cabs. The permanent interaction between many different traffic or network participants can be mapped via the Internet of Things in such a way that information that fairly accurately reflects the current state is available to the general public. This also enables real-time monitoring and control from a distance, which would not be possible without the digital data flow.

Let me give you two more examples of how data has added value that can be used socially or entrepreneurially. When we watch a soccer match on TV, we are inundated with numbers and statistics: possession, ball contacts, the results of the last 20 matches between the two teams, you name it. Where does this information actually come from, and how can the commentator access all this data live during the match? Behind it are specialized companies like Sportcast GmbH, which uses scouting and tracking methods to systematically collect metadata on soccer matches. Managing Director Alexander Günther once said about the importance of data for his company's business model: "We quickly realized that we had to make the collection and also the subsequent description of content part of our service and production mission. This means that a job is only complete when, on the one hand, the finished article is available and, on the other hand, the raw material is populated with the corresponding keywords [1]."

For the second example, let me come back to digitization in the logistics sector, which was briefly discussed at the beginning of this chapter. In intralogistics, the movement data of forklift drivers and order pickers within the warehouse can show where potential is lying fallow. If the past 3 or 4 years are to be evaluated at a logistics service provider, then we might be looking at 5–15 million data records for all picking processes, all stock transfers, all replenishments, and putaways. The data evaluation can show how much distance the forklift driver travels. Does he take the right routes, or can he take a shortcut somewhere? Does it make sense to relocate items? With an ABC analysis, access times can be related to picking frequency: does the positioning of high-frequency items and less popular assortment components make sense in the long term, or can processes perhaps be optimized?

Working with the escalating volumes of data remains manageable because computer hardware and software are evolving in parallel with the volume of data. Today's computing power allows for complex data calculations in real time, as well as predictions and simulations that are valuable for future decision-making. I would be very surprised if you had super or quantum computers in your offices, but as long as Google and Co. are researching the computers of tomorrow, the conventional range of desktop PCs and smart mobile devices is quite sufficient to move your data management forward.

We should think of big data and the IoT together, because everything that has to do with data flow and mobility also has to do with the quality of networking, with broadband connections and 5G networks, and with machine communication between smartphones and other Internet-enabled devices. Before statisticians, scientists, journalists, analysts or, for that matter, their freshly recruited data scientists can draw their conclusions from data and interrogate it in the interests of companies (or organizations or states), the data first has to flow to them. This is done via the Internet of Things, which we can tap into from all sorts of places and then access the data we are looking for without the need for tedious translation and decoding work. The sensors in smartphones, fitness trackers, cars, forklifts, trucks, containers, and ships translate the physical world from which they filter and read information into a data language that can be read and understood on the other end. The devices and their networks join together to form the Internet of Things, in which enormous amounts of data flow back and forth. Often, networking via the Internet of Things first generates the data that complex algorithms or self-learning programs need to form the artificial intelligence that is the subject of Sect. 5.2. After all, it is not only people who can compile information, evaluate data, make comparisons, draw conclusions, calculate alternatives and probabilities, and derive logical consequences. Computers can do the same. And they can now do it much better than us humans. Do you know the law of large numbers? The more cases I examine and which produce a certain result, the more likely it is that the derived explanation or solution corresponds to reality and can be used as a model. If you will, this is the reason why we are collecting more and more data and evaluating it. The sheer amount of data and its evaluation make the result more reliable.

Algorithmics, storage technology, and processor technology have advanced rapidly. Algorithms help to process data according to any criteria and at incredible speed, even under complex conditions, and to include information such as weather, share prices, stocks, or sales in the calculations. This is where the IoT, big data, and artificial intelligence come together. Welcome to the age of digital transformation!

5.2   Artificial Intelligence (AI)

Although the term artificial intelligence (AI) was not coined until the 1950s, the idea of artificial intelligence (AI) has existed for much longer. Inventors and creative tinkerers like Leonardo da Vinci have repeatedly thought about innovations that can perhaps be compared to the self-driving cars of today and tomorrow. Time and again in history, we encounter mechanical beings, from simple slot machines to sophisticated robotic assistants made by watchmakers to the mysterious "Mechanical Turk" of the eighteenth century. The designer, a technophile court official named Wolfgang von Kempelen, gave the audience the impression that his device could play chess on its own. Inside the apparatus, however, sat a human chess player who operated it—much like the puppeteers on The Muppet Show. Early mechanical engineering and future-oriented crafts are not the only sources of intelligent nonhumans. After all, we haven't possessed our prodigious imaginations as culture-creating beings only since the Internet age. Let's take the figure of Frankenstein, who creates an artificial human being in the laboratory. This may only be entertainment in book and film form, but in the creepiness and horror that surround the Frankenstein story, there is, I think, also a bit of fear of humanlike machines: Isn't such innovation against the order of nature? Can we control such machines at all? What will then become of me and my work if smart machines now become a reality? Another interesting figure is that of the golem: medieval scholars create a kind of magical assistant out of clay or other material, who cannot speak or think for himself, but who can carry out commands. The creation of a golem is essentially about AI, if we look at it from today's point of view.

But what does artificial intelligence mean in 2021? Let me quote a compact explanation from a text of the German Physical Society, which I find quite insightful:

> In general, AI is concerned with equipping machines with capabilities that resemble intelligent (human) behavior: in learning, planning or solving tasks. This is achieved with the help of clearly specified and programmed rules or through machine learning. It should be emphasized that there is no such thing as one AI; it is a wide range of methods, procedures and technologies that have been studied for years. These include, for example, natural language processing, knowledge representation (symbolic and sub-symbolic AI) and intelligent software agents. These are computer programs capable of specified, autonomous and self-dynamic behavior. Currently, different intelligent methods are combined (referred to as hybrid systems) [2].

Just as people can be trained to become data specialists, computers can also be taught to handle data sets as cleverly as possible. This is known as machine learning (ML). This refers to special training for computers that process information and data: they are equipped with the right algorithms and fed with data long enough to enable them to recognize patterns, regularities, and laws in texts or images. As a result, the machine can later classify further data input in its special field as known or unknown and compare it with the "knowledge" it has acquired so far. A special field of machine learning and the pattern recognition associated with it is referred to as deep learning. Here, artificial neural networks are used, which are roughly based on the neural structure of the human brain. Similar to the human subconscious, the AI must also be trained. Over time, the system continues to optimize itself. The algorithms used should become more accurate, more purposeful, more reliable, and more powerful as a result of the constant training. This process can be controlled or run, usually using the categories supervised learning and unsupervised learning. Here we are again dealing with an interaction between AI and big data, because the larger the amount of data the algorithms can access, the better the potential optimization of the learning process. We encounter the principle of machine learning every day when we sit at the computer or go online. This includes, for example, the personalized recommendations on sales platforms like Amazon. You know: customers who bought the glittery unicorn also found the sequin backpack in alpaca style interesting. Suggestions for the fastest route when driving are also based on "smart" algorithms, as are the facial recognition of photo software and various automated image processing steps, such as those used by the provider Instagram when filters and conversions for mobile devices are used.

Speaking of "smart" algorithms, currently, the artificial intelligences used are not particularly bright, if you take a closer look. Experts use the term "weak AI" or the English equivalent "narrow AI" to describe this. In their special field, for which they are programmed and trained, computer brains are now increasingly outperforming humans, but when it comes to associating, linking knowledge from a wide variety of fields in a meaningful way, and generally being intelligent, the supposed geniuses very quickly become mere machines again. Personally, I like the term "smart idiots" quite well.

Right now, I'm hearing about new developments, use cases, and potential uses for AI almost every day. Not all of it is useful. Some of it helps individual companies position themselves and make money, but doesn't add much value to humanity as a whole. However, I firmly believe that sustainable applications that cleverly combine AI, big data, and the IoT can help build a better world.

Let's take a look at some examples to learn about the practical possibilities of artificial intelligence. Let's start with some highlights from the last few years:

- Back in 2014, the investment firm Deep Knowledge Ventures (Hong Kong) made headlines for adding an algorithm to its board of directors. The algorithm, called VITAL (Validating Investment Tool for Advancing Life Sciences), was supposed to evaluate databases of life science companies and look for funding trends and investment opportunities. VITAL has since gone away, but the issue of AI for investments has not. For example, there is a fund called ODDO BHF Artificial Intelligence. In the early 2020, the firm behind it proudly advertised that this fund had achieved above-average net value growth of 27% since launch in the late 2018.

- In 2017, Japanese life insurer Fukoku Mutual Life Insurance relied fully on IBM software called Watson to be more efficient in medical assessments and calculations. It's important to remember that Japan is fundamentally more robot- and technology-savvy than Germany. Nevertheless, the case stuck in my mind because at the time, a rather small insurer wanted to cut 34 jobs or almost 30% of the staff in the responsible department.

- In the summer of 2020, the Karlsruhe Institute of Technology (KIT) announced that it had become the first site in Europe to put state-of-the-art NVIDIA DGX A100 AI systems into operation. These computer systems are high-performance servers. Together, the eight accelerators provide a computing power of 5 AI PetaFLOP/s, that is, five quadrillion computing operations per second. The research institution, which is part of the Helmholtz Association, commented not only on the acquired technology but also on the purpose of the research and the motivation of participating researchers: with a view to the Corona pandemic, the new AI systems at KIT could be used to fight it—for example, by speeding up the detection of infection hotspots, predicting spread patterns, or relieving medical staff in the analysis of X-ray images.

- I will come back to the X-ray images in a moment. As a representative of many other AI projects during the Corona pandemic, let me mention another application [3]. A Turkish programmer developed control software for cameras to measure the distance between passersby (keyword: social distancing; other hashtags were deep learning and Python). If the distance is harmless, people are framed with a green square, otherwise yellow or red, analogous to other traffic light displays. Surveillance is, of course, a tricky business. But in my opinion, we would be making a mistake to demonize a technology with surveillance potential on principle just because some regimes and despots use it for their own questionable purposes. Tools are just tools first, even if they can often be turned into weapons. How they can be used more peacefully and still profitably is hopefully illustrated by the following examples.

- Many people I talk to first think of voice assistants like Alexa and Siri when they hear artificial intelligence. It's no wonder, considering that these semi-affordable mass-market products can do things that were not possible with everyday technology until recently. I say, "Alexa, turn on the lights!" and as if by magic, the lights come on. I ask, "Siri, what does 'Baum' mean in English?" and the machine translates for me. If you tend to be one of those who sneer at the power of voice assistants, consider this: it's no small feat for a machine to read the sound waves a human produces by speaking and translate them into words like "Hey," because your sound wave looks different from mine, which in turn looks different from my daughter's. Think about how long it takes you to filter out intelligible sequences from unknown languages. It will be more than a fraction of a second for you, too. Research is currently being carried out into speech assistance systems that are capable of dialog. This means that in the future, the "conversation" with these smart devices will not be limited to question-answer chains and reactions to commands. It will come closer to our human communication, bit by bit.

- Another popular example of AI is the chess computer. At some point, the machine was so good at the game, which is heavily based on mathematics and logic, that it could no longer be beaten even by the best human chess player. Not quite as well known is the AlphaGo gaming computer for the board game Go, which is popular mainly in China. In the meantime, humans no longer stand a chance against this machine either. In contrast to its predecessor, the successor AlphaGo Zero does not feed in data from Go games that have been played, but only the rules of the game. Nevertheless, version 2.0 defeated the predecessor in 100 out of 100 cases. However, such game AIs are invincible only in their field of expertise. They would look bad in any other discipline, while humans can easily master a dozen games at a masterful level. Incidentally, when other Go grandmasters watched AlphaGo's winning game back then, they found some of the computer's unforeseen moves "creative."

I personally find the creativity aspect particularly interesting in relation to computers, software, and algorithms. That has to do with the fact that I was interested in art and also in crafts at an early age. My mother is an artist. She gave me and my siblings many insights into creative work. My father, on the other hand, took me along to construction and modernization work when I was a little boy, whenever there was something to be done on the properties he managed as a landlord. When I now hear people say, "Creativity is reserved for humans, machines lack something crucial for it," then I think to myself: wait a minute! Much of what we call art is actually perfect craftsmanship, mastery of the craft, and so on. For painters, sculptors, and others, cool precision is often also important. I want to give you a few examples of creative achievements by AI that have something to do with the art business, artists, creatives, or the cultural industries:

- Computers have composed music that test listeners could not distinguish from man-made music. Let's keep in mind that a certain Pythagoras of Samos is said to have said the following about music back in ancient times: "Everything is number." And since electronic music can be made with intuitive software without mastering any instrument, it is somehow logical that unfinished works by Beethoven are now declared an AI thing.
- There are also creative AI approaches in the field of word processing software, for example, for screenplays: actor (and singer) David Hasselhoff, whom you probably know, was already involved with AI in the 1980s in his role as Michael Knight in the series Knight Rider. Remember the Smart Watch, with which he could call his high-tech car "Kid." The quirky short film "It's Not a Game" starring this same David Hasselhoff, made in 2017, used AI for the entire script. It was intellectual gimmickry, and I wouldn't exactly call the result groundbreaking. But the director thinks it's possible that 1 day, our entertainment will come

from machines that use computing power and input from creatives to combine data and emotions into art that appeals to people in relevant numbers.

- A third use case concerns the authenticity of art, that is, art analysis: is the "Mill of Wijk" a genuine Vincent van Gogh? An artificial intelligence system that examined the painting shortly before the auction on September 1, 2020, came to the conclusion: with a high probability yes. If you think that the art market in particular is a field where such judgments can only come from humans, I would like to recommend the film Beltracchi. With his imitations of international artists such as Max Ernst, the forger Beltracchi deceived recognized experts of many years. In the case of the van Gogh painting, the appraiser algorithm worked with an ensemble of neural networks that recognizes the style of a painter in paintings. In the case of the "Mill of Wijk," the AI did not detect any anomalies, while it had already been able to identify forgeries in other inspections. According to the Munich-based Alexander Thamm GmbH, which cooperates with the Art Crimes Department of the Berlin State Criminal Police Office, the recognition accuracy for van Gogh is 89%. The model has now unmasked eight out of nine forgeries of the famous painter.
- The British company Engineered Arts has even created a robot artist who paints new pictures. Her paintings have already been exhibited. If you'd like to take a look at this artificial art, search for Aida. Of course, this name is no coincidence: AI as in artificial intelligence, Aida as in the famous opera, and thirdly, it is a reference to the computer pioneer Ada Lovelace.

For companies, AI offers a wide range of possibilities. These concern not only monitoring and managing the current status quo but also forecasts for the future. The more data available for evaluation and the "smarter" the AI application used, the more reliably events can be predicted. This brings us to the area of predictive maintenance and predictive analytics.

Quantity and probability information can be interesting, for example, in combination with robotics and automated processes: robots in production have been around for quite a while, as we all know, but the integration of different software modules, the communication between robots, and the connection of production supply from the warehouse are still partly new territory for us. With integrated internal production logistics, the overarching production control system forecasts which parts are needed at the machine in which quantities at which time and transfers the information to a warehouse management system. This system then initiates picking in the warehouse, transport to production, and provision of the required materials at the machine.

The potential of forecasts relates in particular to the maintenance of equipment, systems, and machines. Maintenance work often takes place on a regular basis, linked to legal requirements, inventories, or other milestones. If the interval is too long, this can lead to interim failures; if it is too short, unnecessary costs may be generated, for example, because skilled personnel check equipment that is still running perfectly. It makes sense for companies to be able to perform maintenance and servicing flexibly. For example, if there is only a software problem (and not a hardware problem), it may be possible to solve this remotely without having to travel to the site. Using automated algorithms is helpful in order to monitor technology and make such decisions, collecting and analyzing data—including machine, device, plant, or production data. Intelligent, real-time data management using AI can help create needs-based maintenance schedules. To improve scheduling for inspections and repairs, AI can be used to analyze audio or image data, for example: Is the gripper arm moving oddly? Does the engine sound as it should? Commercial vehicle and engineering group MAN uses this approach to increase the availability of their own trucks on the roads. The company wants to be able to predict as reliably as possible when a vehicle's critical parts, such as injectors, will fail, which would then lead directly to the vehicle coming to a standstill. The data set setup for prevention purposes incorporated repair records, fault documentation, and telematics data. In parallel, an algorithm was developed to detect "unhealthy" vehicle data in the ECU data. Swiss Federal Railways (SBB) uses an IoT solution from SAP for predictive maintenance of its vehicle fleet. Predictive maintenance is also a promising approach for regional public transport coordination.

Since predictive approaches are exclusively concerned not only with maintenance aspects but also with anticipating supply and demand, this mode of operation of artificial intelligence in conjunction with the IoT is interesting for all kinds of industries: tourism and festival organizers who need to think about the weather or operators of wind power and solar plants and other players from the large field of energy. The German Energy Agency (dena), for example, is coordinating the project "EnerKI—Using Artificial Intelligence to Optimize the Energy System." In this way, it wants to build up targeted knowledge about the use of artificial intelligence in the energy system and make it available to industry, the specialist public, and policy makers. The dena analysis "Artificial Intelligence for the Integrated Energy Transition" states, among other things, the following:

> Predictive maintenance providers for wind turbines promise a prediction of operating element failures 60 days in advance and savings of 12,500 euros per turbine due to avoided maintenance work. AI applications thus not only create added business value, but can also contribute to the integration of renewable energies [4].

There's a lot more to come in the next few years, if you ask me. Let me conclude with another example from medicine to illustrate the interaction between AI, pattern recognition, image data, and the Internet of Things. Think of the importance of X-ray images: if we manage to combine an AI with a strong cloud solution that incorporates millions of X-ray images of the lungs that may or may not show a tumor, the treating physicians have a greater chance of comparing current cases and verifying a guess than if they just consult their "personal database" in their head. After all, how many such X-rays does a doctor see in his career: 1000? 5000? 10,000? In any case, he will be far from the population of experience of all physicians in this field. Moreover, our doctor would have to be able to remember all the images and the patterns of disease associated with them in order to make reliable statements. However, each physician has only a very limited amount of data which he can mentally access. This is where the database of one million X-ray images comes into play. The intelligent pattern recognition software packs the images all on top of each other and recognizes the patterns at a high speed. The system calculates the probable development of the disease and immediately deduces what stage the patient is in. If that seems too contrived, there are already tangible projects in the German healthcare sector that link AI and big data together. Techniker Krankenkasse runs the Pharmacovigilance Monitor, a project that aims to increase patient safety by documenting and evaluating adverse drug reactions. To do this, it uses billing data from around 20 million insured persons and approaches such as deep learning.

5.3   Augmented Reality (AR) and Virtual Reality (VR)

The Internet of Things makes it possible to render events from the real, physical world readable for devices and translate them into a data language so that smart devices and modern machines can do something with the information they receive about locations, temperatures, colors, sounds, and so on. It also works the other way around: increasingly, things in the everything network translate content from the digital, virtual world for us and transform it, for example, into game sequences that we experience or hologram-like images and videos that we can use to visualize something and thus understand it better.

What exactly is virtual reality (VR) and augmented reality (AR) all about? While reality is supplemented with virtual elements on a second channel in AR, we fade out reality in VR and instead immerse ourselves completely in the virtual world. VR glasses, to name probably the most popular device that uses this technology, provide us with a complete new reality that in a sense displaces the physical world. You can think of it as being like watching a movie. A mobile game that uses augmented reality, such as the well-known Pokemon Go, combines elements from reality such as our network of streets and roads with non-real content such as characters from a fictional world. The roots of virtual reality and augmented reality date back to the mid-twentieth century. The first concrete design of a VR system goes back to Morton Heilig. That was in 1956. Only a few years later, Ivan Sutherland invented the first VR glasses. The first steps in the direction of AR were taken about 20 years later, among other things with the prototype "Super Cockpit." This was a helmet that extended the pilot's view with additional information. Just as we look back on 3D glasses as typical accessories of a certain era, VR glasses and VR headsets are the symbol of the new VR era. Microsoft has been offering its HoloLens since 2016. Google meanwhile mainly relies on smartphone applications and accessories: cardboards are cardboard frames with which you can convert your smartphone into VR glasses. Google Lens is currently probably the most important smartphone application for analyzing visual data and recognizing images. The attempts with own hardware were not crowned with success. If you now spontaneously think of Google Glass, its first version had nothing to do with VR or AR and was quite a flop in

Germany. Recently, actual VR glasses were discontinued with the "daydream view" product line. Facebook Technologies, meanwhile, is investing a lot in its VR brand Oculus, whose glasses perform quite well in tests. Old market giants like HP are happily getting involved in the VR business. New players like Shanghai-based Pimax are shaking up the market. (As soon as this book is on the market, the market situation may look different again. Unfortunately, I don't have a crystal ball.)

The success is actually no surprise: we humans like to immerse ourselves in new, foreign, or different worlds. Before VR glasses, there were the movies or computer games that catapulted us into other times and places. Before computer games, there was the analog group play with stories and theatrical elements to break out of our own reality—which was perhaps perceived as too confined. Before movies, there were photographs, painting, and literature in all its facets. In this respect, VR and AR tap into a deep-rooted interest in fantasy and stories by making our world more colorful and bigger. How will these technologies shape tomorrow's economy? Let's start with the story-driven entertainment industry, from Netflix to Hollywood, and with the gaming sector, because the impact there is particularly large:

- Did you buy concert tickets in 2020 and couldn't go to the concert because of the infection control measures to contain the Corona virus? What was a bit of a bummer for you became a serious problem for musicians and singers during the pandemic. A concert experience like that just can't be easily transformed into a digital substitute. Unless ... the singer is called Hatsune Miku: if you only exist virtually and can perform by lip-synching, it's of course easier—even if the problem remains that even a VR star attracts crowds, for which distance rules and mouth protection must of course be considered.
- VR is also interesting to the film industry. The technology can add new depth to documentaries, for example, in the form of insights into the lives of animals and natural phenomena. VR is also expanding the range of special effects for blockbusters and animated films in theaters and home theaters. Have you come across the term 360° video before? If so, you know roughly what I mean. Among others, the 15-min film "The Key" from 2019 has set standards, an experience somewhere between film, theater, travel, and art performance.
- VR is a huge topic in the games industry for consoles, computer, and mobile games. At the end of August, Gamescom 2020 took place completely digitally, like so many trade fairs and major events, but as the "largest computer games trade fair in the world" (quote from tagesschau.de), it reached an audience of millions of professional and amateur gamers, programmers and developers, experts, and interested laymen via the online channels. The event not only had a particularly professional online presence with its own content hub, networking with the popular gaming platform Steam, and the opportunity to move through a virtual exhibition hall very similar to the one otherwise used in Cologne in a specially developed game to experience the trade fair in a playful way. It was of course also devoted to new computer and console games that relied heavily or entirely on VR technology and VR equipment for the gaming experience. These included a game in the universe of Star Wars with flight simulator components

and the game "Medal of Honor," in which you replay World War II on the side of the Allies.

- A certain Mark Zuckerberg of Facebook, whom you may know, is reported to have said: "Like the transition from sharing text to photos and now videos, virtual reality is the future." Think back for a moment, and consider the triumph of Facebook, YouTube, and the online format of video in general before you hastily dismiss the quote as hot air. VR could be the next level of Internet presentation. Who knows?
- Another interesting area of application, which we probably associate more with nostalgia than with the future, is amusement and theme parks. The "VR Nation" recently opened in Berlin—a mixture of Lasertec and virtual amusement park. Sensors on the hands, feet, torso, and head record the movements of visitors, who move in real time as 3D avatars through a 100 m^2 area and experience a game. If you think that's already big, you should take a look at the "VR Star" installation: a Chinese VR superlative on 13,000 m^2.

But even in manufacturing or in the training of quite normal German companies that produce supposedly boring, tangible goods and at first glance have nothing whatsoever to do with such world-building and storytelling, a lot is happening in terms of VR:

- VR glasses can make it easier to instruct employees: when a machine needs to be serviced, service employees wearing smart glasses can be shown step-by-step instructions in 3D. Konica Minolta, for example, uses an in-house product development called AIRe Lens when people need information on the one hand and free hands on the other. Similarly practical: workers at the packing table can virtually see what they are supposed to put in the box next. Cameras film the activities of the hands. The screen adds which parts are next in line. Employees would likely get it right, so picking error rates can be reduced. This can be useful for standard operations and also for deviations from the standard when customers order something out of sequence.
- In cooperation with the Technical University of Cottbus, Rolls-Royce has developed a room for its aircraft manufacturing activities in Germany in which three walls and the floor function as a screen. In this "cave," engineers can, for example, virtually present an engine with over 20,000 parts. Or visitors can use VR goggles and "flysticks" to explore technical details.
- VR also plays a major role in the field of vehicle development. This becomes understandable when you imagine that prototype development is incredibly time-consuming. Thousands of components have to be produced in order to assemble a drivable car. These are time cycles that have to be massively shortened in order to remain competitive. This is why engineers meet in virtual production rooms or prototype laboratories to assemble vehicles from bits and bytes, that is, with virtual components. If the exemplary shift knob is then moved by just a few centimeters, the effects that this has on the seats, rails, but also on the drive shaft become immediately apparent. Moving a gearshift knob has so many effects that

it really amazes laymen. Given the existing technical possibilities, it would be a downright waste to continue to physically implement the construction plans only to be confronted with the errors. Simulations in virtual space can sometimes cut the duration of vehicle development in half.

Lastly, let me mention one possible application from medicine, especially since this is an area that can really do a lot for a better world. Children with congenital heart defects often have to endure stressful examinations and interventions. In the EU project "Cardioproof," researchers at Bremen's Fraunhofer Institute for Medical Image Computing (MEVIS) have developed software that can simulate certain interventions in advance. Initial experience gives hope that this could mean that some interventions could be dispensed with in the future.

The transition between VR and AR is fluid. Some people also refer to both technologies as twin technologies. The following use cases are about AR, that is, augmented reality, or at least this aspect is in the foreground:

- Tablets and smartphones can be essential tools for the craftsman when building a house, namely, when he wants to make his work easier and, instead of taking time-consuming measurements of the wall, consults the tablet, which tells him exactly to the millimeter where the hole needs to be drilled. The system uses comparative values as a guide and calculates the proportions and distances. In this way, it calculates where holes need to be drilled so that the components can be attached correctly.
- AR is also interesting in tourism: apps (2020, e.g., Zaubar) combine city tours and time travel, for example, by making historical images and sound recordings of the Brandenburg Gate available via smartphone when standing directly in front of it. The Babelsberg film studio in Potsdam is turning to AR for set construction. Technicians and fitters use three-dimensional advance visualizations, that is, holograms, and a pair of HoloLens mixed reality glasses. Michael Düwel, the managing director of the art department responsible for scenery construction, said in an interview: "Certainly this work could have been done in the classical way, but it would have taken many times longer for this level of precision." Asked about the future of the film industry, he replied, "We believe that the future of scenery construction lies in the ever stronger symbiosis between traditional craftsmanship and digital technology such as visual effects [5]."
- The Babelsberg film studio is also working with a volumetric studio. Volucap, a joint venture between players from the film industry and the Fraunhofer Institute, is designed to make walk-in films tangible for people. Personally, it reminds me of the holodecks from Star Trek. Do you know them? Thirty-two cameras capture people and objects in three dimensions and create hologram-like models. These can then be inserted into both virtual and real worlds. Just as the aforementioned Berlin VR Park can't quite keep up with the Chinese VR Park, the studios in Babelsberg are of course not quite as state of the art of Hollywood as Universal's film studios.

- For the planning of new company locations, it would be possible to map how the machinery is arranged using augmented reality when setting up a production plant for the first time, in order to plan and optimize the processes, transports, and interactions of the machines. Existing machines can be integrated in the image or superimposed. The view into the tablet is at the same time the view into the future.

Speaking of future predictions, up to now, it was often the case that you could only immerse yourself in the artificial worlds with a jerk or that you felt dizzy when trying out an application with VR glasses or a headset. This so-called motion sickness could become rarer and rarer in the future because, technically speaking, it is caused by delays in data transmission. However, developers and manufacturers are increasingly getting a better handle on such latencies and lags in the age of 5G networks. With a nationwide IoT as a basis, whose data can be transmitted quickly, securely, and stably, many opportunities are likely to open up to enrich our world with VR and AR applications. I write optimistically here about "enriching" because I am convinced that those applications will prevail in the long term from which as many people as possible and our ecosystem as a whole can benefit. Feel free to keep your fingers crossed with me, but please don't just twiddle your thumbs while the world keeps spinning.

5.4   3D Printing

As the name suggests, the Internet of Things lives from things. But what is that actually, a "thing"? You probably think first of Internet-enabled phones, tablets, and laptops and then of larger industrial plants that use some form of software that can be used for modernization and contemporary networking. That's all true, but I'd like to point out another dynamic here related to our hardware. When we talk about devices and hardware in the age of digital transformation, we can't quite avoid the phenomenon of 3D printing. 3D printers and the production processes behind them are modern tools that we can use to produce all kinds of things that companies need: from components and device parts to ready-to-use tools and entire manufacturing complexes. The classic concept of hardware does not go far enough. A printer is not only a device that interacts with software. It can also be used to produce other hardware. In terms of disruptive quality, 3D printing can certainly compete with AI and VR technologies. After all, aside from the fact that such possibilities would once have been relegated to the realm of fantasy, the price of 3D printers has dropped rapidly over the past 20 years, while their speed and accuracy have greatly increased in parallel. Printable materials now include plastics, ceramics, glass, paper, metals, and concrete, as well as synthetic foods and fabrics. A veritable race has broken out for tissue (and comparable materials) in particular, because on the one hand medical products and services can contribute something useful to mankind and on the other hand they can earn extremely good money—at least that is probably the hope or calculation behind the many visionary speeches and research projects. Start-ups focusing on bioprinting have been springing up like mushrooms for some time now. To be sure, there are already market observers and experts who warn against overestimating the hype. I have a quote for you from Capital magazine:

> Whether the first transplantable liver will be printed in ten or 50 years cannot be credibly predicted. The only thing that is certain is that long years of research lie ahead of profit. This is true for almost everyone who is competing in this race to the future [6].

On the other hand, it is also true that some impressive things have already been produced using 3D printing processes. These include prostheses, cars, and components for aircraft. The nonprofit organization New Story, together with the US company Icon, has even printed houses for a settlement in Mexico. The houses were built using a printer called the Vulcan II, which is a proprietary development of Icon and takes about 24 h to build a house, according to the company. The printer applies the cement to build the floor and walls of the house. Printing is controlled via an app, so the team can easily make changes to adapt a house to site conditions, for example. The software that controls the printer also reportedly takes into account the weather and mixes the cement accordingly depending on the humidity to ensure that the quality of the print is always the same. So we would have a software-controlled "thing" that can produce other useful things with the help of predictive analytics, that is, artificial intelligence.

In his book *10x DNA*, entrepreneur Frank Thelen calls additive manufacturing using 3D printing processes "the greatest invention in manufacturing since the hammer and nail." I might not go that far. But it's worth thinking about what it would mean for our products and portfolios if manufacturing could be designed so that smart software could control modern 3D printers in a demand-driven, predictive way. Think about just-in-time production, economies of scale, or spare parts management and warehousing, right down to the loss of sometimes costly raw material that can rarely be used in its entirety with other processes, and it becomes clear: some processes could change significantly here. One conceivable consequence is that manufacturing in the future will be less closed off, less centralized, because theoretically even an average consumer can buy a 3D printer and use it to make certain things for which he can find free instructions and construction plans on the Net. We have already been able to observe this in a negative sense when it came to assassins and extremists apparently using this method to build weapons and bombs. Apart from these extreme cases, which are difficult to prevent, the open source movement, which aims to make code, software, and thus knowledge as globally accessible as possible, is an enrichment for our world. After all, it helps to make people capable of acting even in less educated or wealthy regions. In any case, open-source exchange is an important factor in the context of big data. Companies should be prepared for the fact that they are unlikely to have a monopoly on basic 3D printing functions because of this and will have to set up their unique selling propositions differently. However, another aspect of strategic business management is likely to be even more interesting: if devices are becoming more and more important and device security is also playing an increasingly important role in the IoT, wouldn't it make sense to be able to manufacture as many devices, parts, and components as possible yourself under the greatest possible control? A second objective could be to get to prototypes more easily and quickly through 3D printing. This can be interesting with regard to flexible corporate management and agile methods for idea generation and product development (more on agile methods in Chap. 8).

Currently, there are several 3D printing processes that can be incorporated into the company structure for these or other purposes. These include fused deposition modeling (FDM), stereolithography (SLA), selective laser sintering (SLS), and selective laser melting (SLM). The first methods emerged in the 1980s. In stereolithography, objects are made of light-cured plastic, with a laser hardening the desired surface layer by layer. After printing is complete, the object must be cleaned and irradiated with UV light. In turn, the fusion layering printing technique is most common in printers for home use. It is significantly cheaper than stereolithography. In fusion layering, the plastic is heated, melted, and then ejected from the so-called extruder so that the object can be produced by layers fusing together. After some cooling time, the three-dimensional object is then finished. Hybrid molds and completely new processes will probably be added in the near future. That's how it goes when a technology is discussed everywhere as the technology of the future.

These discussions have long since reached German politics as well. In 2018, there was an inquiry about the competitiveness of the German 3D printing industry. Let me quote some interesting passages from it:

Question 1: How does the German government view the development of 3D printing in Germany? Does the German Federal Government believe that the German industrial location is a world leader with regard to 3D printing and must defend this claim?
Answer: Additive manufacturing (3D printing) has great economic and ecological potential. The classic manufacturing processes for plastic and metal parts are not being replaced by additive manufacturing processes, but increasingly supplemented. Additive manufacturing processes offer opportunities especially for the individualized production of small quantities. The ability to produce quickly, decentrally, in line with demand and with just a few work steps could result in productivity gains in many places and conserve resources. The variety of possible applications is large and concerns almost all branches of industry (e.g., components, prototypes, spare parts, but also solutions such as patient-adapted prostheses). Today, additively manufactured parts are often still considered cost-intensive, but the technologies are steadily gaining maturity. The increasing spread of additive manufacturing processes could lead to technological and structural changes in subsectors of mechanical and plant engineering, tool and die making and their customer industries. New value chains and business models for additive manufacturing are just emerging, partly with new players, partly with existing players moving into new business areas. In the view of the German government, a pioneering role for Germany and Europe in future technologies is of high strategic importance. Germany is one of the world's leading locations for 3D printing technologies, especially for metal-based processes. The German government is committed to

(continued)

ensuring that companies in Germany continue to have the opportunity to push technology boundaries and advance industrial change, in additive manufacturing as in other technology areas [7].

In the same document, the government held out the prospect of promoting knowledge of 3D printing processes, for example, as part of in-company training. Dental technology and the bakery trade were explicitly mentioned here. But it also said in general terms:

In the case of occupations with corresponding requirements, the accelerated introduction of digital technologies into training with a view to skilled workers for small and medium-sized enterprises is being flanked by the Federal Government. [...] In addition, the BMWi is funding investments in digital equipment for ÜBS in the area of continuing education and training so that they can offer high-level qualification measures with a digitalization focus. With the help of the funding, 3D printers, among other things, will also be integrated into training and continuing education courses. This is an important basis for the use of 3D printers in company practice.

How German industry is coming to grips with 3D printing processes and the idea of additive manufacturing can be seen, for example, at Siemens. Among other things, the international technology group is cooperating with the machine manufacturer BeAM on CNC machines for control technology and software for creating what are called digital twins. The corresponding press release states that the rapid industrialization of additive manufacturing goes hand in hand with a digital transformation and can only come to fruition through close collaboration between experts from the fields of software and hardware as well as the area of industrial 3D printing, as this collaboration, so to speak, exemplifies. Uwe Ruttkamp, Head of Machine Tool Systems at Siemens Digital Industries Software, said: "By using digital twins across the entire value chain from virtual design to the real component, digitalization also ensures the highest efficiency, productivity and data transparency of the entire production process as well as the highest quality of the manufactured component [8] in additive manufacturing."

Siemens is also significantly involved in the MindSphere World association, which is only 2 years young. MindSphere is a cloud-based IoT operating system from Siemens. One of the first members is EOS GmbH, which sees itself as a pioneer in the 3D printing industry. EOS stands for Electro Optical Systems. The company, based in the Munich area, offers equipment, materials, and solutions in the field of laser sintering technology, which is of great importance for 3D printing. Tobias Abeln, Managing Director of Technology and Development (CTO) at EOS, is convinced: "In the context of Industry 4.0, a constant digitalization of production is taking place [9]." Industrial 3D printing offered by his company enables "completely new degrees of freedom in design and manufacturing" and is increasingly being used in series production.

To better understand the interaction between 3D printers and the possible uses of additive manufacturing with the Internet of Things touched on here, let's take a look at a few exemplary products from the printer:

- A company called Nano Dimensions has succeeded in 3D printing electronics for IoT-enabled devices. These included an IoT transceiver just a few millimeters in size and special torque sensor applications, such as those used for smartphone finger sensors or motion sensors in surveillance devices.
- Others are trying their hand at materials that are particularly suited to the situation, from smartwatches to aircraft parts. If sensors installed in aircraft can provide reliable data on material condition, outside temperature, air pressure, kilometers traveled, etc., this data can be combined and used to manufacture future parts: maybe component X needs to be a bit more cold-resistant, while plastic B needs more flexibility. If a smartwatch shows signs of wear or annoying inaccuracies, the data on use behavior could possibly reveal weak points that were not yet known during production.
- Intelligent coffee management is also conceivable, to return to the historical connection between the Internet of Things and coffee drinking. Suppose you were to pour a portion of your energy drink into a sink equipped with a smart drain sensor every day; it could tell your colleagues about you via the IoT. Maybe the smart 3D printer will suggest that you print your next coffee cups a little smaller or larger.

In conclusion, we should not think of 3D printers as individual objects. It is better to think of them as components of a networked world that can continuously evolve and adapt thanks to permanent data exchange and optimizing software. If we then extend the radius from the smart home to an international corporation or consortium that joins forces, it becomes clear that the combination of the IoT and 3D printing has a lot of potential.

References

1. *Unfold Magazine*, Issue 1, 2019/2020, p. 75.
2. Deutsche Physikalische Gesellschaft. (Ed.) (2020, August). Artificial Intelligence for the Future of Europe. Physikkonkret No. 47, Physics and Information: Special issue on the occasion of the 175th anniversary of the DPG. https://www.dpg-physik.de/veroeffentlichungen/publikationen/physikkonkret/physikkonkret-47
3. https://github.com/KubraTurker/Social_Distancing-CV
4. German Energy Agency (dena): artificial intelligence for the integrated energy transition. Classification of the technological status quo and structuring of fields of application in the energy industry. Status: 09/2019. https://www.dena.de/fileadmin/dena/Publikationen/PDFs/2019/dena-ANALYSE_Kuenstliche_Intelligenz_fuer_die_integrierte_Energiewende.pdf
5. *Unfold Magazine*, Issue 1, 2019/2020, p. 113.

6. https://www.capital.de/wirtschaft-politik/organe-aus-dem-3d-drucker
7. Federal Ministry for Economic Affairs and Energy (BMWI): Kleine Anfrage der Abgeordneten Reinhard Huben, Michael Theurer, Thomas Kemmerich, u. a. und der Fraktion der FDP betr.: "Konkurrenzfähigkeit der deutschen 3D-Druck Industrie", BT-Drucksache: 1914629. https://www.bmwi.de/Redaktion/DE/Parlamentarische-Anfragen/2018/19-4629.pdf?__blob=publicationFile&v=2
8. BeAM and Siemens intensify collaboration in industrial 3D printing in the field of Directed Energy Deposition. Siemens AG Press Release, 19 Sept 2019. https://press.siemens.com/global/de/pressemitteilung/beam-und-siemens-intensivieren-zusammenarbeit-beim-industriellen-3d-druck-im
9. https://3druck.com/industrie/eos-foerdert-integration-von-3d-druck-ins-iot-1970197

Prepare IoT Projects Successfully

Even though I only touched on the developments and technology trends of the future in Chap. 5, I hope it has become clear that we can do an incredible number of useful things for our economy and the society of tomorrow with networks of smart, Internet-enabled devices. At this very moment, one of these ideas may be maturing in your head: how you can offer your customers real added value through the Internet of Things, how you can make your production more efficient, or how you can use IoT to make the world a little safer, more comfortable, healthier, or more livable. Because an idea is the beginning of everything. A certain Cicero (not CIO) put it this way:

> The Beginnings of all Things Are Small.
> Attributed to Marcus Tullius Cicero

I hope that with this book I can inspire you to use the potential of IoT profitably—and not just for the drawing board, if you know what I mean. That is my appeal to you.

Of course, in only very few cases is it possible to move smoothly and easily from the initial idea to implementation. What's the best way to handle your idea for an IoT project? How do you proceed without spending many months and thousands of euros on a project when you don't even know beforehand whether it will be a success or whether customers, colleagues, or business partners will see an improvement in the process, business idea, or business model? On the one hand, it is clear that an IoT project, like other IT projects in a corporate context, is a business project. You can definitely fall back on best practices when it comes to resource planning, for example. On the other hand, IoT projects in the Industry 4.0 environment have a much higher technology content and more hardware issues, which makes it different from a typical implementation project for ERP software, for example.

Although Fig. 6.1 does not necessarily invite people to dream and get creative, it clearly shows how broadly the use cases can be spread when a corresponding survey

A. Holtschulte, *Digital Supply Chain and Logistics with IoT*, Management for Professionals, https://doi.org/10.1007/978-3-030-89408-5_6

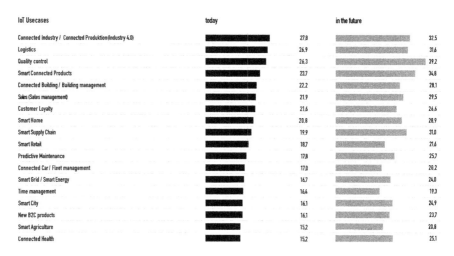

IoT Usecases	today		in the future	
Connected Industry / Connected Produktion(Industry 4.0)		27.8		32.5
Logistics		26.9		31.6
Quality control		26.3		39.2
Smart Connected Products		23.7		34.8
Connected Building / Building management		22.2		28.1
Sales (Sales management)		21.9		29.5
Customer Loyalty		21.6		26.6
Smart Home		20.8		28.9
Smart Supply Chain		19.9		31.0
Smart Retail		18.7		21.6
Predictive Maintenance		17.8		25.7
Connected Car / Fleet management		17.0		20.2
Smart Grid / Smart Energy		16.7		24.0
Time management		16.4		19.3
Smart City		16.1		24.9
New B2C products		16.1		23.7
Smart Agriculture		15.2		20.8
Connected Health		15.2		25.1

Fig. 6.1 Use cases for IoT (source: Mauerer, Jürgen et al. Internet of Things 2019 Study. p. 11)

is carried out among companies. The overview is taken from the "Internet of Things 2019" study and shows the fields and segments in which the more than 300 companies surveyed classify their current and future IoT applications. There is no such thing as a "killer" application, as the authors of the study put it so well. Rather, the spectrum is large and will remain so in the future. For example, in connection with COVID-19, I came across various IoT applications, many of which sound very exciting—from distance measurement via camera to monitoring body temperature to the official corona warning app.

The study also contains other interesting findings on IoT projects. Almost 70% of the companies were satisfied or very satisfied with their respective projects, while the share of companies that were "rather not" or "not at all" satisfied was only 6%. At this point, I would venture to say that satisfaction had something to do with both good (or bad) preparation and realistic (or exaggerated) expectations. Such expectations concern, for example, the idea of when the project will bear visible fruit (see Fig. 6.2).

As you can see from Fig. 6.2, patience is often required: in a quarter of the projects, the added value only materialized after 3 months and in a further 28% only after a year. In case you're wondering at this point how exactly to measure success, the top five indicators for the companies surveyed in this study were (in descending order):

- Productivity increase.
- Cost reduction.
- Increasing sales.
- Reduced downtime/increased utilization.
- Better image values for the company.

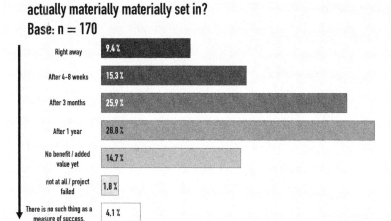

Success measurement: When did the benefits / added value of your IoT project actually materially materially set in?
Base: n = 170

Right away	9,4 %
After 4–8 weeks	15,3 %
After 3 months	25,9 %
After 1 year	28,8 %
No benefit / added value yet	14,7 %
not at all / project failed	1,8 %
There is no such thing as a measure of success.	4,1 %

Fig. 6.2 Project runtimes and performance measurement (source: Mauerer, Jürgen et al. Internet of Things 2019 Study. p. 12)

Chapter 7 provides numerous concrete use cases for IoT in smaller and larger projects. Of course, I was not personally involved in all of these projects and therefore cannot give you a detailed account of what the preliminary work looked like in each individual case before the project was finally launched on day X, and unfortunately I also do not know how satisfied everyone involved was in retrospect. I go into more detail about controlling for use cases in Sect. 6.3. However, there are a few success factors for IoT-based applications that can be used as a guide right from the start:

1. **Specialization is good**: Do not try to do too much at once! It's better to focus on a specific use case. To do this, you could focus on a weakness or void that has prevented your company from being more profitable so far. But strengthening strengths also works.
2. **Leverage insider knowledge**: Use the expertise available in the company to further strengthen your advantage with new functionalities, even if this chapter is a lot about design—with IoT, data, and useable information play the decisive roles.
3. **Don't forget the offline world**: Applications in the industrial sector sometimes have to function in places with poor Internet connections and have to be designed accordingly. Offline performance should therefore be taken into account right from the start of development in order to avoid disruptions.
4. **Service mindset**: Put yourself in the shoes of users and customers to ask what exactly they get out of your application or innovation. Some projects may make processes easier for companies internally, but they don't necessarily make life

easier for other stakeholders (more on the service perspective in the following sections).

5. **Keep applications flexible**: Making your digital application scalable and adaptable to changing market conditions and user needs could pay off in the end. So also consider possible adaptation requests and sales models (licenses, white label).

6. **Bring supply to digital platforms**: In today's platform economy, platforms and communities are important links between supply and demand. As well-known and easy-to-find points of contact on the web, business platforms and digital marketplaces reach a number of customers simultaneously. Used skillfully, in-house and external platforms increase visibility and can improve the value chain for IoT projects.

In addition, for the preparation of IoT projects, you can fall back on a method that has already been tried and tested by others, for example, by me, and found to be good. The method I am referring to is called design thinking, and I have been able to use it successfully several times in my work as an IoT solution architect at SAP SE and as a chief technology consultant for various international strategy consulting companies. The procedure, which I will describe to you in more detail in a moment, has proven itself in various constellations. It helps to concretize ideas and quickly launch an IoT project in the Industry 4.0 environment. Design thinking is very effective for clarifying important questions well before the actual start of the project, often including questions that were not even on the radar screen. Before we delve deeper into this method, I would first like to give you a somewhat more general understanding of design in Sect. 6.1, because this also has implications for IoT projects.

6.1   Design Thinking According to Rams

For an IoT system to fit in smoothly and feel good in terms of functionality and handling, you should give some thought to design. You may be wondering what the topic of design has to do with the data-driven and often intangible Internet of Things. Well, even IoT systems, which are certainly very technical systems, involve interaction with humans at some interfaces. We have already addressed this in Chap. 2: the Human Machine Interface (HMI).

Dieter Rams, a multi-award-winning industrial designer who is responsible for consumer products at the Braun company, says that you can't understand good design if you don't understand people.

Rams' ten principles of good design are:

1. Good design is innovative.
2. Good design makes a product usable.
3. Good design is esthetic.
4. Good design makes a product understandable.

5. Good design is unobtrusive.
6. Good design is honest.
7. Good design is durable.
8. Good design is consistent down to the last detail.
9. Good design is environmentally friendly.
10. Good design is as little design as possible ("back to the simple").

So how can these principles help you build a really good IoT solution? By relating the points to an IoT system, you arrive at the following analogies:

1. An innovative IoT solution solves problems for which there was no solution before. As a side effect, this IoT solution also enables other use cases, for example, because the data obtained opens up completely different and new business models.
2. To make an IoT solution useful, you need to focus on the users and consider in advance how they will interact with the user interface, for example.
3. Esthetics really have no place in such a technical environment, do they? "Anyone looking for esthetics should probably look at nude paintings rather than ranting about IoT systems!" This assumption is not entirely correct. We also create esthetics, for example, by designing an appealing user interface that the user likes to use.
4. The solution should be understandable despite all its esthetics. The user should intuitively know how to operate the solution and how to make certain network and security settings, for example, without having to search for a long time.
5. The unobtrusiveness of an IoT system with a good design is shown by the fact that you don't actually notice the IoT system because it fits perfectly into your operations and processes.
6. But what could be meant by "honest" with regard to an IoT system? As with any solution or product we purchase or develop, we should have confidence in the IoT system on the one hand, and, on the other hand, the IoT system should not promise us functionalities that it ultimately fails to deliver.
7. You can ensure the longevity of a good IoT system by taking three steeps: First, the components should be modular, as described in Chap. 2, and you should be able to replace technologically obsolete components. Second, the software application and processing programs should meet the modern requirements for an IT system. Especially in the area of security, IoT systems must always be kept up to date. If adaptation or optimization is no longer possible due to the components, programming language, or network technology, then some components or even the complete IoT system must be replaced. Thirdly, the components must also be downward compatible.
8. The details of an IoT system are very important, especially in the area of user interfaces and user experience. Imagine that you, as a mechanical engineering company, want to generate extended customer benefits through additional digital services based on your IoT system and offer a software service in addition to your machines. This must be fully adapted to the expectations and

requirements of your customers at the human-machine interface. Always analyze the behavior of the user. Every detail is important here.

9. You ensure environmental friendliness by relying on durable components and
the possibility of reusing components. Compatibility of existing and new
devices also contributes to environmental protection, since this means that in
the event of a defect, you really only have to replace the components that are
really beyond saving. Plus, you'll still save money if you make sure you design
an extremely lean IoT system. Think about how you can do without components
or, if necessary, use and reuse data from sensors before you install components
in one place for tasks that could actually have been performed by other
components.

10. As Rams says, it doesn't have to be complicated. Think as simply as possible,
and don't make a science out of designing your IoT system!

Before we move on from Dieter Rams' thoughts on design to the approach of
design thinking and its application in the corporate world, I would like to get you in
the mood with some nice quotes from Albert Einstein and Steve Jobs. There's really
no need to introduce these two, but I'm committed to service thinking, so I'll do it
anyway. Steve Jobs founded the American technology company Apple. He always
had the user in mind and designed parts, circuit boards, components, and entire
devices with a consistency down to the last detail "from a single mold." The trust in
Apple's products is still very high. In 2003, almost two decades ago, the New York
Times quoted Apple founder Jobs, who was still alive at the time, with these words:

> Most people make the mistake of thinking design is what it looks like. People think
> it's this veneer—that the designers are handed this box and told, 'Make it look good!'
> That's not what we think design is. It's not just what it looks like and feels like.
> Design is how it works.

The physicist Einstein managed to make his extremely complex research results
and theories suitable for the masses and thus establish a broad interest in physics in
society. Two quotes are attributed to him that fit very well with the approach of
design thinking:

> You can never solve problems with the same mindset that created them.
> If I have an hour to solve a problem, I spend 55 minutes on the problem and 5 minutes
> on the solution.

The second quote is very helpful to me as a design thinking coach and to my
clients in design thinking workshops when some impatience creeps in with the
participants. Often, some particularly solution-oriented and motivated participants
ask me when we will get to the solution. Often the client has already held a few
workshops himself or the participant in question has already designed a solution.
However, that is not the point at all in the first place. Design thinking is a process in

which actually up to 80% of the problem, the people involved, the circumstances, side effects, the market, and the person with all its characteristics are illuminated. We thus make sure that we don't disregard anything that would have been relevant to the new product, service, etc. afterward and come to the solution with all these insights very late in the process. If you attend a design thinking workshop, get involved. You will see how well the result fits the requirements of your customers, colleagues, and users.

6.2   Design Thinking: Better than Brainstorming

Before my several years of training as a design thinking coach at SAP, I would not have believed the power this approach has to help understand and solve problems. In the various training camps (referred to as Method Camps, D-Camps, Coach Camps, and Skill Drills), we learned special methods of problem analysis, questioning techniques, moderation, and group interaction. In contrast to classic brainstorming, the design thinking approach has more depth because it takes more time to understand the different facets of a given initial situation and because thoughts are less linear. It also takes into account the wealth of experience and ideas of multiple people. This helps prevent thinking from becoming too one-sided because, for example, one person might think only about profit or another might think only about the technical details.

Design thinking may seem playful at times and sometimes even allows for silly moments, but that shouldn't obscure the fact that this approach is strictly systematic and has results as its goal. However, the looseness, informal atmosphere, and open space design, which I'll discuss in more detail in a moment, help participants give free rein to their ideas. It can not only be a welcome change to think without rigid rules, ingrained routines, or blinders. It also often leads a group further. Humans are already conditioned by evolution to adapt, to go new ways, and to invent new tools—these abilities are basically the starting point for design thinking. That's why you can actually use the thinking approach in all kinds of contexts, regardless of the subject, industry, or field of study. You can even use it to solve conflicts in the family. Nevertheless, as I said, there is a framework, a system. You will always find four to six successive phases that structure idea generation and collaboration in facilitated design thinking. Personally, the model with six phases appeals to me the most. As you can see in Fig. 6.3, it usually starts with a challenge and, if you don't stop early, ends with prototyping and testing. In the following, I will explain the phases in more detail and give you a few tips from practice.

6.2.1   Design Thinking Phases at a Glance

The challenge is, in a sense, a critical stocktaking with the aim of changing or renewing something. It contains a precisely formulated description of the problem so that those involved can think about how this specific situation can be mastered.

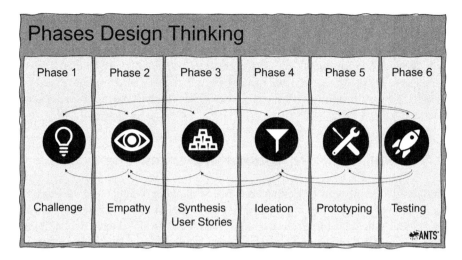

Fig. 6.3 Phases in design thinking (source: digit-ANTS GmbH)

Phase 1 is first about gaining a general understanding of the problem and its facets. The first ideas for solutions and thoughts are collected and also written down. It has proven advantageous to use different colored sticky notes and to bold or underline key words in the second step. A challenge like this doesn't have to be squeezed into a short, snappy sentence, even though in the age of Twitter and 5-s attention spans you probably kind of wish you could. On the contrary, a challenge can and should be multilayered. It can have several levels. When elaborating and formulating, you can take an analytical or disruptive approach: in the analytical approach, the actual processes in the company are often examined with the help of methods from business process modeling (BPM). For example, business processes can be depicted graphically in order to discover neuralgic points in a value chain: Which processes repeatedly encounter difficulties? Where in the chain are particularly many different departments involved? If bottlenecks always occur in the supply of goods to the production line in a supply chain, you could clearly identify this weak point using this method. In the disruptive approach, you look at the company from the outside with a what-if perspective. In doing so, you often assume the worst-case scenario with a little touch of humor. A fitting question could be: How will we lose all relevant partners and customers in 10 years? Ideally, this way of thinking will enable you to identify threatening competitor offers to which you can respond early on with your own services. A retail company that is always in a price war with its competitors should perhaps ask itself why customers buy from it in the first place instead of going to the competition. Perhaps it would be better in the long term to leave the price war to the others and set out on a path to becoming the service and quality leader, because this way you have better chances in the long term.

In the logistics sector, for example, a challenge for design thinking could be: "How can our company reduce logistics costs by 10% without compromising quality, while at the same time making the product range more diverse?" A slightly

1. Create and customize the challenge

Example in the area of construction materials:

"In a tough competitive environment, which is increasingly characterized by eCommerce, how can we reduce handling costs in logistics on the one hand and create added value for our customers on the other hand so that they are willing to pay slightly higher prices?"

Fig. 6.4 Example of a challenge (source: digit-ANTS GmbH)

more complicated challenge for the beverage industry might involve logistics and production alike: "In an increasingly complex environment with growing product container diversity, how can logistics cost-effectively meet the high customer and sales demands while supplying production operations with empty containers and stock materials on time and in sufficient quality and quantity?" Well, do you have a headache now? At least with design thinking, you wouldn't have to mull it all over on your own. You would have help. If, on the other hand, this is still not complex enough for you, you're welcome to add the aspect of where the production plants are located and what location issues logistics would have to take into account at a suitable point in this process. In any case, the production employees' perspective on the question would probably be different from that of the logistics specialists. Production would presumably ask: "How can production operations produce and supply the required quantity of products on time and in high quality in an increasingly complex environment with growing product and container diversity, taking into account the economic aspects of batch size and setup time optimization?"

What I want to say is that a challenge is not limited to a single requirement or question. After all, the solution is assigned to a group that can confront different sub-problems with diverse skills. If your people enjoy this sort of thing, feel free to make references to famous teams from film and television such as the A-Team, the X-Men, or, as far as I'm concerned, the companions from The Lord of the Rings.

In **phase 2**, the participants should put themselves in the shoes of other people. This is why you will find the term empathy in the phase model in Fig. 6.3. The design thinking group asks itself, for example: How does a forklift driver from the central warehouse actually feel when he starts his workday? And how does the forwarding manager feel at his workplace? The development of fictitious characters, referred to as personas (see Fig. 6.4), which represent a group of employees in the respective positions, vaguely resembles the work of a criminal investigation profiler, because one also gets into the psyche of the characters a little: Could the working conditions for the forklift driver be improved? You develop personas who face particular challenges and formulate corresponding needs. The forklift driver might think to himself: "When I start my shift, I often have to look for a forklift because it is not parked in a set place. And most of the time it's empty, too." Now this may sound a bit trite. But the realization that the man has to deal with this problem on a daily basis could inspire constructive thinking among workshop participants. Sometimes one is surprised at how close the horizon is in everyday life and work. The world remains a limited one for each and every one of us, even in the Internet age. Looking at the challenge through the lens of a shipping manager, one might ask, "From my position, how can I lower process costs in picking or reduce returns?" Occasionally, this second phase is referred to as the research phase or the 360° phase because its purpose is to research and get the most comprehensive view of the defined challenge. The team gathers information while examining the challenge from different perspectives. How intensive this second phase will certainly depend to some extent on the composition of the team.

Phase 3 is intended for developing user stories based on the personas conceived and the needs expressed by them. The employees and users involved in the IoT application have their own perspectives, their own user stories, and customer journeys (see Figs. 6.5 and 6.6): When do you even come into play? Where do you reach "pain points," i.e., critical points and moments that disrupt the flow of the application or project and ultimately perhaps counteract the user as a whole from this individual perspective? For the overall picture, the observations and assumptions about the different personas created should be combined. Some use analogies of puzzle pieces or mosaic pieces for phases 1 and 2, which are now to be put together to form an overall picture. In any case, a kind of synthesis of the first two steps occurs in this third phase. The thoughts have gotten a bit out of hand. Now the flow of thoughts is channeled again somewhat, and a framework is created for the planned IoT project.

In **phase 4**, first ideas are collected, which then have to be filtered and linked (see Fig. 6.7). The moderator decides how strongly to push the idea generation phase. There are basically two tactics here: divergent thinking has something childlike about it and is often supported with movement games. In the meantime, one collects as many options as possible. Another variant is convergent thinking. Here, one selects more strongly from the beginning, selects solution approaches, and combines according to logical criteria. Either way, a funnel is formed, figuratively speaking, into which all ideas flow—and (again) with the stopwatch running. The moderator makes sure that the workshop does not drift into aimless spinning and that the best ideas are filtered out in a clustering process. An exciting question is also how to deal with the results of this workshop phase. Later, during the implementation of the problem solutions and innovations discovered through design thinking, people who were not present at the workshop just might object. For this reason, I would recommend communicating the results in a meaningful way and bringing them to the attention of the responsible departments as soon as possible.

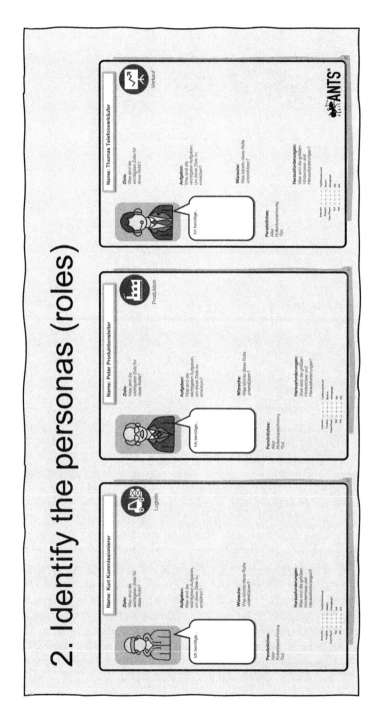

Fig. 6.5 Identifying the personas (roles) (source: digit-ANTS GmbH)

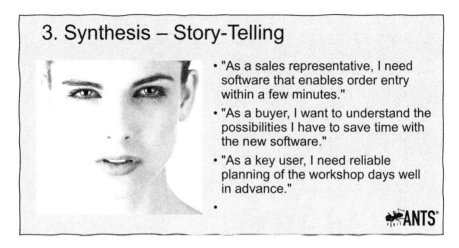

Fig. 6.6 Synthesis: storytelling (source: digit-ANTS GmbH)

Fig. 6.7 Developing user stories (source: digit-ANTS GmbH)

Phase 5 (prototype phase; see Fig. 6.8) is unfortunately skipped or omitted in many workshop formats, probably because it is not easy to implement. However, this is a missed opportunity to really get something out of such a seminar. A prototype is to be created from the insights gathered so far. In contrast to the rapid prototyping and minimal viable product/service approaches (see Chap. 8), design thinking aims less at the concrete market launch of products. Here, the end result of prototyping is a testable product, service, or software solution in the broadest sense. A prototype in the sense of design thinking can also be located on the conceptual or planning level. For example, if the goal is a just-in-time supply concept for manufacturing or for filling empties at a brewery, schedules and rules could be

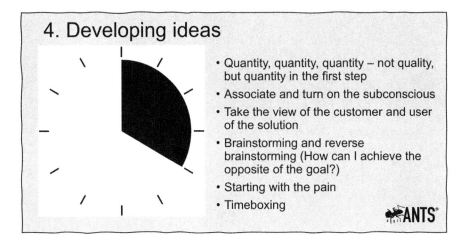

Fig. 6.8 Developing ideas (source: digit-ANTS GmbH)

defined here, for example, that the supply vehicle has priority over other suppliers or empties collectors in the plant's own yard. It would also be possible to implement a concrete action plan to cut logistics costs by reducing the variety of items and to reduce setup times in production. At the end of prototyping, it might turn out that new processes would be needed for this. When prototyping software, a capable developer or programmer could be brought in to put it all together. However, for the first round, an analog prototype would also do in which the screen masks (user interfaces, UIs) are drawn on paper. From the UIs, the processes and underlying software functionalities up to the software architecture could be derived in later steps.

No matter how intensively you project yourself into the customers of the present and future with your personas and corresponding empathic analysis, no design thinking team can really validly predict whether a new offer will be accepted and have chances on the market. In **phase 6**, which follows prototyping, you should gather reactions and feedback (see Fig. 6.9). This can be done using conversation, interviews, or questionnaires. It is important that you present your prototype, its potential, the targeted area of use, and the premises you identified in the workshop. For example, you could talk to the sales team and field service in a first round and then expand the testing circle bit by bit: from the picker to the driver and the dispatcher and the transport logistics manager to the shift supervisor, maintenance staff, and electrician in production. Ideally, depending on how these conversations go, the prototype will be developed and adapted iteratively. There's no question about it: this is a lot of work that goes well beyond a workshop, and that's why companies are always put off by it. But basically, this step is the sensible and final transition to the level of the entire company where before you could let off steam for a while under laboratory conditions. Testing can even have event character if you get involved on it. A good feedback phase can open up great opportunities to expose

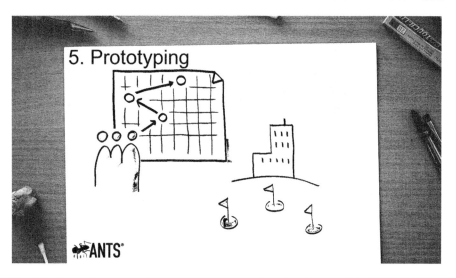

Fig. 6.9 Prototyping can also be a picture or a process flow chart (source: digit-ANTS GmbH)

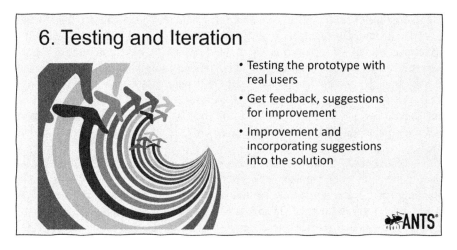

Fig. 6.10 Testing and iteration (source: digit-ANTS GmbH)

potential customers to the prototype and better understand their needs. Addressing
customers in this way and involving them in new developments are probably not bad
ideas from a modern sales point of view (Fig. 6.10).

6.2.2 Tips for Successful Implementation

Although I know of successful and somehow memorable workshops in which design
thinking was tried out or used in depth, in theory such a workshop can also go

terribly wrong if you set it up incorrectly. To save you from that, I want to give you some basic tips here.

For joint reflection and problem-solving to succeed in the context of design thinking, both the composition of the team involved and the atmosphere and design of the rooms are important. Often, the requirements of several areas intertwine when dealing with issues for a company or an industry. An interdisciplinary group evaluates situations and problems in a more multilayered way than a single person can. Design thinking is a game of ideas that you play together, not against each other. Therefore, it is important to take a stroll off the beaten track. If one of the participants is not open to alternatives, this will sooner or later slow down the whole team. Let's assume that a medium-sized company in the automotive industry wants to offer end-to-end status monitoring of its vehicles as a service. Its goal is to transmit error messages directly to the service department and thus be able to help customers more quickly. In order to work through and discuss this in a sensible manner, it is advisable to bring together employees from vehicle development, service, spare parts logistics, and IT. The workshop should be attended by people who are likely to contribute relevant knowledge and skills to the success of the project.

In addition to the composition of the team, the room situation should also be taken into account, because it definitely has an influence on the way colleagues get along with each other. Instead of meeting in a conference room with heavy tables and a rehearsed seating arrangement, it's better to meet in open spaces that don't constantly remind those involved of the day's business and allow for flexible sitting, standing, walking, and grouping for the next few hours. Lightweight, portable, and wheeled equipment can go a long way here. For inspiration, feel free to look at New Year's speeches by the German president or even stiffer acts of state from other countries and then try to do the opposite if possible when selecting and staffing spaces for your design thinking. Standing tables are better than piles of desks and neutral rooms better than the boss's meeting room.

Don't start with existential projects right away. Design thinking can even be a crisis management tool, if used correctly, but that requires a certain amount of experience, I would say. Of course, creative sessions can always have a serious background. But existential pressure and creative problem-solving are only compatible to a limited extent. Therefore, during the design thinking session, the atmosphere should distract from urgency rather than reminding of it. For creative solution finding in design thinking workshops, it is important to be able to speak openly in the group. Empathy and trusting collaboration contribute significantly to success. I have ended many DT workshops on the first day after a few hours because the teams were not open to each other and there was fear, inhibition, and competition between the participants; therefore, no meaningful result could be expected.

6.3   Reality Check for Use Cases

Since I'm convinced that good IoT projects will make our world a better place in the long term, I may sound a bit naïve to you now and then. However, in my opinion, visionary thinking, the search for creative solutions to problems, and entrepreneurial action are not mutually exclusive. Without new and original ideas, we would have a different economy with much more product piracy and fewer strong brands, brandings, and entrepreneurial figures. Without a good dose of business sense, however, great ideas rarely amount to much. As a married man with a family, I am of course familiar with the saying "Let he who commits himself be tested forever." My wife could confirm that I also know the motto "Trust is good, control is better" from home. It can cause you almost as much trouble as it can save you, as I've learned. But for new IoT projects, a little control may be in order. Once a promising idea for a use case has been found, it should be checked to see how it can be implemented in terms of software and hardware, which prerequisites the company does not (yet) fulfill, and whether or not the whole thing is economically viable. This can also be integrated—at least in part—in a workshop with design thinking. However, if you want to separate this or if design thinking is not a viable method in your case, you could alternatively fall back on the project management and controlling steps that have proven successful in comparable projects. Keep in mind that most IoT projects are dynamic and will involve innovation as software components evolve, for example. For this reason, it may be advisable to work with tools from innovation controlling if you want to document and check a use case in this way.

Among other things, there is a multi-part, free series with helpful checklists on successful innovation management at the RKW Competence Center. This is a nationwide networked organization, funded by the Ministry of Economics, that supports companies during their startup phase and also during the next steps, especially when it comes to modernization. There you will find, for example, a compact introduction to innovation controlling (https://www.rkw-kompetenzzentrum.de/innovation/faktenblatt/erfolgsfaktor-3-das-innovationscontrolling/einfuehrung).

You could also use an approach by Nikolas Eckhardt and Ingo Meironke, two authors on the staff of the international management and technology consultancy Campana & Schott. The two suggest three sub-steps after the successful search for ideas in order to test the feasibility of implementation:

1. Identify the right technology.
2. Create a maturity model and perform an efficiency check.
3. Validate concepts.

The first sub-step, determining the appropriate technology, means matching and allocating data processing layers for considerations with regard to IoT. Should we process the information in the cloud or via edge computing? Does the processing and response to the information need to be real time? What information should be compulsorily uploaded to the cloud for evaluation?

For the second control step, which concerns efficiency and maturity, Nikolas Eckhardt and Ingo Meironke look at three areas:

- Maturity level of digitization.
- Status quo of the IT infrastructure.
- Possible obstacles due to internal processes.

To determine the degree of maturity with regard to digitization, you should look at where data and information are still being recorded in analog form and entered manually. It's also important to check the access rights to the data inventories in each case for the data processing steps that have already been digitized. I would also include the topics of data protection and data security, as well as General Data Protection Regulation (GDPR) compliance. The status quo of the IT infrastructure includes the computing power of the computers and networks involved as well as security aspects for hardware and device software (keywords: security by device and security by default). For the third step, which considers the internal processes, the people are probably the decisive factor. Get an idea of the knowledge level and time capacities of the employees you want to involve in the IoT project. As several surveys have shown, it can be difficult for small- and medium-sized enterprises (SMEs) to find employees with the required knowledge and skills (in-house and external). Typical of several publications, Fig. 6.11 shows an interesting survey result from the Internet of Things 2019 study.

By far the biggest organizational challenge in the IoT use cases, as you can see in Fig. 6.11, was a lack of IT professionals. Position 4 in the left-hand table is also worth noting: 21.4% of over 250 companies surveyed were missing key skills from their own workforce. On the right-hand side, in the table on technological hurdles, you will again find "IT systems with outdated operating systems" that cannot be patched, as well as the integration of devices, sensors, and actuators into the IT infrastructure, each with more than 20%. You already know this from Chap. 5. Let me briefly address both challenges—capable people and outdated technology—in the following sections.

6.4 Partners and Support for IoT Projects

If you want to tackle a new IoT project, you don't have to do it from A to Z on your own. Most smaller companies lack the resources for this in at least one place. There can be many advantages to getting outside support.

When preparing, for example, it can be helpful to engage a professional facilitator for ideation, especially if you are engaging in design thinking. For collaborative thinking and creativity, as I described earlier, it is important not to give any one voice more or less weight than another. When in doubt, any alpha dogs need to leave the event if shy people won't open up otherwise. Because of group dynamics like this,

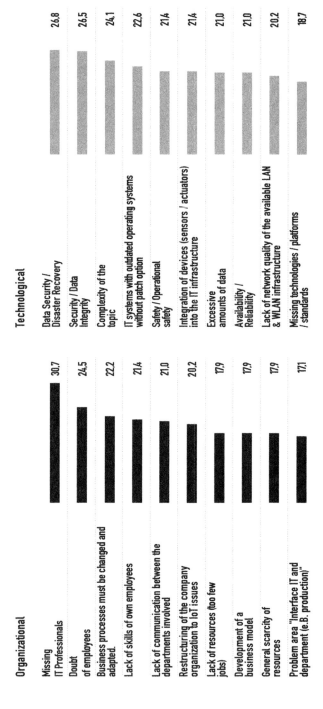

Fig. 6.11 Challenges for IT projects (source: Mauerer, Jürgen et al. Internet of Things 2019 Study, p. 15)

Organizational

Missing IT Professionals	30.7
Doubt of employees	24.5
Business processes must be changed and adapted.	22.2
Lack of skills of own employees	21.4
Lack of communication between the departments involved	21.0
Restructuring of the company organization to IoT issues	20.2
Lack of resources (too few jobs)	17.9
Development of a business model	17.9
General scarcity of resources	17.9
Problem area "Interface IT and department (e.B. production)"	17.1

Technological

Data Security / Disaster Recovery	26.8
Security / Data Integrity	26.5
Complexity of the topic	24.1
IT systems with outdated operating systems without patch option	22.6
Safety / Operational safety	21.4
Integration of devices (sensors / actuators) into the IT infrastructure	21.4
Excessive amounts of data	21.0
Availability / Reliability	21.0
Lack of network quality of the available LAN & WLAN infrastructure	20.2
Missing technologies / platforms / standards	18.7

you need a moderator or facilitator who, on the one hand, can stand back and let the others do their thing but, on the other hand, is able to intervene and mediate at critical moments. This can be someone from your own ranks or a professional brought in from outside. Two arguments, which you should simply weigh up in terms of cost-benefit for your particular situation, speak in favor of help from trained coaches and facilitators: for inexperienced design thinking coaches, it may be difficult the first time to find the balance between a realistic challenge, practical personas, and an entertaining, humorous workshop situation. For those instances, you can call on people like me. Second, it will take some time for someone on your staff to be adequately trained. If you are in a hurry, it will probably go faster with external help.

Apart from the brainwork, you may also need new devices or machine components for the planned IoT project that you cannot manufacture yourself (see also Sect. 6.5). In this case, of course, the good old network will help you. However, you can also benefit from the fact that some IoT platform providers are also involved in enterprise networking. At SAP, for example, you can draw on existing networks and scouting for IoT projects. Employees in the Walldorf-based company's Data Space in Berlin now have more than 5 years of experience in scouting and working with startups. A program called SAP.iO is designed to accompany and facilitate use cases. One way to do this is to extend the functionality of SAP's standard software with innovative solutions from startups. Another is to give founders the chance to position new solutions with SAP customers. So if you happen to use SAP software, you can try to find technology partners through such channels. Similarly, other large networks are organized out of Germany. There is no harm in researching companies such as Bosch, Siemens, ABB, or the sensor manufacturer SICK. Such large providers with an electronics and sensor focus usually have reliable and scalable solutions ready to help you roll out quickly.

If you want to research vendor-neutral hardware manufacturers for a planned IoT project, you can proceed as follows:

- Search for companies in the online business networks XING (for the German-speaking region) and LinkedIn (for the international region) and contact the responsible persons there.
- Use specialized websites and online platforms to find startups for collaborations, for example, at startupdetector (www.startupdetector.de), Crunchbase (www.crunchbase.com), Startbase (www.startbase.de), Gründerszene (www.gruenderszene.de), or deutsche-startups.de (www.deutsche-startups.de).
- Analyze the membership structure of the International Organization for Standardization (ISO) committee on IoT in more detail to find potential partners in relevant technical groups. The website of the International Electrotechnical Commission (IEC, http://s-prs.de/v747239) lists the members of the international committee ISO/IEC JTC 1/SC 41 Internet of Things and Related Technologies. This is the technical group that developed the ISO/IEC 30141 standard on IoT reference architecture (see Chap. 2).

As you've probably noticed, the amount of research gets higher with each bullet point. The spectrum from "We'll pull this off on our own for now, it's just a little test balloon" to "This will catapult us to the next level if we pull it off with a really good partner" is certainly quite large. I will say a few more words about the sense of long-term, strategic partnerships that affect the entire corporate and innovation strategy when we take a closer look at IoT strategies (see Chap. 8). But even on a project-by-project basis, smaller, external support can provide the crucial help needed to successfully get an IoT application off the ground.

6.5   Buy New or Upgrade?

I have already briefly touched on the phenomenon of retrofitting when talking about the integrated and separate sensor systems for IoT devices and the features of IoT platforms that can speak for or against an implementation. Now let's expand on that a bit more with a view to IoT projects. Enterprise-wide, it's often overkill to clean out all the old devices and completely replace them with new ones. After all, it's impossible for many companies to simply radically replace all existing equipment with a new generation of smart devices. In most cases, it is more appropriate to integrate the older machines and devices into an IoT system rather than managing multiple areas in parallel within the enterprise-wide world of machines and devices. It is unrealistic, especially for small- and medium-sized companies, to completely renew production systems. If the current systems are still fully functional, one naturally wants to use them as long and as fully as possible. Those who have only recently invested in new, unfortunately not yet (fully) IoT-capable hardware might shy away from further investments in networking and harmonization. Often, the acquisition costs for recommended new models and equipment exceed the budget. And setting up completely new factories or production halls right away would require not only liquidity but also property and personnel management that is more likely to be found in stock corporations and large corporate groups.

This is why SMEs in particular like to resort to the aforementioned retrofitting in order to bring existing systems and modern IoT systems into line with each other. The term retrofit is composed of the Latin retro for backward or directed into the past and the English fit for our adaptability in the sense of Darwin's survival of the fittest. The retrofit approach encompasses machine updates and plant modernization, especially in industry. In terms of IoT, retrofit means retrofitting machines already in operation with new functions. For example, many machine sensors can be connected to IoT modules so that control data or production data can be used in real time and in the sense of Big Data. This could be information about temperature or humidity, for example. For such retrofitting, we need an efficient bridging technology that enables machines to feed understandable and usable data into IoT networks and modern IT platforms. We need adapters, boxes, gateways, and middleware, where the solutions rarely have vendor-neutral names but are usually already branded by the name. Three examples from Bosch's product world are the Transport Data Logger (TDL), the Cross Domain Development Kit (XDK), and the Connected Industrial Sensor

Solution (CISS). A Stuttgart-based company was able to use XDK to bring together data from additional sensors in the production environment, route it through the network, and connect it to the existing production control system. These data relate to temperature, pneumatic pressure, and vibration. This is where we come back to predictive maintenance as a form of artificial intelligence in data monitoring for condition monitoring (see Chap. 5). With TDL, the Galleria Nazionale d'Arte Moderna e Contemporanea in Rome was able to monitor the transport of a painting. By attaching the Transport Data Logger to the shipment, all environmental influences of the cargo were recorded, transmitted via Bluetooth, and visualized via a mobile app. According to Bosch, the client saved about 30% in costs compared to the sensor devices used previously but was kept up to date on relevant positions and environmental influences at all times. And while I'm promoting Bosch here, the traditional company has also reportedly managed to catapult a lathe from 1887, which the founder himself is said to have worked on, into the age of Industry 4.0 via an IoT gateway. If you think about it for a moment, you might just start dreaming again: Is retrofitting possibly an option for adding a dimension to recycling, upcycling, and producing less scrap worldwide? It would be great if technology gaps could be closed on a global scale, ideally through sustainably produced IoT bridge technology.

For track and trace applications in transportation, such as the delivery of the painting mentioned above, retrofitting with small mobile adapters is of course particularly useful and correspondingly widespread. But even stationary hardware located on the shop floor, in the factory, that was not developed and commissioned with the current state of knowledge about machine languages, data readability and data security, can be retrofitted so that it meets current standards and is once again compatible with modern solutions.

Such retrofitting naturally brings a few challenges:

- Retrofitting cannot disrupt ongoing operations too much. After all, you don't want any production downtime or delivery problems.
- For an IIoT platform to communicate efficiently with the connected devices and machines, the machines must not fail to communicate with each other. Now, however, the medium-sized IT landscape with its many specialists and individually built-up know-how is rather heterogeneous when we think of machine control, file formats, interfaces, and the like. Where humans can rely on interpreters and translators, the machines need help in the form of drivers and patches that restore lost compatibility.
- If the machines then deliver comprehensible information and data, you have to be careful about who can see and use this data and with what access rights. I have already said a few words about data protection and data security in connection with IoT platforms and multi-cloud strategies. Even retrofitted company hardware can become a GDPR problem if you simply let things/data run there.
- In addition, a centralized IT structure with an IoT platform to which all devices are connected is probably a more interesting target for hackers than isolated machine software, because they cannot get anywhere efficiently from this

"isolated solution." So when we bring new things onto the network, the traffic routes should be sufficiently secure.

On the other hand, the advantages of retrofitting are not limited to cost issues. There's also the space argument: nowadays, IoT components are usually so space-saving that you don't need to expand your production buildings, while the actual industrial plants and machines have not yet shrunk quite as dramatically as our data carriers, for example. If you use the retrofit approach, your workforce can continue to work with the familiar equipment as usual. Experience shows that training for upgraded equipment is not as costly as training for newly purchased equipment. Upgrades are simplified. Software can be updated not only centrally, but possibly remotely. Some machines and systems achieve better energy efficiency after being upgraded by retrofit, since they are only started up when necessary.

In this chapter, you learned how to prepare IoT projects. In Chap. 7, I will introduce you to various IIoT use cases. On the one hand, these are intended to provide you with inspiration for finding your own application possibilities, and on the other hand, they are intended to deepen your practical insight by providing you with very concrete information about what is already made possible by IoT today.

Use Cases for the Internet of Things

7

In this chapter, I would like to present the benefits of the IoT based on specific use cases. The majority of the use cases comes from the areas of logistics and production. They provide inspiration for possible IoT applications that can be used to implement Industry 4.0 scenarios in companies.

We will take a closer look at the following use cases in this chapter:

- **Driverless transport vehicles**
  In the first use case (see Sect. 7.1), I present driverless transport vehicles and the corresponding control systems (automated guided vehicles, AGVs), which are now not only used to optimize intralogistic transport processes but are also revolutionizing the entire production chains and lines with their flexibility. One example of the use of AGVs in production is the connection of freely arranged machines in a modern group technology manufacturing.
- **Container management**
  In the second use case in Sect. 7.2, you will learn how container fill levels can be transmitted in real time and what this means for logistics as well as supply and disposal processes. You can also use corresponding technologies in production supply to generate real-time transparency about the inventory situation for bulk goods or liquids. As an example, I will present how a waste disposal company detects the fill levels of glass containers by means of vibration patterns and schedules its fleet of trucks to empty the containers according to demand.
- **Corona warning app**
  In Sect. 7.3, I would like to introduce the functionality of the Corona warning app. This is an interesting IoT use case that covers some important privacy and information security issues. Your smartphone becomes an IoT device when you activate this app, capturing movement patterns, contacts, and other characteristics in real time and sharing them via a cloud platform.

© The Author(s), under exclusive license to Springer Nature Switzerland AG 2022
A. Holtschulte, *Digital Supply Chain and Logistics with IoT*, Management for Professionals, https://doi.org/10.1007/978-3-030-89408-5_7

- **Track and trace in logistics and production**
  In Sect. 7.4, you will learn how to track goods, commodities, containers, and vehicles globally and in real time using the IoT. Tracking can be used in production, transport, and intralogistics.
- **Smart glasses in production and logistics**
  As soon as information is displayed in the field of vision of a maintenance technician, warehouse worker, or production employee, he can be guided in his work and have both hands free. The fact that the smart glasses used here can transmit what the wearer sees to another maintenance technician in real time results in interesting use cases and various advantages in production and logistics (see Sect. 7.5).
- **Object recognition and identification with the IoT**
  In Sect. 7.6, I will show you the opportunities that arise from the use of object recognition in production.
- **Maintenance and servicing in production**
  Certainly the best-known example of the IoT in production is predictive maintenance by recording and analyzing sensor data on machines. Since this use case is not only well known but also highly relevant, I explain the context and application in Sect. 7.7.
- **The IoT business models in mechanical engineering**
  In Sect. 7.8, you will learn how the use of the IoT systems in production in general and in the manufacture of tools and machines in particular can result in new business models. For example, the IoT system can help to rent machines to customers in the form of a leasing model through clever analysis of sensor data.

7.1   Driverless Transport Vehicles in Production and Logistics

This section describes the current situation and the architecture of automated guided vehicles (AGVs) and their integration into higher-level corporate software. In this case, the warehouse management system and, if necessary, the production planning system still play a central role as enterprise software and integrated information system. These systems form the skeleton in terms of master data and synchronization of value flow, goods flow, and information flow.

Staff shortages, the merging of production and logistics, very small series and requirements for modular production, flexible manufacturing structures, and the demand for digital logistics and manufacturing have led to an increase in demand for driverless transport vehicles in recent years.

Now that the technology is very mature in terms of physics, however, the IT concepts of automated guided vehicles (AGVs) on which vehicle integration is based seem to be lagging behind. Instead of integrating the higher-level control system into the existing software systems, additional system layers are being pulled in today. As a result, the potential that could arise from the use of AGVs is not being fully exploited. With a contemporary Industrial Internet of Things (IIoT) system architecture, modern concepts can be implemented relatively easily, and data can be processed at the points in the system where it makes sense from a performance and quality point of view.

The time is ripe to rethink the integration of driverless transport vehicles into the existing software and system landscape, because the need to use driverless and autonomous industrial trucks will continue to grow for the following reasons:

1. **Difficulties in finding qualified personnel in production and logistics**
   The shortage of personnel in logistics is an issue that has been known for some years now among truck drivers. For some time now, it has also been difficult to fill vacancies with qualified personnel in intralogistics. According to the job survey conducted by the Institute for Employment Research (IAB), the research arm of the German Federal Employment Agency, there were 82,000 vacancies in logistics in the second quarter of 2018. This is a record level.
2. **Merger of production and logistics**
   The areas of production and logistics can no longer be considered separately. Particularly in the automotive and mechanical engineering industries, work is carried out in three shifts, which means that personnel costs account for a significant proportion of production and logistics costs.
3. **Clock-synchronous deliveries**
   Deliveries are made just in time or even just in sequence to the production machines. There is no space at the machines to buffer material. Therefore, the material flow must be highly integrated into the demand situation at the production machines, and the machines must be supplied and readied on the dot.
4. **The need for flexible production forces manufacturers into modular production**
   In the field of automotive production, the first modular manufacturing processes are already being implemented. The fast pace and individualization of products (keyword: one-piece series) are the issue here, as well as the market's requirement to implement innovations agilely on the product. This leads to the fact that AGVs are replacing the production line and can also directly take over warehouse and logistics activities after the production process is completed.
5. **The search for digital, innovative IoT use cases in connection with Industry 4.0**
   Another development is that companies are looking for IoT use cases for innovations in the course of the digital transformation in logistics and production. They are finding them in the area of automation and autonomization of internal transport and warehouse processes and, of course, in the area of modular manufacturing.

7.1.1 Initial Situation

In intralogistics and production, goods are moved—and for the most part still by people on industrial trucks. Where it makes sense and is possible, goods have increasingly been stored in automated high-bay warehouses and automated small parts warehouses in the past.

But what has to be done when transports between source and sink cannot be standardized in this way? What has to be done when tugger trains travel very individual routes and stations or when material supply and disposal between machines in modular production is very individual? What has to be done if the supply and disposal of production has to react flexibly to changes and different sinks? And what has to be done when production lines have to be rebuilt within minutes?

In these areas, driverless transport systems (AGVs) are the ideal solution. The system usually consists of driverless forklift trucks, a master control system, sensors for determining the location and for recording the plant and hall topology, transmission technology between the vehicles and the master computer, and the peripheral systems (automatic warehouse, traffic lights, gates, loading stations).

In terms of vehicles, forklifts, tugger trains, under-run FTFs, and under-run tractors are the most common representatives of the genre. In the assembly area, AGVs are also used as mobile workbenches and can replace the assembly line in series production.

Original equipment manufacturers (OEMs) in particular have recognized that new vehicle series in automotive production also require the use of new production processes and are cautiously introducing new concepts and technologies related to AGVs.

The vehicles are integrated on the software platform (AGV control station). It controls the communication among the vehicles and supplies the vehicles with orders. It stores the information about the plant and hall topology. It controls the traffic flow and receives status messages from the AGV controllers and peripheral equipment such as traffic lights, gates, loading stations, and automatic warehouses.

Furthermore, the control station level ideally also offers the following functions:

- Display of the material flow in real time.
- Simulation of the travel paths.
- Integration of machine information (MES).
- Optimization of intralogistic processes in coordination with the WMS.
- Communication with FTFs of all common manufacturers.
- Integration of the automatic warehouse.
- Control of traffic lights and gates.

In many specifications, the requirements for the master controller are greatly neglected, although this is where the core of the functionality lies. In addition, it is not uncommon for the master control to require its own server.

The manufacturers of driverless transport vehicles offer suitable control stations for their vehicles, which are usually still installed on-premise at the customer's data center or directly in a dedicated computer in the warehouse. Contemporary approaches in the cloud are still rare at present. In addition, these platforms do not fit the vehicles of other manufacturers. It is therefore currently common practice to buy the FTFs and the software platform from one manufacturer—a typical lock-in effect.

The manufacturer of the AGV supplies not only the vehicles but also the control station software, which is usually only suitable for vehicles from his company. Vehicles from other manufacturers cannot be integrated into the software at all or only with great difficulty.

7.1.2 AGV Control Station: Brand Self-Made in the Cloud

For the reasons mentioned above and because some customers want to make themselves independent, many customers are taking matters into their own hands: in digitization projects, dynamic teams of logistics experts and software developers on the customer side are now developing their own IoT software platforms, which are then intended to unite the integration of different vehicles on one platform— usually in the public cloud. Often, they also develop their own driverless transport vehicle at the same time.

Here, three fundamental problems arise again and again:

1. A solution operated in a public cloud can reach performance limits with an unfavorable strategy regarding storage temperature (see Sect. 2.1.2) and due to the limited bandwidth via the Internet. The bandwidth requirements are at least comparable to the requirements of an automated warehouse placed on the warehouse control computer, provided that all information is to be processed in the cloud. You should therefore urgently make a plan in advance as to which data you want to keep in the cloud, which in Edge and which in Fog.
   (a) A high proportion of the intelligence resides on the devices themselves, yet feedback and control require high levels of communication. Check exactly which data must be processed where and which can be outsourced.
   (b) The number of AGVs in a network multiplies the amount of data that the higher-level controller must receive and process. The requirement for data transmission in milliseconds is not uncommon here.
2. Individual innovation projects prevent a uniform standard that integrates FTFs on one platform. This standard in the interface from the vehicle to the platform is long overdue. The German Engineering Federation (VDMA) has launched the first part of the VDMA OPC UA Robotics Companion Specification. With the obvious and widespread scenarios of initiative asset management and condition monitoring, the German Engineering Federation is trying to recommend certain standards here in its guideline VDMA 40010-1:2019-07. The guideline can be downloaded at https://www.digit-ants.com/2019/09/10/opc-ua-companion-speci fication-for-robotics-opc-robotics-part-1-vertical-integration.
3. It follows that in addition to the standardization of interfaces and agreement on which decisions should be made at the AGV level, there is still a lack of standard software today, an "AGV control tower" with standardized interfaces into inventory management and warehouse management.

The Burden with the Specifications

Due to the poor integration of the manufacturer platforms with the FTFs of other manufacturers, customers are becoming massively dependent on one manufacturer. This dependency is also facilitated by the fact that customers offer software and hardware together in one package in almost every project as a matter of course. This is fatal because it prevents suppliers of an independent platform for AGVs from gaining access to the market in the first place. From the point of view of the bidder, this procedure is understandable, since the bidder wants to have only one contact for the AGV trade and cannot and does not want to take on the coordination of hardware and software.

What Levels of Control Are Really Still Needed?

In many specifications, the potentials that could result from an integrated platform as an AGV control tower fall by the wayside. The requirement in the specifications for an AGV control unit, which often communicates directly with the AGV control units two levels below the warehouse management system and one level below the warehouse control computer, comes at the expense of functionality and flexibility, because the optimizations at the different levels mean that the overall result is no longer optimal (see Fig. 7.1).

7.1.3   Success Through Simplification

By reducing the number of systems and system levels and cleverly integrating and linking the interfaces at the warehouse management level, decisions can be negotiated directly at the top level. In SAP Extended Warehouse Management, for example, the material flow control system (MFCS) is integrated into the warehouse management level through the MFS module. Following the model, it makes sense to also integrate the master control of the driverless transport vehicles on this level. In this way, decisions can be made holistically for the material flow on a single level. All the information then only has to converge at this level. This means that, in addition to automatic high-bay warehouses, other peripherals such as gates and traffic lights can also be integrated into the control system.

Of course, if the assembly line is replaced by AGVs, the flexibility and the software allow it to be moved a few meters to the right or left, or the manufactured parts can be transported directly from the end of production to the sink or to different sinks. But these are by no means all the possibilities offered by the use of AGVs in an integrated scenario. An integrated control station could react to disruptions in the operating sequence because it has all the relevant information at its disposal.

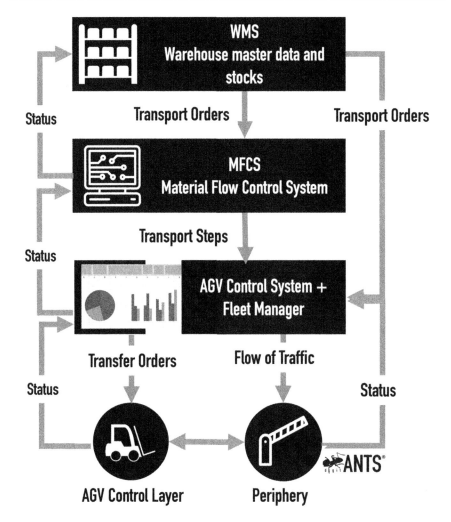

Fig. 7.1 Traditional control levels in automated guided vehicles (source: digit-ANTS GmbH)

Practical Example

If an AGV drives to a picking storage location to pick up a part for production and, contrary to expectations, the location is empty, the AGV would wait for replenishment. In an integrated scenario, in which the AGV guidance system is integrated in the warehouse management system, the following steps could be triggered by the AGV:

(continued)

1. Post a zero inventory in WMS, since the bin is physically empty.
2. Trigger a replenishment to the picking storage bin.
3. Search for an alternative picking storage bin in the WMS with stock.
4. Create a transport request in WMS from an alternative source.
5. Move to the alternative location, and confirm the transfer order later.

The example shows that the possibilities, if you take a closer look at them, are much more than the mere automation of supply. Through clever integration, events could further automate booking processes and decisions. Stakeholders can easily gain this insight if all stakeholders are involved in the project planning and design of the facilities. One stakeholder is always central IT, since it must ultimately maintain the systems and ensure their operation.

Corporate IT Must Be Integrated in Tenders
The tenders often reveal very little about the requirements for the integration platform and the control system. Furthermore, the tenderers say little or nothing about how the solution is to be integrated into the IT infrastructure, which components and functions are to run in the IoT cloud, which in Edge and which in Fog. This is because the requirements have so far often been formulated purely from a warehouse and production perspective, and the IT department is rarely involved in the tendering process. However, if the "driverless transport vehicles" project is to be treated as an IoT innovation in the area of digital transformation in logistics and production, processes and functionalities must also be viewed disruptively. This is strongly recommended in order not to merely equip an "evolved," partly question-able material flow with new technology. Rethink the processes and warehouse movements based on the newfound capabilities. What would stop you from letting the AGV automatically re-sort the stock continuously during quiet phases when there is little utilization in the warehouse, in order to always have an optimal ABC distribution of your stock in the warehouse? In modern fully automated high-bay warehouses, this is standard nowadays.

Think and Go New Ways
Disruptive means that processes are fundamentally questioned, and, in the wake of market changes and consumer demands, the company, logistics, and production must also follow new business models. Replacing conveyor belts with driverless transport vehicles is not enough. Often, revealing creativity in the flow of materials requires methods such as Design Thinking to get away from the old structures a bit. The method comes from software development and helps to look at the processes from the end user's point of view and thus to find the necessary functions for an optimal path from the user's perspective. The method can be used to find additional use cases like the one in the previous example, because it creates an open climate for bringing ideas to the table that might otherwise remain unspoken in the minds of the participants.

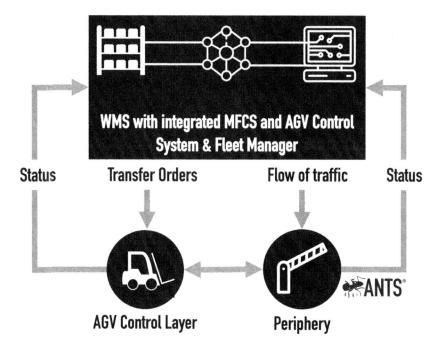

Fig. 7.2 Target image during integration into the warehouse management level (source: digit-ANTS GmbH)

Ideally, the hardware and software are put out to tender separately after a detailed clarification of requirements. This allows the best provider to be selected for each trade. However, this is precisely why IT must also be involved in the tender process. Three advantages could be achieved by separating hardware and software in the tenders:

1. Disclosure of the vehicle manufacturers' interfaces and integration points could be made a condition for participation in the tender, and standards could thus be created virtually as an aside.
2. The customer obtains independence from the manufacturer of the FTFs.
3. The development of standard software for supervisory control with appropriate integration at the control level of the AGV and at the warehouse management and inventory management level would be pursued.

Conclusion
In efforts to use FTFs in material flow, contemporary controls should be used, and the FTF should be understood as an IoT system. This allows you to decide how to operate which AGV devices and at which level in the IoT system architecture you process the data, according to the IoT reference architecture. The control levels should be minimized and ideally integrated on one level (see Fig. 7.2), since this

allows you to map integrated scenarios and automations that make material flow and booking processes more efficient. The tenders for control station software and vehicles should be separate and coordinated with regard to the requirements for the interfaces and the IoT system architecture. The central IT department must be at the table for this. When defining the requirements, modern methods such as Design Thinking should be used to identify the use cases. During implementation, an agile approach could help you a lot to initially go live with certain areas in production and warehousing and to get returns from your investment very quickly.

7.1.4   Architecture and Components

Table 7.1 gives you an overview of the entities and components required for automated guided vehicles.

Table 7.1 Required components and entities for driverless transport systems

Entity	Type	Description	Technology
Warehouse worker	Human entity		
Driverless transport vehicle	Device		
Cameras	Sensor		
Laser	Sensor		
AGV control station and user interface	Software system	Visualization and possibility of intervention by personnel	
Warehouse management system with user interface	Software system	Creates and confirms transfer orders within the warehouse based on stock removal, putaway, transfer, or production staging needs and picks for deliveries	WMS (integrated information system) fed by the ERP system
Warehouse control computer/ material flow control	Software system	The warehouse control computer directly influences the control units, for example, PLCs of conveyors in the warehouse	
Enterprise network	Network	Enterprise network that provides access to edge components and the cloud application	
Gateway	Gateway	Establishes internet connection or connection to the warehouse control computer, depending on which optimizations are to be made and where	
Cloud service AGV	Service	Optimization	
Software service AGV in edge	Service	Optimization	

7.2 Container Management in Real Time

Glass is considered environmentally friendly because it can be easily recycled. However, recycling requires both collection and recycling. Glass is collected in the private environment in cities and municipalities in throw-in containers. These are emptied regularly by disposal companies, and the used glass is transported away so that citizens can throw in new used glass again. So far, so good. Oh no, wait, the story is just beginning. How efficient do you think the emptying of the containers is? Are they always full to bursting when the truck drives by to empty them? Yes, sometimes they are, and sometimes they were full many days before they were emptied, so the waste glass piles up or lies smashed on the street and sidewalk. Often, however, the containers are only filled to a fraction. The Bochum waste disposal company and start-up Zolitron Technology GmbH from the most beautiful city in the Ruhr region no longer wanted to put up with this state of affairs. The disposal company's main problem was that when scheduling the vehicles, it had no idea what situation the driver would find at the containers.

7.2.1 Problem

"Honey, can you please take the waste glass to the container when you're out to get rolls from the bakery? Our waste glass box is bursting at the seams," my wife calls as I'm putting on my shoes and about to start walking. Well, what the heck, I'll just take the stupid box with me. Arriving at the container, I see a picture of horror and destruction. Everywhere bottles and glasses stand and lie on the containers, on the ground, and in the boxes next to the containers. The poor person who has to clean up the mess afterwards! Probably the container service and the city street sweepers will have to do that. Splinters and broken glass block my way to the openings of the glass bins. Well, it's no use anyway, because the containers are full to the brim. I consider whether I should simply put my glass beside the other glass too. Or should I look again opposite the supermarket, where there are more containers? I start to think: How can it be that the container services don't notice that the old glass is piling up here and that emptying the containers is long overdue? Are they on strike, or what's the deal? Well, the container services today all empty the containers according to a fixed schedule. They don't know whether the container is full, empty, or overflowing when they do the scheduling. This leads to the fact that such a chaos can arise at the glass container. But what is certainly just as annoying for the disposal company is when the containers are actually still empty and are nevertheless approached for emptying.

As you can see, this is an area where optimization could be made so that emptying is only done as needed. Otherwise, the entire business amounts to a waste of resources. What might a Design Thinking challenge to this problem look like? Perhaps like this: How can we ensure—even in times of high fluctuations in the volume of empties—that used glass is collected on an as-needed basis and that used glass containers are emptied so that citizens can throw their used glass into the containers at any time? This question is intended to serve as the basis for a solution and the possible path to an IoT solution as the basis for the further exemplary procedure in the Design Thinking process.

7.2.2 Solution Design with Design Thinking

As an example, imagine you were faced with the problem described above, wanted to design a solution, and proceeded according to the Design Thinking method. In order to better understand the problem and the parties involved, you should first identify the personas, that is, the actors involved and the people affected by the situation, and describe them in the form of a profile.

Which people are affected by the situation in this case? Yes, of course, first of all every single one of us as a private person who simply wants to get rid of our waste glass. Let's call this persona Peter. Armin, the resident who has to look at the mess every day, is interested in finding a solution. He always keeps his own property perfectly neat. The lawn and hedges are accurately trimmed, and the paved paths are clean and free of weeds. But this horrible sight of the glass waste disaster across the street ruins everything. People in town are already saying that order and cleanliness are slowly going downhill in this neighborhood. Horst, meanwhile, is afraid that the value of his well-kept single-family home is in jeopardy. Then there's Michael, the employee at the municipal depot, who has to clean everything here. The city mayor Brigitte also wants a solution, since the city has to must answer for the costs of cleaning at the end. The person who however surely has the most interest in a solution is the driver Frank, who empties the containers, as well as the dispatcher Dirk, who schedules the vehicles to empty the containers and has to coordinate cost-optimized routes and times. Managing director Gustav of the container service has to reduce the costs for emptying this year. This was decided by the service's supervisory board.

Since this is a book about IoT use cases in industry, I suggest we take a closer look at the three people with the most interest in a solution. These are the CEO Gustav, the dispatcher Dirk and the driver Frank. To give the persons a face and bring them to life as personalities, we create the personas' profiles in the first step.

When creating the profiles, this is how I usually proceed with the Design Thinking teams in my projects:

1. We choose a distinctive name for the persona. In the future, the persona will always be called by this name, which makes the whole thing very personal and human. You can imagine that just finding the name in the group leads to shared laughter and joy.
2. We choose a suitable avatar picture or paint a portrait ourselves in the profile.
3. We fill in the profile under the heading Goals. It is important that the goals are to be seen in the long term. We are talking here about the points against which, for example, the managing director is measured. Many people become aware for the first time at this stage of what the actual goals of a particular role in the company

actually are. What gives a lot of information about the roles within a company is if you take a look at the official descriptions, such as those published by REFA [1], and put them next to the categories of your finished profile. This will give you a good impression of how the company and the colleagues present actually define certain roles compared to the "standard." Perhaps fundamental follow-up discussions will arise here, but they are not purposeful in this round.

4. We now fill in the profile under the heading Tasks. In every workshop, I'm asked what the difference is between goals and tasks. The question is justified because we quickly conflate the two in our everyday lives. I then always explain: goals are long term. Tasks are the concrete activities that the person undertakes to achieve the goals. An example: the goal of a business manager is, for example, to secure the order situation. A concrete task that makes this goal possible is acquiring new customers and ensuring that the needs of existing customers are satisfied.

When looking at the profiles, the first thing that stands out is that they are created independently of the use case presented later (see Fig. 7.3). It is important to understand where the people and role owners normally come from, what makes them tick, and what else moves them. This has two benefits: we get to know the stakeholders and people involved better, and we have the chance to identify topics that we can do "on the side" for the person that would not involve any additional effort worth mentioning as a result of the IoT innovation.

In the second step, we let the people speak and formulate their wishes. We do this, as described in Chap. 6, with what are called user stories.

Examples of User Stories

Managing Director Gustav:
As a general manager, I need a solution that increases the cost efficiency of emptying containers while showing me where I have potential for optimization.
I need a technology that fits into the existing software architecture, extends it with contemporary technologies and provides new innovative functions. This technology should already provide extensibility for further use cases without costly retrofitting.

Dispatcher Dirk:
As a dispatcher, I always need up-to-date information about the fill level of the containers at the sites so that I can schedule the vehicles to empty the containers as needed.

Driver Frank:
As a driver, I need information on what situation awaits me at the next container location so I can assess whether there is still enough vehicle capacity to accommodate the additional waste glass.

Name: David Managing Director

Goals:
What are the main goals for this role?
* support operation
* develop the strategic orientation of the company
* Positioning and investments for product and technology innovations
* Use of staff and equipment
* Securing order entry
* Expansion and care of customer and supplier relationships

Tasks:
What are the most important tasks to achieve these goals?
* Discussions with clients about current relationships and services
* Evaluate new possibilities for process optimization
* Observing what market competitors are doing
* Analysis of work processes
* Financial planning, sales planning, cost accounting
* Promotion of employees

I need...

a solution that gives transparency about the situation outside and meets the increased requirements of our customers.

Wishes:
What could support this role?
* Data to plan the business
* Good employees who lead their role in the interests of the company
* Technology that supports business processes
* Cost reduction in logistics and vehicle fleet
* A supervisory board that better understands our problems in operations
* Customers who pay on time

Personal:
Age: 54
Role designation:
Managing Director
Container Service

Challenges:
What are the biggest obstacles and challenges?
* Lack of transparency of the situation on the road and at the container
* Increasing cost pressure
* Increasing customer expectations of our service

Fig. 7.3 Profile of the managing director with his goals, tasks, wishes, and challenges (source: digit-ANTS GmbH)

7.2.3 Solution

The solution is as simple as it is ingenious. The waste disposal company USB Bochum GmbH in the heart of the Ruhr area has implemented the requirements described above in a project together with the Bochum-based start-up company Zolitron Technology GmbH. The collection containers have been equipped with vibration sensors for level measurement. How can vibration sensors be used to measure the fill level, the technically interested reader may now ask, when it is also possible to work with optical monitoring?

Good question. The answer: the vibrations on the outer shell of the metal containers, to which the sensors are attached, vary depending on the fill level. The sound image and its change over time depending on the fill level can therefore be used to calculate and interpret how full the container is (see Fig. 7.4). The information is then transmitted to a cloud platform via the mobile network. The software in the cloud platform detects whether a container is so full that it needs to be emptied. The technology makes it possible to avoid overfilling at container locations and schedule emptying them at an early stage.

In the cloud platform, the information is consolidated, and follow-up activities are triggered. The driver and dispatcher receive real-time information on the situation from the container yard. The driver is equipped with a tablet PC in his vehicle. The dispatcher's planning software sends the information to the driver's tablet via the cloud. The driver and dispatcher can see on their user applications which containers need to be emptied before the regularly scheduled time.

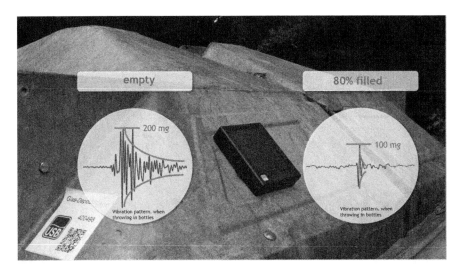

Fig. 7.4 The sensor unit is mounted on the outside of the container and detects the vibrations during glass insertion. Pattern recognition, which calculates the fill level, takes place in the cloud platform (© Zolitron Technology GmbH)

The sensor unit is installed on the outside of the container. This enables energy supply via a photocell. This has the advantage that no maintenance is required to replace batteries. This would not even be possible with an ultrasonic or optical-based level measurement method, since the measuring unit required for this would have to be installed inside the container. According to Zolitron, the sensor units require very little energy. The service life of the sensor units is given as approximately 10 years. What is still quite easy with a glass container is already more difficult with a used clothing container, since very clear vibrations have to be measured when throwing in glass. This is somewhat more difficult with textiles.

Other use cases for container fill levels can also be implemented in the construction industry and actually all other industries where container fill levels have to be recorded. In principle, liquids or powders and bulk materials in containers can also be measured. Here, it is not so much the vibration during insertion or pouring that is relevant, but the sound patterns of the container at different fill levels. We know this from the phenomenon of a water glass, which has a different sound when bumped at different fill levels.

However, further use cases could also be realized with the glass containers. The sensor units are additionally equipped with temperature sensors and GPS modules. This information is of great value to municipal depots and their winter road maintenance services. If the temperature falls below a certain level at a certain area, then the gritting vehicles could be scheduled here as needed. Furthermore, the sound sensors in the sensor units could be used to measure the volume of traffic due to the emitted noise and adjust traffic light controls for traffic routing accordingly.

The Advantages of the Solution at a Glance
- Reduction of kilometers per ton.
- Savings through clean streets.
- The tenders will be simpler, and the data will be more detailed (depot containers are normally tendered every 3 years).
- Construction site logistics: the construction site comes to a standstill when there is no more material.
- There are lower disposal costs and more inventory transparency in the construction industry, since half-full silos can be sent to the next job site within a construction company and do not need to be disposed of.

7.2.4 Architecture and Components

Table 7.2 provides an overview of the entities and required components for the IoT container solutions.

Table 7.2   Required components and entities for container solution with the IoT

Entity	Type	Description
Driver	Human entity	The driver who controls the pickup vehicle
Dispatcher	Human entity	The dispatcher who schedules the vehicles and drivers
Vibration sensor	Sensor	The vibration sensor which sends the vibration pattern to the control unit
GPS module	Sensor	The GPS module which transmits the location information of the container, which together with the fill level, if necessary, results in collection and emptying of the waste glass
User interface dispatcher	Software system	Visualization, planning support, and possibility of intervention by personnel
Mobile driver app	Mobile software application	Real-time information on container fill levels and order completion feedback
Enterprise network	Network	Enterprise network that provides access to edge components and the cloud application
Cloud service	Service	Optimization
Transport management system	Software application	Planning and control of transports
Telematics system	Cloud software	Real-time transmission of vehicle position, vehicle status, transport order transmission

7.3   Corona Warning App

During the Corona pandemic, we witnessed a live use case for the Internet of Things in Germany and even made use of it ourselves: the official Corona warning app of the Robert Koch Institute. Even though the app caused a lot of discussion in the run-up, in the following I will try to look at it as an IoT use case in the most factual way possible.

The respiratory disease COVID-19 was declared a global pandemic by the World Health Organization (WHO) on March 11, 2020, having already been classified as a Public Health Emergency of International Concern at the end of January. In mid-June 2020, exactly 3 months later, the official German Corona warning app, with the Robert Koch Institute as provider on behalf of the German Government, was available for download in app stores. As you probably remember, there was criticism of the supposedly slow development time, which was justified, among other things, with references to reliable functionality and the German as well as European data protection standards.

The stated aim of the app is contact tracing. It is intended to inform users retrospectively whether they have come into contact with an infected person. The goal of app use on the provider side is to be able to trace and interrupt infection chains. For individual users, this overall societal motivation is joined by the individual gain in information and time: a warning from the app can help us react early to an infection that has not yet been detected. During a pandemic, however, these two levels can hardly be separated, because if I protect myself, I also protect my fellow human beings.

To come to the Internet of Things in this use scenario: infection control via app entails the hope that technology and automated processes can take over tasks that are not possible for us humans in this form. Riding on a crowded bus or getting caught in a crowd at the train station, you can't and won't ask everyone you share air or health-related areas with about their Corona status. The whole thing becomes completely impossible if we consider that, as an ill person, you only find out that you have been infected after such encounters (I don't want to imply here that he or she consciously risks infecting other people with verifiable Corona disease). How should one then retroactively locate and contact all the people one might have accidentally infected?

But since 90% of people carry a smartphone around with them all the time anyway, on which the Corona warning app provided free of charge is now active, a movement pattern could be automatically created via the IoT and a database created in this way. This would make it possible to determine which persons I came so close to in the past few days—in the relevant period before I was officially tested positive—and notify them that there was a risk of infection. So, as a precaution, the app sends an automatic warning to all these people's mobile phones so that they can be tested or take meaningful action. I don't need to elaborate here on how important the time factor is in containment. The German federal government puts it this way in the FAQ for the warning app:

> The previously manual process of tracking infections is greatly accelerated by this digital assistance.

Based on our experience to date, we know of course that the ideal case described above hardly ever works smoothly in practice. Theory and practice are rarely congruent.

Let's first take another look at the steps from the user's point of view before we look at weaknesses and problems with the functionality.

First, we download the app from an app store (see Fig. 7.5). This is either the Apple platform or Google Play for Android devices, because the RKI app uses the interfaces of the iOS and Android operating systems, that is, the interfaces provided by Apple and Google with their respective protocols (DP-3 T and TCN). In the next step, I can make some basic settings as a user: the app was designed to be multilingual from the start. After the launch, there was initially a choice between German and English. Since the beginning of July 2020, more than 20 languages were selectable during the download, including Turkish, Romanian, Arabic, Vietnamese, and Chinese. This is also due to the fact that the app should not only be available in the Federal Republic of Germany, because strictly national thinking inevitably falls short when it comes to a pandemic in a globalized, mobile world, and Germany is acting accordingly here as an EU member.

DIE CORONA-WARN-APP:

HILFT INFEKTIONS-KETTEN ZU UNTERBRECHEN.

Jetzt die Corona-Warn-App herunterladen
und Corona gemeinsam bekämpfen.

Fig. 7.5 The Corona warning app of the Robert Koch Institute (source: Robert Koch Institute)

While the language selection is relatively large and also includes easy language and sign language, the accessibility is somewhat lower in terms of device diversity. For one thing, the user interfaces of the app are clearly designed for smartphones. They are not adapted to tablets or smart wearables. For another, there were limitations with Internet-enabled phones. Since they have to interact smoothly with Google and Apple interfaces, both the age of the phones and the cooperation of manufacturers such as Huawei with the American IT giants played a role here. As of mid-October, the status was such that the application should run on IOS 13.5 from the iPhone 6 s and on Android-based smartphones from the Android 6 operating system.

A particular challenge with an app that shares such sensitive health data is and remains data protection. This starts even before the download: for German citizens, use of the official app is voluntary, while other countries compel their citizens. Second, after the download, I have to become active as a user and consciously allow the app to use my mobile phone as a tracking device without determining its location in terms of infection protection. The default setting is in fact a cautious one, because the developers have taken the principle of privacy by default seriously.

Data protection worthy of the name includes app users having control over what happens to app data (privacy by default).

The third and probably most important limitation concerns anonymity. As an app user, I can't find out which people are using the app, who has a positive test result in the app, and who I have come so close to that the smartphones have assessed this encounter as relevant for infection. We only ever receive this warning in encrypted form, just as we use the app ourselves without having to enter personal data. The attribution is done by the things in the Internet of Things and software communication, not by the human users. When tracing smartphones, changing Bluetooth keys are used every 10 min. They are changed at such short intervals to make it even more difficult to recognize individual pseudonyms.

In addition to the commissioned companies (SAP, Telekom) and subcontractors, data protection experts from the government cosmos such as from the German Federal Office for Information Security (BSI) and the team of the German Federal Commissioner for Data Protection were involved in the app development from the very beginning. In addition, the source code was made public in the spirit of open source so that civil society and scientists could also get involved. What is technically possible is not always politically desirable. For this app, there was basically a trade-off between human rights and speed in development as well as tracking: I may lose valuable time as an individual for protective measures because the app warning may not be in real time. But this also prevents people from being branded with a kind of digital Corona sign and having their dignity and integrity violated. On the one hand, this protection of identity concerns the behavior of one's fellow human beings, according to ethical and legal considerations; on the other hand, as an EU citizen in the twenty-first century, one should be protected from inappropriate state surveillance even in times of pandemic. On these points, for example, the German app goes beyond the otherwise comparable app in Singapore.

If we take another look at these requirements, the 3 months of development time may no longer seem so long, even if countries like China have once again pushed the whole thing through faster. In any case, Linus Neumann from the Chaos Computer Club described the Corona warning app to media such as tagesschau.de as a "mammoth project the likes of which humanity has never seen before." In retrospect, we can also see that app development in other countries had to be partially interrupted or even aborted because mistakes were made.

From a purely technical point of view, the smartphone apps communicate via the Internet of Things using wireless technology, so that the privacy problems that would be caused by tracking the location of mobile phone users can be avoided. We're talking about signal exchange between moving devices, which has to be cheap and efficient and shouldn't put such a strain on smartphone batteries that users shy away from the app because of it—in other words, even more requirements. For the Corona warning app, the choice fell to the Bluetooth Low-Energy (BLE) standard, which led to applause, but also headlines like this one in the Handelsblatt: "Difficult distance measurement via Bluetooth: Why the Corona warning app is an experiment."

If an encounter occurs, short-lived random codes are exchanged between the users concerned and stored on the devices for 14 days. The Bluetooth technology includes two parameters, encounter duration and distance measurement, for which calculations are run. Both the distance between devices and the time duration of critical distances are calculated. For the software integrated in the app, encounters with a Corona-positive tested person who exceeds a threshold of various measured values are considered risk encounters (see Fig. 7.6).

A typical reassuring message, provided that the "risk determination" was activated, reads as shown in Fig. 7.7.

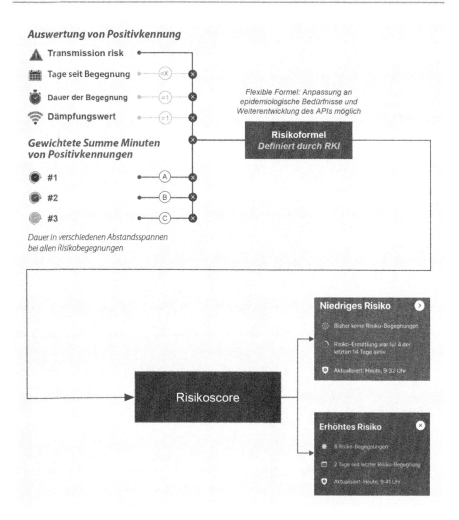

Fig. 7.6 App calculations according to a scheme of the provider RKI (source: https://www.rki.de/DE/Content/InfAZ/N/Neuartiges_Coronavirus/WarnApp/Funktion_Detail.pdf?__blob=publicationFile)

So here we have a free mass-market app on behalf of the government that meets the highest privacy standards, is easy to use, and can still do something to help contain the Covid pandemic—an extremely exciting use case that involves many important IoT aspects.

However, it is not yet possible to give a final verdict because the pandemic is unfortunately not yet over as this book goes to press. The app will continue to be adapted and revised. User behavior is also changing. But I will at least try with an interim conclusion. The German Government itself drew a mixed 100-day balance in September 2020: Health Minister Jens Spahn spoke of the "most successful Corona

Fig. 7.7 Sample status
message of the risk
determination (source: https://
www.rki.de/DE/Content/
InfAZ/N/Neuartiges_
Coronavirus/WarnApp/
Funktion_Detail.pdf?__
blob=publicationFile)

app in Europe by far." The government assumed around 18 million downloads by
that time. Nearly 5000 citizens had informed their contacts after a positive test result
with the help of the app. (By mid-October, there were about 10,000, according to the
RKI.) This had alerted thousands that they might be infected. On the other hand, it
was apparently the case that every second app user who tested positive for Corona
did not store this test result in the app in such a way that contacts could be notified

accordingly. There was a lot of external criticism of the app. The following points are probably the most important:

- **Synchronization:** The app did not work properly on various Apple devices. During the summer, there was apparently no contact verification for several days up to as much as 2 weeks. Users also reported disruptions in connection with the update to the iOS 14 operating system version.
- **Data flow:** Ute Teichert, Chairwoman of the German Federal Association of Public Health Service Doctors, publicly criticized the app as hardly helpful in practice. Since the app's data is not automatically forwarded to the public health offices, she said, the app is pretty useless for the daily work of public health offices, because it is extremely rare for an app user to contact the offices about a warning.
- **Reach in Germany:** Only part of the population uses the app, the others may not (too young), cannot (device too old), or do not want to (voluntary). Above all, not all infected people use the app at all or as intended.
- **International networking:** A Corona warning app for the whole of Europe is hardly feasible due to technical and political hurdles. The German app and technically comparable apps from other countries also record the Bluetooth codes of other Corona apps when traveling abroad. However, there is still no interface between the national server systems for the exchange of warnings across national borders. While anonymized data is stored on the devices in Germany and only sent to contacts in the event of an infection, the data for France's Stop Covid app is stored on central servers. For the interaction with the Swiss app, on the other hand, agreements are lacking at the political level.

If we look even further outside the box and look at similar apps around the world, we find even more differences in the technical implementation and political attitude regarding pandemic apps. In addition to contact tracking, data collection, and citizen information, as implemented in Germany, quarantine monitoring is a particularly important feature. I would like to present some examples, for which I used the website https://netzpolitik.org, which is particularly informative in terms of Corona apps: the government-developed Polish app Home Quarantine works with selfies that citizens are asked to upload during a quarantine period. Taiwan relies on radio cell interception, for which the state cooperates with mobile operator Chunghwa. In Hong Kong, tracking wristbands and the StayHomeSafe app are mandatory for a transition period when entering from Europe and the United States. The app is then linked to the mobile phone number and collects Bluetooth, WiFi, and GPS data which is automatically transmitted to the police.

In China, digitization had its own scale and momentum even before the pandemic outbreak. The country has the highest density of mobile devices in the world, if the figures are correct. With the services WeChat and Alipay, it has super apps with billions of users, which are also being included in the digital pandemic response across the board. In this way, a state-verified phone number can be linked with QR codes and thermal imaging cameras to create a control infrastructure that would not be possible in Germany even if the majority wanted it. This brings us back to my conviction that the IoT will make the world a better place.

Before we move on to the next use case, let me say something: of course, locating and tracking people through a central authority using smartphone technology can also lead to government surveillance and repression if it falls into the wrong hands or falls prey to an appropriate political agenda. However, older tools like knives and hammers can be used to do good or bad: eat, build, make art, or kill. The dark side of Corona apps and the misuse of the IoT functions should make us thoughtful, but not technophobic. Although many difficulties were still evident in Germany and elsewhere in 2020, I am optimistic that the Internet of Things can still contribute a lot to pandemic and epidemic control in the future.

7.4   Track and Trace in Logistics and Production

As will have become clear in the previous sections, the Internet of Things is of particular importance for logistics. Networking affects pretty much every good we can store and deliver, order, and ship. The IoT is an integral part of today's modern warehouses because it simplifies processes, increases efficiency, and boosts productivity. Real-time control of logistics processes based on the IoT data is also interesting outside of engineered and thoroughly organized warehouses: our supply chains are rarely short and manageable in times of complex just-in-sequence as well as just-in-time conveyor deliveries, eBay, Amazon, and Alibaba, and in view of the global movement of goods. They are often global, with many intermediate stations and transfer points. At the end of the chain, at the destination address, we have someone more and more frequently every day who has heard of shipment tracking and wants to be informed at all times on their mobile device whether the delivery will arrive on time or not. For many, it is a piece of micromanagement to balance the workday, family planning, daily commutes, and receiving the parcel—this service also strikes a chord with our mobile age.

We can roughly distinguish three areas of logistics that are relevant for real-time tracking:

- **Inbound logistics**, that is, the delivery of material and the processes of subcontracting.
- **Intralogistics**, that is, the movement of goods from goods receipt via the warehouse and production to goods issue.
- **Outbound logistics**, that is, the delivery of finished goods to customers or business partners.

In the following, we will take a closer look at the use case of track and trace for areas of intralogistics and outbound logistics. Before we get to the use cases, let me return to my vision, that is, we can make our world better and more livable with the right use of the IoT. What are we talking about when we talk about more efficient, smarter logistics? You'll find people arguing that we already consume way too much. If we optimize logistics even further, it will lead to even more traffic, even more exhaust, even more waste, and even more energy consumption for smart devices, even though what we actually need is less of everything. This thinking should be taken seriously. I have children ages six and eight to whom—even if I wanted to—I could not credibly explain that the Fridays for Future movement is nonsense. I would say, however, that these are two different issues. Awareness of sustainable consumption, of a greener economy, and of renewable energy is something we all need, worldwide, and fortunately younger people (and committed seniors like David Attenborough) are working on this on many channels.

But this does not change the fact that we live in a globalized, commodity-intensive world and that people on the whole do not want to and cannot change their consumption habits. I know this very well, since I have been living vegan for 2 and a half years now, and there are countless sensible reasons in every respect (animal welfare, health, resource consumption, and CO_2 emissions) for doing without or at least reducing the consumption of meat and other animal products. Everyone must start with themselves and act as a role model. Nevertheless, logistics, traffic, and transportation are necessary and part of our reality today. Accordingly, when it comes to using the IoT and other future technologies such as artificial intelligence and VR, our motivation matters. Smart, agile logistics also has a future because it is more compatible with the perspective of future generations. One factor that can still be used to convince people very quickly today is cost. The costs per shipment or delivery item in a smart logistics chain are significantly lower than in supply chains organized traditionally and without technology.

The "business as usual" approach is losing its fans on many fronts in society as a whole. Issues such as environmental pollution and nutrition are, in turn, strongly linked to logistical processes. Perhaps we really do need to learn to get by with less again. Until that happens, we should definitely try not to waste resources in logistics either. That goes from superfluous journeys when delivering and unloading to packaging and storage space. I am sure that we humans will have more scope to rethink and shape things if we take care to ensure transparent supply chains and the greatest possible insight into the underlying processes.

7.4.1   The IoT in Intralogistics

Warehouses have always been places where people have made their work easier with tools and new technology. Just think of the classic forklift truck or electronic signatures and sorting systems. In this respect, it should not surprise you that we find a large field of application for the IoT and many exciting use cases in intralogistics.

In my book *IoT with SAP*, I already pointed out the need to take a holistic approach when using the IoT. The IoT must be integrated in an ERP system such as SAP; otherwise, the use case is often just a show case to demonstrate that the basic technical feasibility is there and offers a relatively superficial benefit without impacting the core processes of the company. This is because an innovation technology such as the IoT does not create real innovation. Innovation with the IoT in intralogistics can only arise if innovation technology and integrated information systems such as WMS, ERP, TMS, and MES interact optimally with each other. Otherwise, the IoT will only create further isolated solutions that hardly contribute any value to the overall system. Intralogistics in particular offers us diverse opportunities for integration and transformation in the direction of the IoT, virtually without the installation of additional hardware. Already today, the warehouse world is characterized by integrated information systems, such as warehouse management systems, ERP integrations, database solutions, material flow controls, programmable logic controllers (PLCs), and automatic high-bay and small parts storage systems, as well as robots and automatic packaging systems. In addition, intralogistics was the first sector to introduce and productively use mobile data collection, contactless identification via RFID, voice guidance, and voice recognition such as pick-by-voice and pick-by-light.

Vast amounts of data are continuously and incessantly generated and processed in the warehouse management system and the ERP system. These are some examples:

- Goods receipt (notification, receipt, deconsolidation, quality inspection, putaway, inventory confirmation).
- Outgoing goods (order management, retrieval, picking, consolidation, packaging, shipping, staging, delivery confirmation).
- Returns.
- Scrapping.
- Internal processes (stock transfer, replenishment, transfer posting, inventory, slotting, rearrangement).
- Resource planning and employee scheduling.

Using the IoT lets us make the flow of goods within the warehouses much more transparent to the outside world and react much faster to changes.

Application examples of the IoT in intralogistics include drones and self-driving load units, which I have already presented to you in Sect. 4.3 in connection with warehouse management software. More generally, automated guided vehicles (AGVs) are an important building block for an automated, self-organizing warehouse in the 2020s. These mobile robots, which we as average consumers know in a similar form as self-propelled vacuum cleaners or lawn mowers, have the goal of ensuring fast and flexible warehouse movements, reducing transport damage, and, let's not kid ourselves here, saving on personnel costs. If a company wants to ensure the smoothest and fastest possible material flow in intralogistics, this has a lot to do with a continuous flow of data: route-optimized control of AGVs and robots by a smart transport control system can shorten travel times and minimize unproductive machine idle time. The IoT in such a system can and may theoretically "work" around the clock—not us humans, of course, since no shift system in the world can cope with that in the long term. Such transport robots are now available for almost every intralogistics task. They can move boxes and containers and transport pallets and sometimes even objects weighing several tons. And most importantly, they replace the classic conveyor belt or conveyor line between machines. Yes, you heard me right: they replace the conveyor belt. But why should an AGV, which is significantly more expensive to purchase than a 10-m conveyor line, now take its place? Well, as you have already seen in the previous sections, with AGVs you can design the transport routes between the machines very flexibly and adjust the material flow and the preparation and processing steps after each work step. In times of batch sizes of one piece, this is essential, since in production each product ends up having a completely individual machining process.

Just because robots have a lot going for them doesn't mean human employees will disappear from warehouses, because a truly intelligent employee naturally has some advantages over a smart machine, especially since humans use other IoT devices to assist them.

Also interesting for use cases from intralogistics is IdentPro GmbH from Troisdorf in Rhein-Sieg-Kreis district. The company's self-declared mission is to offer digital solutions that make the intralogistics of every company sustainably successful. I would like to take a representative look at the IdentPro Track service, which we find in the intralogistics of BMW and Warsteiner, among others. In each case ERP and warehouse management software from SAP is used, to which the new IoT functions have been connected. The combination of beer brewer and carmaker is a bit unfortunate, because drinking beer and driving a car are not compatible. But, all joking aside, automotive logistics and the beverage industry are of course highly exciting sectors for IoT applications.

Real-Time Navigation and Booking of Warehouse Tasks in the Automotive Industry
Let's first take a look at the use case at BMW. The group wanted a paperless material flow with automatically triggered bookings in the ERP system for its VZ-2 supply center at the Landshut site. Other goals included the best possible utilization of the transport capacities used and guaranteed correct deliveries to internal and external recipients. To achieve this, the 2017 innovation was to do away with barcode scanning by forklift drivers, which was apparently too error-prone or inefficient. The solution from Troisdorf relies on what is called contour-based laser localization and works in such a way that the drivers of more than 20 classic forklifts for the wide and the narrow aisles can carry out the internal transports scan-free. This warehouse's forklift guidance system included a driverless system in addition to these human-controlled machines. Lasers are attached to all of these vehicles, detecting the surrounding contour and permanently determining the current position of the vehicles in a digital warehouse map. According to the company, the accuracy is ± 10 cm. When loading units are set down, their individual x, y, z coordinates are determined for each individual loading unit and stored in a central database. The localization laser provides the x, y values, while a height sensor on the mast contributes the z coordinate to the current height. This makes the barcodes for

localization superfluous, so to speak. By the way, we are talking about a warehouse with around 18,000 storage spaces and an area of almost 50,000 m^2.

According to the provider, this is how the software works: the transport orders created with the help of the SAP software are automatically transferred from the Troisdorf-based company's system. "There, they pass through an [...] integrated optimizer, which distributes the transport orders to the vehicles in the best possible way according to configurable criteria such as priority, travel distance and double play. The forklift drivers receive the orders on their forklift terminal and are navigated to the requested load units (source). The pallets/containers are automatically identified during pickup and compared to the transport order. If the pickup is correct, the forklift driver is guided directly to the destination (sink); if the loading unit or sink is incorrect, he receives an error message" [2]. This would effectively prevent incorrect deliveries.

Real-Time Locating System in Beverage Logistics
The IdentPro Track software was also a sensible option for the Warsteiner Group as a forklift guidance system, especially to avoid empty runs. Here, more than 30 vehicles were involved at the two locations in Paderborn and Warstein. One obstacle for the drivers in the warehouse was that empty pallets do not have a unique identification (Serial Shipping Container Code, SSCC). As a result, it was sometimes difficult to efficiently coordinate the flow of materials, in this case the movement back and forth of empty and full beverage crates on pallets. There was also a lack of transparency regarding the inventory situation in the warehouse.

If you can't record the empty crates and pallets quickly and easily, this naturally also influences the subsequent processes that build on them. So the question arose: how do you get the physical things mapped in the digital world in such a way that people with software really benefit from automated data traffic? In this case, a quick-filter process helped: At the forklift terminal, employees enter which empties and how many of them they are picking up with a few clicks in the system. In the corresponding user interface, ready-made menu selections, such as for container size and bottle type, speed up this input. Above all, sample images are integrated into the input mask for quick comparison (Fig. 7.8).

Even production removal can now be carried out without scanning processes. During belt removal, which involves up to 12 pallets at a time per step, the forklift control system automatically obtains the loading units—or handling units (HUs) in SAP language—of the pallets from the warehouse management software from SAP. In this case, it was desirable for Warsteiner Logistics to combine the collection of full loads as cleverly as possible with the delivery of empties in a double play. Since the storage, retrieval, and transfer of the full pallets can also be realized without scanning barcodes, and feedback to the warehouse management software is automated here, empty runs can be prevented. For the overlapping logistics between the two locations, the software can also visualize how exactly the respective trucks or trailers are loaded with the help of loading diagrams. Anyone who has ever seen how such things are handled in the old-fashioned way with shouts plus a piece of paper and a pen will not dispute the sense of such innovations (Fig. 7.9).

Fig. 7.8 Forklift drivers are guided to the pallets they are to pick up at the beer producer's block storage facility (© IdentPro GmbH)

Fig. 7.9 Forklift truck during production belt removal: after picking up the six pallets, the IoT system indicates the location where the full load is to be stored in the block storage system with centimeter precision (© IdentPro GmbH)

As a partner in this modernization project for the beverage industry, an SAP consulting firm was on board that specializes in SAP's warehouse management solution and has already implemented projects for the Paulaner Group. If such or similar companies are also of interest to you as partners, I can recommend the LogiMAT trade fair (more on strategic partnerships in Chap. 8).

> Incidentally, this real-time locating system (RTLS) with the integrated forklift control system is not an IoT application that necessarily communicates on the Internet via a cloud platform. The main part of the application is operated in Edge, since a fair amount of information exchange is required in real time. In addition, the design and architecture of an RTLS and forklift control system in intralogistics involve the question of what information is useful outside the warehouse, that is, in the cloud. It is therefore common for these systems to operate for the most part outside the Internet, sending only the essentials to the cloud. Nevertheless, I count these applications as part of the Internet of Things because they can and will be integrated into global supply chain structures.

For the large companies selected here as examples, BMW and Warsteiner—and for many somewhat smaller companies as well—the logistics processes are not limited to the warehouses in Germany or at other locations. After all, the goods will eventually reach the customer or at least the point of sale for end customers. Section 7.4.2 deals with this part of the supply chain and outbound logistics.

7.4.2   Theft Monitoring in the Warehouse with the IoT

Can you imagine that the IoT can help you in warehouse management to secure against theft and also give your partners an assurance about stored goods? Let's take a look at a use case described in the ISO/IEC TR 22417:2017 standard, where goods in a warehouse are monitored and tracked using the IoT.

The use of this IoT system enables a constant evaluation of the assets in the warehouse complex. Banks can require such a system for granting a loan, so that the assets in the warehouse can be used as collateral for the granted loan and are monitored. The system can be used to ensure that goods can be moved only after proper authorization.

If a company that owns warehouse goods wants a loan from a bank, it can use the stocks in the warehouse as collateral for the money borrowed from the bank. To do this, the owner must first have the inventory valued and confirmed by the warehouse manager. This valuation and confirmation from the borrower is used by the bank officer to assess whether or not the bank can take the risk of the loan. In this scenario, the bank has a very difficult time assessing whether the information is accurate or falsified or whether the goods have already been illegally removed from the warehouse. The bank has hardly any way to monitor the activities in the warehouse after the loan has been disbursed and, in case of fraud, could be left liable for the risk.

The bank's security could be greatly enhanced by an IoT system for real-time inventory monitoring. The following information is captured:

- Movement of stocks in the warehouse.
- Time of storage.
- Timing of the outsourcing.
- Weight of storage units, handling units, and loading units.
- Stock types.
- Quantity per storage unit, box, HU.
- Exact storage place and location in the warehouse.
- Identity of employees who move, store, and pick up goods.

If materials, boxes, stocks, or load units are removed from the warehouse without authorization, an alarm is triggered that first informs the security personnel but also the lender.

Table 7.3 provides an overview of the entities of an IoT monitoring system in the warehouse according to ISO/IEC TR 22417:2017.

7.4.3   Tracking in Global Supply Chains

If we look at global supply chains, the exchange of information via the Industrial Internet of Things is also of immense importance today. The business partners involved understandably want to know at an early stage if there are delays, if goods have been damaged en route, or if they have to respond to unforeseen events with alternative approaches. If all parties involved are networked in such a way that data can flow in real time from one end of the network to the other, this creates the much-discussed transparency within logistics chains, end-to-end visibility in the supply chain. Or, to put it another way, the everything network makes logisticians' hearts beat faster all over the world. Of course, we are no longer living in the Middle Ages, where we might have learned too late about a lost harvest because the messenger had an accident on the long way to those who needed to know. But it is already the case that the increasing networking of devices all over the world has given us possibilities for organizing and carrying out our logistics and transport processes that we did not have even a generation ago. We can remotely track the current location of a shipment because sensors and tags on the goods or even on the means of transportation provide us with this data 24/7. In addition, we can monitor the condition of the goods using the IoT sensors. Whether or not cold chains are being maintained is no trivial matter for food and for medicines. Vibrations caused by roads, by reloading or by weather influences, are also of interest to transport and logistics companies. Here, the big data principle for digital transformation from a business perspective applies again: real-time data from the IoT sensors only really has business added value if I can relate it to my entrepreneurial actions, in this case

Table 7.3 Entities of an IoT monitoring system in the warehouse according to ISO/IEC TR 22417: 2017

Entity	Type	Description
Stock	Physical entity	Crates, pallets, boxes, loading units, storage units, handling units
RFID tag	Physical entity	RFID tags attached to cartons and containers contain the recorded information about goods
RFID reader	Sensor	RFID readers collect all information about the goods. RFID sensors read identities of the tags
Electronic scale	Sensor	The electronic scale records the weight of all goods individually or in boxes or containers
Sensor with UWB module	Sensor	The location of the goods in the warehouse can be calculated and recorded using sensors with a UWB module
Laser radar	Sensor	The laser radar detects contours when stock is put away. The system detects contour changes and triggers an alarm as soon as a deviation is detected, which normally occurs when storage units are moved
Alarm controller	Digital system	The alarm controller triggers a sound and light alarm when storage units are removed or relocated without permission and also sends alarm information to the cloud platform
IoT gateway	IoT gateway	The IoT gateway connects sensors, sensor nodes, and RFID tags. It sends information read by RFID readers and other external networks to the cloud and manages the local network
Online monitoring service	Cloud system	The online monitoring service records and stores information about goods in the warehouse, name, supplier, storage location, and weight. It registers workers (name, ID, employee number) going into or out of the warehouse. It manages warehouse information and provides information service for the bank and the company. It can provide security service if needed
Resource access system	Cloud system	The resource access system connects to third-party systems and collects data on real-time price information of the commodity. It matches value of collateral with value of loan in real time for the bank
Information resource database	Cloud system	The information resource database categorizes all sensor and device data and links them to inventory data. It stores this data and provides interfaces for authorized data exchange with other cloud services
Maintenance system	System	The maintenance system ensures stable and safe operation. It records all operating states, device conditions, and maintenance services
Rule management system	System	The rule management system describes and verifies the rules for trading the insured and lent goods

my business data for logistics processes. The difference hopefully becomes apparent by imagining a traffic jam. The dispatcher in charge doesn't need to know to the minute where truck 12b is moving, rolling, or standing. But he wants to know the following: are we on schedule or at least still within the scheduled buffer, or will it become critical at the next station? If we are talking about a fleet of trucks heading for the container port in Hamburg or Duisburg, the software should be able to link the position of the cars and the status of the container ships (departure times, loading capacities). As a dispatcher, a smart solution would help me maintain an overview without having to put a lot of effort into contacting the drivers, shipping companies, and other parties involved.

Here, the potential also entails a challenge: for supply chains with sections using highways, ports, and ships, there are usually several players. On the one hand, there is the sender or shipper, with whom the end customer in many cases initiates the actual order. On the other hand, there are the logistics service providers, such as DHL in Germany, who take on the transport order. These in turn often commission other service providers, especially for transport. Nowadays, professional transport services are not limited to the activity, "I load a car, drive from A to B and then unload." In many cases, public authorities, insurance companies, or banks are also involved via the ports, train stations, and other transhipment points.

If the world were straightforward, all these players would have software and hardware from SAP, Microsoft, Oracle, Infor, or other major vendors, and everything would mesh perfectly. Well, dream on! As far as I know, the industry is more like this: the IT infrastructure is made up of diverse systems from each player, and you have to pick up the phone sometimes for info. Producers, for example, use an ERP solution to manage customer orders and goods production. Logistics service providers such as DHL usually use specialized software to plan shipments. It is said that they also use partners and subcontractors who have their own systems for planning and executing orders, for example, because the factors of price and reliability are still somewhat higher on the list of selection criteria than questions of IT harmonization. We have just had an example from intralogistics, where an SAP solution and specially developed software have to harmonize.

Of course, everyone involved had an interest in working together efficiently even before the Internet of Things became so important. Ever since we've been able to exchange data and information electronically, companies have been doing the same. The established solutions and routines involve many point-to-point connections, online bookings, and the like. But the comprehensive networking and the technical prerequisites for overarching real-time data management are often not yet there. In order for the companies involved, suppliers, shippers, etc. to be able to view the status of the logistics processes and call up all relevant information in real time, a modern system landscape would be needed. Cloud-based solutions that could also be accessed by users outside the company's own organization would be good. Ideally, these solutions would enable communication with each other so that there is no need for parallel emailing or telephone follow-up. Standardized interfaces are essential for data exchange. The appropriate digital data analysis tools must be integrated for forecasting and predictive analytics. All of this brings us back to the "things" in the Internet of Things, because they are, after all, the things that are ordered, shipped, and tracked: the products, the packages, the boxes, the racks, the refrigeration units, the containers, and the ships, trucks, semitrailers, and rail cars.

Let's not kid ourselves: customer expectations in terms of quality, punctuality, and reliability of goods shipments are high. This is reflected not least in the massive criticism of DHL deliveries in Germany: if the parcels don't arrive, if the shipment tracking data doesn't reach the end customer, the customer quickly gets angry. In global competition, no company can afford this in the long term. Logistics companies are under additional pressure resulting from the factors of price and environmental awareness. Regardless of whether B2B or B2C: those who are accustomed to favorable conditions thanks to giants such as eBay, Amazon, and Alibaba are reluctant to pay higher prices. The IoT also increases speed: the possibility of online ordering around the clock from anywhere in the world on the one hand and the already established premium offers for express deliveries on the same day on the other hand do not exactly provide for deceleration. At the same time, the industry has to deal with the CO_2 emissions of logistics processes, because climate change can no longer be ignored and the debate about it will certainly not stop at this industry of all industries. Just as a scenario: Amazon customers can choose for their product whether they prefer the fastest, the cheapest, or the most environmentally friendly delivery. In order to be able to implement this in logistics and transport processes, one would probably need very well networked databases on the one hand and an agile form of process management that enables flexible control on the other.

Track and trace for the global supply chain is important not only with regard to end customers, however, but also because of safety regulations and other political requirements. Since 2019, for example, an EU directive requires pharmaceutical companies to ensure that the path of their medicines is traceable. All packaging elements—from the blister pack and folding box to the shipping box for intermediaries and the pallet for wholesalers—must be marked with a clearly identifiable serial number. For track and trace to work, it must be possible to document along the entire supply chain when the status of a packaging unit changes. There it is again—transparency from the manufacturer to the end customer. In practice, this leads to questions such as: How do you collect the relevant data? And how do you store it? Just as the Internet of Things cannot be conceived of without people interacting with and using things, networking, tracking and tracing via track and trace is as much about things as it is about people. The desired end-to-end visibility is hardly possible without an end-to-end IT infrastructure that can be accessed by all stakeholders. Connectable cloud solutions, but also blockchain technology with its decentralized IT architecture that is particularly difficult to manipulate, are currently the most promising solutions for the new problems.

In the short study [3] "Track and Trace Technologies at a Glance," published in 2019 by a research team from the Fraunhofer Institute for Industrial Engineering (IAO), the researchers distinguish among four processes:

- Optoelectronics.
- Transmitter-receiver systems with RFID.
- Real-time locating systems (RTLS).
- Environment with blockchain technology.

We are familiar with optoelectronics from the supermarket checkout, for example: scanners are used to read the barcodes on the products. This means that digital data is converted into light signals and light signals are also converted into digital data, the other way around. Scanners or cameras illuminate the object and receive the light, which is reflected back. This makes the information behind it "visible" and retrievable. Optoelectronic processes score points with their great suitability for applications in rooms and buildings, high accuracy, and comparatively low cost. The study authors dare to predict that barcodes will remain the most widely used element of optoelectronic processes in the future. With regard to 3D codes, they see great development potential in terms of the interaction of the IoT with virtual and augmented reality.

Transmitter-receiver systems work with digital signals that enable communication between a transmitter and a receiver. The information is exchanged via electromagnetic waves, usually with the help of microchips or antennas. These are also referred to as RFID systems (Radio Frequency IDentifiers). The maturity of this process is similar to that of optoelectronics. However, it has two advantages: first, visual contact between the elements' sign and camera is not necessarily required, and second, such a transmitter-receiver system usually works somewhat better outdoors. Systems that operate with real-time locating do not require the transmitter and receiver to be in close proximity. Instead, both elements are continuously connected to each other. This, of course, is wonderful for real-time object tracking. GPS navigation systems, WiFi applications, and Bluetooth communication usually work according to this principle.

Tracking again works differently with the help of a blockchain architecture. Here, the object and state are not recorded in a tangible way, but are entered into a blockchain network with a digital identity. What transactions are for digital currencies such as Bitcoin, Ethereum, or DeFi would be events/actions within the network that concern the whereabouts and state of an object. The authors are understandably cautious here because blockchain is still a fairly unknown quantity. However, they also state the following: arguments such as the universal suitability, the degree of automation and the range, and, above all, the high information content with the low susceptibility to errors speak in favor of the use of blockchain technologies in the environment of tracking and mobility.

7.5   Intelligent Data Glasses in the Warehouse and in Production

Many companies now rely on data glasses and augmented reality in warehouse operations. These are often referred to as smart glasses. You'll find examples of what such glasses look like at https://www.wareable.com/ar/the-best-smartglasses-google-glass-and-the-rest.

Do not confuse smart glasses with VR glasses. With VR glasses, the user is visually cut off from the outside world and puts a smartphone-sized display on their nose. With smart glasses, we're talking about augmented reality, which means that you augment the real world with the information that is superimposed in or in front of your eye.

Routes and paths can be displayed in the eyeglass displays. Images of objects can be displayed there, making it easier to find them. Material-relevant information, such as quantities or sizes, can also be displayed here. Since voice input has improved significantly in recent years, I would venture to predict that voice functions will become even more established in intralogistics. In this way, an employee could confirm that he has picked up or delivered goods without having to have his hands free for a long time. Perhaps you have also heard of the pick-by-vision picking process. This means that the smart glasses interact with the objects in the warehouse; each product has a barcode that the glasses can scan. Compartments, shelves, or specific warehouse areas could also send an optical signal to such glasses, when practical. Companies like DHL have been experimenting with such AR glasses for a while. However, time will have to tell whether or not the benefits from such methods outweigh the disadvantages and whether or not alternative methods will not become more widespread. The disadvantages include the fact that such interactions require uninterrupted network/WLAN coverage in the warehouse and reasonable battery management for the data glasses. In addition, scanning via glasses does not yet always work well or immediately. Furthermore, this technology is not suitable for all employees without problems: some people get dizzy from the AR applications, and people who wear their own glasses often need extra equipment.

Let's take a look at a specific use case from production and use it as an example to bring together the necessary IoT components in accordance with the IoT reference architecture. This use case, which is also covered in the ISO/IEC TR 22417:2017 standard in standard section 7.10, among others, describes how a factory worker receives information on the shop floor via smart glasses when setting up and adjusting a machine. Smart glasses are used in factories to:

- Provide information to users.
- Scan barcodes via a camera, so that the user can see specific information based on individual customer requirements.
- Can enable precise positioning during installation or maintenance.

Smart glasses display information and instructions to production workers in your field of view on the inside of the glasses so they can keep their hands free for assembly or maintenance work. Some models have a camera. With this camera, wearers can share what they see with colleagues around the world and receive instructions via the display or audio transmission. So it's also possible for an employee on site to wear the glasses without really having detailed knowledge of

Table 7.4 Required components and entities for the IoT use cases with smart glasses

Entity	Type	Description
Production or warehouse worker	Human entity	The person who wears the smart glasses and receives important information about the work and logistics process through them
Smart glasses	Portable device	The glasses worn by the employee, which capture information via the integrated camera and provide the user with instructions and additional information via the display
Camera	Device	The camera captures information such as barcodes or objects
Display	Device	The display superimposes information for the user in the field of view
User interface	Software system	Supports voice, touch, and gesture commands
Enterprise network	Network	Enterprise network that provides access to product data and assembly instructions
Cloud service	Service	Product data and work instructions in the repository

the machine they're working on. This allows a remote service technician to diagnose and obtain information about the equipment without visiting the plant.

These are the advantages of using smart glasses:

- Increased productivity.
- Minimization of errors.
- Increased occupational safety.

Smart glasses belong to the category of wearables, which means that they are devices that we as humans can wear on our bodies. If you want to use smart glasses in production or other areas, always bear in mind that the wearable devices have a camera and often also a microphone installed, which can be intercepted in the event of a cyberattack or may reveal confidential insights into product data or other sensitive information.

Because of the previously listed sensors for video and sound, acceleration, speed, and location, these devices are also able to collect information about their human users. Again, make sure that you comply with the relevant personal data protection laws and do not collect or store data unnecessarily—and if you do, make sure that the relevant cloud services comply with the data protection laws applicable in the country of use.

Table 7.4 shows the required components and entities for the IoT use cases with smart glasses.

208   7 Use Cases for the Internet of Things

7.6   Object Recognition with the IoT

Another exciting application area for connecting the digital and real worlds is object recognition using the IoT. As a use case, I would like to present a case of optical object recognition, which my co-authors Martina Mohr and Michael Stollberg describe in more detail in our book *IoT with SAP*. We can neglect some details concerning software functions and program code at this point. What is interesting for us is the application area as such.

Recognizing objects in images is increasingly becoming a task for artificial intelligence (see Chap. 5). Whether we are talking about stationary objects, that is, photos, or objects in motion, that is, videos, in pattern recognition, identification, and detection, software and algorithms are already doing a good job in many cases today, taking the pressure off us and opening up new possibilities. New technology is turning real objects into data material in the digital world—whether we're talking about people being filmed in public places in the context of social distancing, objects being passed by a self-driving car, goods in the warehouse being tracked by camera technology, or a camera recording where the transport vehicle is at any given moment. I don't have to explain to you that camera technology is ubiquitous these days. Digital photography has long since replaced analog photography and film processing, which I personally remember from my early days at the daily newspaper Westdeutsche Allgemeine Zeitung. We only have to look at how widespread camera assistants in cars and, above all, smartphones with integrated cameras are. Nor do I have to convince you that images are now ubiquitous on the Internet. Of course, all of this also plays a role for the Internet of Things, including corporate context and the crime scenes of Industry 4.0. In connection with warehouse management software (see Chap. 4), I told you about drones that, equipped with a camera, fly through the warehouse. If you think back to your first encounters with the Internet (or to Chap. 1), we are quickly back to the webcam and the first coffee machine on the Net. Seen in this light, it is almost compelling that optical object recognition with modern camera technology now has a firm place in the Internet of Things. The cameras that are responsible for the visual data in such IoT settings take over tasks that previously had to be performed by human eyes—much in the same way that we can also partially outsource hearing to sensors for acoustic recognition. In some cases, the digital eyes see better than ours; in any case, they are not so quickly exhausted. What's more, visual status monitoring for shelves, machines, or product components can be transformed into an automated process through networking via the Internet of Things.

For the specific use case that I will present in the following, pattern recognition via algorithms is relevant, with the help of what are called convolutional neural networks (CNNs). These networks consist of different layers. The convolutional layers are particularly important for optical recognition. As Martina Mohr aptly summarized in our book *IoT with SAP*, a CNN essentially consists of a sequence of filter applications on an input image. On the image of the real object—the primal input, if you will—several filters are applied in the first layer step. The output for the next layer sequence is called a feature map. This is repeated step by step. The first

Fig. 7.10 Object detection with YOLO version v3 (source: https://commons.wikimedia.org/wiki/File:Detected-with-YOLO%2D%2DSchreibtisch-mit-Objekten.jpg)

layers usually generate feature maps in which many details of the original image are still recognizable. The more sequences are run, the more abstract the image stacks become. A feature can then be derived from data on sizes, edges, and distances. In my colleague's example, it is a handle that could be used to distinguish a cup from a glass. But it could also be a bottle cap that allows you to distinguish a Flensburger beer bottle from a Beck's Blue with a crown cap or a shirt from a blouse. There are several variants of such CNNs. For our application, however, a basic understanding of the YOLO architecture is sufficient at this point. Here the abbreviation stands for "you only look once."

The YOLO method for image recognition is powerful enough to detect objects on video recordings with a latency of 22–51 ms. It is designed to detect objects in motion as quickly as possible. YOLO does this by dividing the incoming image into a certain number of cells and determining for each cell one or more bounding boxes. These are simply rectangles that are placed as a frame around objects (see Fig. 7.10). The rectangles each have an image position, so they can also be tracked in motion. In addition, the software determines for each box whether it contains objects. If so, it also tries to categorize the objects, which of course requires training data beforehand.

Our use case is optical object recognition using a camera and YOLO technology in the IoT. The specific scenario involves monitoring a turntable that is intended as a station for polishing on a typical conveyor line. If irregularities occur here, the object recognition via the IoT should report this in real time, if possible, in the sense of condition monitoring. In this case, irregularity means: the stones intended for polishing fall off the belt, or the defined quantity of stones on the turntable is clearly too high or too low.

What Do You Need for Such a Setting?
In addition to the camera, the IT architecture here includes an IoT platform in the cloud and an AI computer that generates structured data from the images. The filmed objects could not send data directly to the IoT without the camera, because they are not equipped with the necessary sensors. I am mentioning this here so that you can once again be aware that data traffic in the Internet of Things does not take a direct route in many cases, but rather via intermediate stations such as the camera in this case. In addition, we need a bit of a child's toy for our use case. You don't believe that? Then you've probably never heard of the fischertechnik training models for Industry 4.0. The company's own advertising states:

> With fischertechnik, many of the things that will be important in a smart factory can already be simulated and tested today—and, above all, demonstrated in a compre-hensible way. The IT department uses the connection to a cloud to make data from the factory available in real time. The technicians monitor the plants and machines remotely via their smartphones and mobile devices. Production reports progress to the connected systems via integrated sensors in order to automatically derive the next steps, for example, triggering the order to organize the replenishment of goods or sending the pickup order to logistics. Industry 4.0 applications can be ideally simulated and grasped haptically with fischertechnik, deepening learning and under-standing on the path to digital transformation. [4]

The simulation models, which are based on the brand's building block system developed as recently as the 1960s, now include high-bay warehouses, sorting lines, and vacuums. For the SAP colleagues' use case, a training model is in use for a conveyor line with a turntable and polishing station. The goal behind this "test setup" is as follows: if the material flow via the turntable does not run as planned, a service message is triggered in the system so that a maintenance technician can head for this weak point as quickly as possible.

The process steps for this use case look like this:

- A camera permanently films the station and sends an image of the turntable to the YOLO neural network every 5 s.
- The YOLO AI continuously evaluates if everything is okay or if there are any anomalies.
- The status that the algorithm evaluates and transmits in this way appears as a sensor value on the IoT platform.
- In this case, it is the SAP Leonardo software bundle that creates a digital twin and links it to the sensor. However, many other cloud platforms are also capable of mapping this use case.
- Critical values automatically trigger an action that results in a service ticket.

As far as training the AI is concerned, you could in principle also use AI services that have already been trained, here for image recognition or for other use cases. Various companies have launched initiatives to offer their partners and customers ready-made solutions that only need to be trained with their own images (or the required data sets). These include Intel, SAP, and Amazon Web Services. In our example, however, the training is part of the use case.

In the training phase, pictures are taken of the turntable and the polishing station in operation so that YOLO can be trained to recognize the normal condition and identify deviations from it. For this purpose, the camera is placed above the polishing station of the simulation model. In this setting, the requirements for the camera to be used are relatively low: the images are scaled to 608×608 pixels when processed by YOLO. A USB interface is also required to send the images to a laptop. This is also part of the standard program of today's cameras, as far as I know. If speed were an elementary aspect, one could optimize the image transfer between a camera and a computer here by using a camera with a computing module with an integrated graphics processing unit (GPU). Further processing takes place on the local computer and in the cloud, in this case with recourse to scripts in the Python programming language. The code contains, among other things, some if lines, that is, if-then formulas for conditions that are fulfilled or not fulfilled by the stones on the turntable.

Here we are back to the paradox of artificial intelligence that has no idea: the AI model doesn't know what to recognize. The human must first define it. In optical object recognition, we would naturally start from our eyes and the observations we ourselves make optically. What looks like a defect to us is also defined as defective in the appropriate language for the algorithm. What represents the desired state to us must also be written down. Here, the notation also includes labeled images, that is, images that have already been classified for the CNN. Object recognition, which was simulated in the case of our use case, is not yet particularly complex because only a few simple objects had to be identified in a constant environment. For those involved, 100 images were enough to get the whole thing working in a way that satisfied everyone. As a guideline, however, the colleagues rather recommend the following: "As a rule, you should use 1,000 different images per class (here: normal state and error state) for training."

Closely related to the application area of object recognition are use cases in the areas of maintenance and repair, which also fall under the terms predictive maintenance and predictive analytics. We will take a closer look at these use cases in Sect. 7.7.

7.7 Maintenance and Servicing in Production

If we can realize optical or acoustic object recognition through device networking and data exchange via the Internet of Things, this will also open up new possibilities for the application areas of maintenance and repair. I already mentioned the technician who receives an automated maintenance order as soon as anomalies occur in

Sect. 7.6. As is often the case, there are no patents on the terms, but the difference between reactive and preventive maintenance/repair should be relatively clear. Most people probably replace a light bulb only when it is broken. With a car, on the other hand, regular maintenance in a workshop is more common, so that the stoppage due to a defect does not occur on the highway 700 km from home.

Many experts add three further concepts to these classic maintenance concepts, which can hardly be realized without the Internet of Things:

- **Condition-based maintenance:** The current condition of a machine or system is taken into account for maintenance work. For this purpose, the responsible persons usually use data from sensor and control systems.
- **Predictive maintenance:** Analysis algorithms predict when maintenance will be necessary by comparing current condition data with "trained" empirical values.
- **Intelligent maintenance:** This is predictive maintenance 2.0, so to speak. In addition to predictive algorithms, data analytics and artificial intelligence are used. The long-term goal is independent maintenance of the machine systems, if possible without human intervention.

This all sounds exciting and sensible, but it describes more where the journey is headed than where German industry currently stands across the board today. Up to now, a high manual effort has been relatively characteristic of the processes for operating industrial plants. This also applies to maintenance routines and maintenance processes. It is not uncommon to find a kind of triangular trade in connection with industrial machinery and equipment: there is the manufacturer side, that is, the OEM (original equipment manufacturer); the machine operators or users who, for example, use the OEM products in production; and the specialized service providers who often take over tasks such as assembly and disassembly, maintenance, and servicing. When I buy equipment as an operator, I usually receive instructions from the manufacturer on how to install and how to use the equipment. Close your eyes for a moment and imagine these documents: What do they look like? Could it be that you are now thinking more of paper in telephone book format and not necessarily of modern machine-readable documents? In addition, you have to assume that only a few machine operators are fully committed to monoculture. I haven't found a study on this, but I would tend to assume that most companies have acquired a mix of equipment from various OEM sources over the years. So in the worst case, an engineer or maintenance provider has to dig through a lot of paper to maintain a more complex plant, because if you find someone who has the experience to do it, you can't pay that machine wizard. What would be desirable is a kind of digital library that contains all the relevant information about a plant and that can be accessed by the operator and the manufacturer as well as the service provider when needed, but building such a library is not possible without a major effort. The library would have to follow the principle of single source of truth (SSOT), that is, a universally valid set of data that claims to be correct and can be relied upon.

Another factor that can cause huffing and puffing is time and resource management: maintenance work often takes place on a rotating basis, coupled with legal requirements, inventories, or other milestones. You've seen this before with bottle banks, which were emptied at regular intervals even when they weren't full. If the interval between maintenance is too long, this can lead to intermittent failures; if it is too short, unnecessary costs may be generated, for example, because specialist personnel are checking equipment that is still running perfectly. It makes sense for companies to be able to perform maintenance and servicing flexibly. For example, if there is only a software problem (and not a hardware problem), it may be possible to solve this remotely these days without having to travel to the site. To monitor technology and make such decisions, collecting and analyzing data—including machine data, equipment data, plant data, and production data—using automated algorithms is helpful. Intelligent, real-time data management via AI can help create needs-based maintenance schedules. To improve scheduling for inspections and repairs, AI can be used to analyze audio or image data, for example: Is the gripper arm moving oddly? Does the engine sound as it should? Specially developed sensors can monitor equipment and products acoustically, for example. If there is an unusual operating noise, this may be an indication of defects or malfunctions that could lead to a failure. In production, for example, a blunt saw blade could be identified via machine technology. The interaction of sensors, drones, cameras, and intelligent software today provides us with pretty good data pools that can also be used for reliable forecasts. The preceding initial situation pleases people like me because there is something to optimize. Operators and service providers can improve their business processes for maintenance and repair. For manufacturers, if you think about it a little further, there are new services in the digital environment and even more flexible sales models, such as pay-per-use.

The following examples give you an overview of how predictive analytics and predictive maintenance are already being used or how they could be used:

- For beverage logistics and the bottlers used there, predictive and intelligent maintenance could make production and logistics more flexible: if the bottler could access the sales volumes of the last 10 years, it would be possible to make a decent forecast for the future for every single product sold. Of course, certain factors have to be factored in. The weather is changing, for example. It's getting hotter, and people are drinking more. But deriving a pattern from the past would certainly be helpful for current planning.
- We can already find some use cases in traffic management. The commercial vehicle and mechanical engineering group MAN relies on AI functions to increase the availability of its own trucks on the roads. The company compiled a data set in order to predict as reliably as possible when critical parts in particular, such as injectors, will fail on a vehicle, which will then lead directly to it coming to a standstill. This data set included repair records, fault documentation, and telematics data. An algorithm was also developed to detect "unhealthy" vehicle data in the ECU data. Swiss Federal Railways (SBB) is already using an IoT solution from SAP for predictive maintenance of its vehicle fleet. Other similar projects are underway in regional public transport.

- IoT-based predictions are also of interest to health data and health tech companies: a team from Mount Sinai Emory University's Icahn School of Medicine, together with project partners, was apparently able to prove that a certain protein protects against Alzheimer's disease using models based on predictive analytics:

> To better understand how genetic factors impact Alzheimer's disease risk and development, the group built predictive network models of late-onset Alzheimer's disease by mining DNA, RNA, protein, and clinical data. By integrating DNA variation with additional types of molecular and clinical data, more complex, holistic models of disease can be constructed and mined to elucidate regulatory and mechanistic drivers of disease and points of therapeutic intervention, researchers said. [...] These predictive analytics models enabled them to identify key regulators of Alzheimer's disease and spotlight VGF, the only key driver of a suppressed response across all datasets. VGF is a neuronal protein that regulates memory, and levels of it are reduced in the brains and cerebrospinal fluid of patients with Alzheimer's disease. [5]

The IoT and more modern maintenance approaches are a huge topic for the energy transition, as the following examples show:

- The Climate Change AI group (https://www.climatechange.ai) has published a paper [6] that makes suggestions for the use of AI in climate protection for 13 areas. Often, the focus is on predictive maintenance. Using a database to calculate the most efficient driving routes possible saves emissions at the end of the day. Data-based forecasting with the help of the IoT could also be a solution for better utilization of power grids.
- The German Energy Agency dena is coordinating the project "EnerKI—Using Artificial Intelligence to Optimize the Energy System." In this way, it wants to build up targeted knowledge about the use of artificial intelligence in the energy system and make the knowledge usable for the economy, the specialist public, and politics. The dena analysis "Artificial Intelligence for the Integrated Energy Transition" from fall 2019 states, among other things: "Providers of predictive maintenance for wind turbines promise a prediction of operating element failures 60 days in advance and savings of 12,500 euros per turbine due to avoided maintenance work. AI applications thus not only create added business value, but can also contribute to the integration of renewable energies [7]."
- The Hamburg-based company Kaiserwetter specializes in the evaluation and correlation of customer data in the renewable energy sector. For example, it evaluates the data from wind farm components or solar power plants to make normal values and deviations from turbines and the like available at the click of a mouse. The benefit for operators is obvious: if everything runs smoothly, they have control in real time without the need for a technician to be on site. It also makes benchmark analyses with anonymized competitors possible, which is sure to interest one or two companies. For these services, the company pulls data

directly from customers' plants and processes it with the help of software. Up to now, automated annual reports made this way have taken around 3 days. If the managers' visions come true, it will 1 day be just 3 s.

- Researchers at the Karlsruhe Institute of Technology (KIT) are developing self-learning frahling sensors as part of the PrognoNetz project to improve the utilization of high-voltage lines. The sensors are to model the cooling effect of the weather in real time. Wilhelm Stork, head of microsystems technology at KIT's Institute of Information Processing Technology, explained, "This allows the amount of electricity transported to be increased by 15–30% under favorable conditions, that is, low outside temperature or strong wind [8]."

- The Danish energy group Ørsted is dedicated to the topic of smart metering and data-based business with electricity from renewable energies. Maintenance using the IoT data also played a role in this. For example, one question that has many implications is: when do you send a ship to an offshore wind farm for a repair? For that, you have to consider the weather and safety constraints, as well as the investment cost and time factor. If it were possible to connect the analog devices in such plants and factories to the Internet of Things, the data inventory for condition control and monitoring would provide as accurate and comprehensive a picture as possible. This would then allow a more informed decision to be made between the options.

Simulations are an integral part of many approaches you learn about in business studies. Today, computational simulations in business practice can do amazing things with data, especially if they are cleverly designed and, perhaps soon, even coupled with artificial intelligence as a standard. The Internet of Things can provide crucial information for business decisions to set the course for the future. I am sure that there will be many more use cases for condition monitoring and maintenance processes.

The IoT Architecture
Let's now look at a use case where we build an IoT platform for monitoring motors in a production line to monitor preventive maintenance for the motors. The motors are connected to our IoT system via sensors. We can use push processes to automate the processes and thus also order parts via the supply chain in case of the need for maintenance. The use case is described in detail in the ISO/IEC TR 22417:2017 standard (standard section 7.16). The IoT-supported use of predictive maintenance results in the following advantages:

- Optimization of the availability of resources.
- Increased throughput.
- Minimized unplanned downtime.
- Reduction of maintenance costs.

Process Steps and Processes that the IoT System Must Support

1. The user receives motor information on performance and can thus trigger predictive maintenance processes.
2. The IoT gateway creates data from the acquired information in Message Queuing Telemetry Transport (MQTT) format, an open network protocol for machine communication, and sends this data to the API of the predictive maintenance and quality assurance application. The application runs in a cloud service.
3. API and IoT devices are authorized in the cloud service.
4. Data is transferred to the predictive maintenance and quality assurance application in the cloud.
5. A real-time check is made for exceptions, conditions, anomalies, and need for action.
6. The workflow and asset management integration are triggered. The technician is notified.
7. There is complete automation of the process as a cloud service.

Table 7.5 lists all entities required for the use case, describes their type and how they work, and provides notes on the underlying technology.

7.8   The IoT Business Models in Mechanical Engineering

In today's society, especially within the upcoming generation of decision-makers and entrepreneurs, we see a clear trend towards the sharing economy. This new mindset of entrepreneurs also has an impact on the business models of companies. A high capital commitment through the purchase of a new production machine is becoming increasingly unattractive, as the payback periods for investments are also shortening. This means that classic business models have to be rethought, and, for example, a mechanical engineering company has to provide innovative business models for financing its equipment for customers.

The ISO/IEC TR 22417:2017 standard describes in section 7.19 an IoT system that technically maps machine finance leasing. This system monitors the performance and key figures of a machine in real time and tracks the position of the machine in order to transmit this information to banks offering machine leasing. At the same time, the operator is able to read, collect, and evaluate the information from the machine components. Among other things, this would enable predictive maintenance and minimize downtime, but that's not the point here. What is interesting, however, is that we can use this data for statistics, performance data, and determining average operating costs. The transparency helps the operator safeguard his plant and helps the bank minimize risk.

This model also makes a somewhat more far-reaching financial business model conceivable: use-based billing for machine operation. We know this from the use of

Table 7.5 Technical components according to ISO/IEC TR 22417:2017 (based on the IoT reference architecture)

Entity	Type	Description	Technology
Technician	Human entity	Maintains the motors in the line	
Supervisor (production manager)	Human entity	Responsible for the production process of the line	Central production control tower
Motor	Physical entity	Monitored for performance and faults	
Sensor on motor	Sensor	Monitors the functions and values on the motor	
IoT gateway	IoT gateway	Collects motor sensor data and forwards it to cloud services and applications	Note transport protocol for internet connection (here MQTT for sending to cloud service)
Device registration	Database	Stores and enables registration of device identities in the IoT system	SQL database
Predictive maintenance and quality application	Software application (cloud application)	Software application that analyzes incoming sensor data, compares it with historical data, and triggers follow-up actions such as maintenance	
Central production control tower	User interface for end users	End-user application, which should be graphically appealing and help the supervisor to quickly identify any need for action on the production line	

heavy construction machinery. If you rent an excavator, then 8 h of machine running time per day is included. If the excavator is operated for more than 8 h/day, each additional hour costs extra. Imagine now charging by hours of operation or even by output rate. Let's take a sheet metal press as an example. There is a per-unit charge for each fender that the machine produces for the OEM in automotive production. This shifts the OEM's risk to the machine tool builder. When business is booming, more parts are produced, and machine costs go up. If production has to be scaled down, then machine costs drop as well.

Table 7.6 shows the technical components required for this according to ISO/IEC TR 22417:2017 (based on the IoT reference architecture).

Table 7.6 Technical components according to ISO/IEC TR 22417:2017 (based on the IoT reference architecture)

Entity	Type	Description	Technology
Temperature, vibration, motion sensors	Sensor	Captures data from machine components, for example, battery level and temperature	
GPS device	Sensor	Real-time position data of the machine for the service application	
Alarm controller	Sensor	For machine theft or malfunctions (reports an alarm or warning to the service platform)	
IoT gateway	Gateway	Connects sensor, alarm controller, and RFID readers, collects information, and manages the local network	
Internet connectivity	Network		
Resource access system	Cloud system	Connects to third-party systems to retrieve data (this includes the machine manufacturer's ERP, warehouse management, production planning, and MES systems)	
Information resource database	Database	Categorizes sensor and device data and stores them	
Machine monitoring and tracking system with user interface	Cloud system	Provides machine operating status data, data analyses, and visualizations and prepares them in user interfaces for end users, machine manufacturers, machine users, banks	
Maintenance system	Cloud system	Observes safe, stable operation, records operating and equipment conditions of all machines, and provides maintenance service	
User authorization management system	Cloud system	Provides users with access to information according to their permissions	

References

1. https://refa.de/berufe
2. IndetPro GmbH.
3. https://www.iao.fraunhofer.de/de/presse-und-medien/aktuelles/objekterkennung-fuer-innovative-logistiksysteme.html
4. https://www.fischertechnik.de/de-de/simulieren/industrie-40
5. Kent, J. (2020, August 20). Predictive analytics models detect Alzheimer's-protecting protein. Online article. https://healthitanalytics.com/news/predictive-analytics-models-detect-alzheimers-protecting-protein
6. Tackling climate change with machine learning. 5 Nov 2019. https://arxiv.org/pdf/1906.05433v2.pdf
7. German Energy Agency (dena): Artificial intelligence for the integrated energy transition. Classification of the technological status quo and structuring of fields of application in the energy

industry. Status: 09/2019. https://www.dena.de/newsroom/publikationsdetailansicht/pub/dena-analyse-kuenstliche-intelligenz-fuer-die-integrierte-energiewende

8. Karlsruhe Institute of Technology (KIT): Artificial intelligence improves power transmission. PrognoNetz: Self-learning sensor networks for forecasting the load capacity of overhead power lines—adapting operation to weather conditions makes optimal use of the grid. Press Release 055/2019. https://www.kit.edu/kit/pi_2019_055_kunstliche-intelligenz-verbessert-stromubertragung.php

From Project to IoT Strategy

In Chaps. 6 and 7, we saw what IoT applications can look like in practice and how to prepare for a use case with your own company. Most of you would probably agree with me when I say that IoT projects are not a flash in the pan. The first project—whether it was successful or not—is soon followed by another. You may now be thinking something like "Well, sure, I guess it's like that for you as an IoT consultant, but things are a little different for us." I'll say two things about that: in my day-to-day work as a consultant and advisor, it's important to me that projects I'm involved in are a success. I don't want you to think that I buzz from project to project like a wasp in a beer garden (I'm much more comfortable with ants. That's why my company is called digit-ANTS GmbH). From my perspective as a consultant and companion, however, I can of course keep a close eye on what is happening in the German economy with regard to IoT. Some have a lot of catching up to do; others are proactively leading the way. In any case, the companies are on the move. This brings me to the second part of my response: How will you get around integrating IoT-enabled devices and applications into your company and business model in the long term? There are people who have adopted a kind of defensiveness that reminds me a bit of old friends. Back in the day, they would say in a tone of conviction, "I don't need a cell phone. What would I do with it?" Now they all have one, and a smart one at that, and they themselves have to smile about their former attitude.

How I position myself as a company in the IoT sector certainly has a lot to do with the industry and the size of the company. But in my experience, it is also often a matter of psychological issues, the willingness to change, and the attitude toward innovation. We are already familiar with technological advances such as those we are currently experiencing, thanks to the development of computers and data storage media. However, the Internet age has another quality of its own in terms of density, speed, and global dimension. One can rightly feel overwhelmed by this. But my appeal would be: try to help shape the changes. For myself, I have experienced that willingness to change pays off. When I started my own business, the reaction was often: Why didn't you prefer to continue working as an employee? For some, this

A. Holtschulte, *Digital Supply Chain and Logistics with IoT*, Management for Professionals, https://doi.org/10.1007/978-3-030-89408-5_8

question also spoke of a certain fear of change. When I switched to a vegan diet in my private life, it was even more extreme. Some simply didn't believe me; others rightly reminded me that I myself used to rant about vegans. Well, you can manage to surprise yourself and others. If Bosch can connect a nineteenth-century lathe with modern sensors to contemporary IoT platforms, why shouldn't any other company be able to move with the times and bring its inventory into the world of tomorrow?

Broken down to a specific company, questions about IoT orientation can certainly be answered, even if they seem complicated at first. The Internet of Things can and should become part of the overall strategy, especially since companies in Germany are a structural driver of innovation anyway. You can read about this, among other things, in the study "Research and Development in Government and Industry, Germany, in International Comparison," which is part of the series "Studies on the German Innovation System" at the Center for Economic Policy Studies (CWS) of the Institute for Economic Policy at Leibniz University Hannover. It states:

> In Germany, two-thirds of the funding for research and development (R&D) comes from the domestic economy. It is thus far more dependent on the economy than in most other European countries. Only in Japan, Korea and China is this proportion even higher. R&D in universities and non-university institutions in Germany is financed to an above-average extent by business, which is evidence of relatively intensive R&D cooperation between business and government in Germany by international standards [1].

According to the authors, in figures it looked like this: In 2016, more than 90 billion euros were spent on research and development in Germany. More than two-thirds of R&D funds were spent on conducting R&D in business. Only in Japan, he said, was business R&D spending even more concentrated in large companies than in Germany. Small- and medium-sized companies, in turn, would determine the breadth with which R&D is anchored in the economy with their R&D activities. I would like to quote a passage from the study on the relationship between R&D departments in companies and innovation processes and on the distinction between the terms innovation and R&D:

> Entrepreneurial R&D depends very much on a high level of education of the workforce and the performance level of scientific research. Highly skilled workers are needed not only for business R&D activities, but also to absorb scientific findings. On the other hand, new technologies also need to diffuse, industrial research results need to be translated—into technological inventions, into product and process innovations and ultimately into sales, value creation and employment. This requires additional innovation activities and expenditures as well as investments in property, plant and equipment. In this respect, it is clear that R&D only represents one aspect of the innovation process, namely the "primary input". However, there are also many companies that develop and introduce new products or production processes without carrying out R&D. Therefore, R&D is not a synonym for innovation [2].

Even if the publication goes into further depth with regard to the distinction between R&D and innovation, for example, with the help of what's called the Frascati Guidelines, this should suffice for our purposes here. Returning to our topic of IoT, let's take another look at a somewhat more concrete trend study entitled "The Internet of Things in German SMEs: Significance, fields of application and status of implementation." As already mentioned in Chap. 3, 161 experts with "decision-making authority in IoT projects or other digitization initiatives" answered questions for this study in fall 2018, some of which touched on strategic aspects. Under the heading "Big goals, no rush," we find an interesting summary of the statements with which the companies surveyed assessed their own situation and the market and industry situation with regard to IoT.

> SMEs are pursuing big goals. For 36%, fully automated processes in operations and in transport and logistics are absolutely no longer a vision, but a realistic scenario that is being worked on. For another 36%, this statement still applies in part. This is a remarkable result that underlines the significance of IoT for SMEs: Without IoT, full automation in operations, production, logistics and transport would not be possible at all. However, it seems that there is not quite such a hurry to network vehicles, devices and products. 45% of respondents confirm that they are not working flat out to network their "things" within the next 12 months. Another 41% want to do so partially [3].

The way it looks in my personal conversations, the majority of SMEs have had IoT on their agenda for a while. But, of course, this varies from industry to industry and company to company. For the latecomers, it is important not to fall too far behind, not to wait too long with the first significant IoT project. For the trailblazers who have already implemented some IoT use cases, new services at Level 2 become a challenge, for example, apps and digital assistants or predictive maintenance and energy management based on IoT sensor data.

In this final chapter, I am concerned with strategic thinking and action in connection with the Internet of Things, because as I have already described, the decision for an IoT platform, for example, is often a strategic decision. In the following sections, we will look at some important levers for a holistic IoT strategy. In Sect. 6.2, I already introduced design thinking as an agile method for idea generation and project preparation. In Sect. 8.1, I deepen the view with a presentation of other agile methods. Scrum, Kanban, rapid prototyping, and the minimal viable product are useful tools for implementing IoT projects and developing market-ready prototypes, products, and services under today's conditions. In this chapter, I would also like to give you some ideas on how you can build a sustainable digital business model, form strategic partnerships for IoT services, and reconcile the necessary willingness to innovate with what you have built up and achieved so far.

8.1   Implement Agile Projects

Agile methods have been a topic for years, even if they have only found their way from the English-speaking business world to German SMEs with a certain delay. As a management consultant and project manager, I have experienced that many German companies have difficulty with flexibility, with changes, with the famous courage to take a step back. They have become accustomed to a different approach over decades—and change is an art in itself, for individuals as well as for a group of people, especially for people in organizations and institutions. After all, the clichés about German thoroughness, about our depth of planning and obsession with detail, all have a kernel of truth. After all, Germany is not only the land of poets and thinkers but also the land with the TÜV and the technical guidelines, the DIN standards and forms, the meticulous engineers, the insurance companies, and the lawyers. However, high-quality standards and the "Made in Germany" of the twentieth century are now no longer enough to remain competitive, because today's competitors can produce inexpensive copies at breakneck speed that are difficult to challenge on a global scale. What individual market players have developed over years of planning may be adapted, branded and successfully sold by others in much less time. Keyword: disruption. Agile action is therefore a fundamental building block for the management, logistics and production of the future.

Agile methods that help companies do this include Scrum, Kanban, minimal viable product (MVP), and rapid prototyping, which we will take a closer look at below. Usually, such agile methods are contrasted with what's called the waterfall method. The waterfall method means that projects are divided into several phases. These phases build on each other and are consistently worked through in the course of the project in a previously defined sequence. Once a phase is completed, the result is no longer questioned or even reversed. Typical phases in IT are conception, design, technical implementation, roll-out, and support. The name "waterfall method" has become established over the years. While the term may still evoke positive feelings in you, because you may think of beautiful nature or your last vacation when you hear this word, others speak of one-way planning to illustrate the rigid and inflexible nature of linear planning. Everything flows stubbornly in only one direction, with no alternative routes to take and no way to turn around and row back to the starting point. This involves risks: you can quickly become a slave to determined planning if preparation and implementation consist of inflexible stages and phases that strictly build on each other. It is better not to jump off moving trains. But do you really know where your company will be in 3 years? Why start a multi-year project now that consumes high costs for planning when everything is changing so quickly and you may not even be able to keep track of the project's timeframe for your company?

The waterfall method was and is used primarily in hierarchical structures. I would not say that it is completely outdated nowadays. The waterfall offers the possibility of planning extensive projects precisely and executing them reliably. The software group SAP has developed its own waterfall model with the proven Accelerated SAP (ASAP) method. SAP has not completely removed Accelerated SAP from the menu;

it continues to serve alongside agile alternatives and has also developed into a new method, SAP Activate, which was developed for the implementation of complex integrated SAP ERP systems. In 2019, I went to SAP to get certified as an SAP Activate Project Manager. I found it very interesting how an agile project method can help implement such a complex software product like SAP S/4HANA. You will realize by the end of this chapter that it is not so easy to take an agile approach to an integrated information system, an ERP system, because the modules for finance and materials management cannot be implemented in a completely detached and independent way. After all, we're talking about integrated software, and a movement in materials management always has an impact on value flows in the financial areas.

These agile methods have a few advantages over the more immobile waterfall-style planning and implementation method:

- User behavior can no longer be compared with that of 20 years ago. The speed at which customers and providers communicate has increased dramatically.
- Planning mania down to the last level of detail can lead to companies developing past the market and ultimately no longer being able to react quickly enough because they lack flexibility. Many industries and submarkets have become more complex, making it impossible to plan every single step with all its dependencies in detail and to define follow-up activities.
- In agile project management, the planning cycles are significantly smaller. The philosophy of "trial and error" becomes an integral part of development.
- Users are involved at an early stage, which has the advantage of being able to see directly whether products and services are accepted and to incorporate feedback into development very quickly. This saves a lot of money because development is done for the market and not without it.

"Operating agilely" also has something to do with modern corporate management, corporate culture, and management style. Those who embrace agile methods show their people that they are thinking about hierarchies and employee participation, about motivation and team spirit, about work climate and needs, instead of hiring employees according to a pattern in order to immediately put them in drawers for the next years or decades. After all, it's about changing routines, roles, and ways of working once in a while, adapting to new circumstances in order to achieve the best possible results as a company. This brings us to the topic of smart leadership, which I can unfortunately only touch on in this book.

Even if you cannot imagine your own company working consistently with agile methods for idea generation, product development, project management, or other processes, I advise you to familiarize yourself with design thinking and the other approaches presented in this chapter. Be (and remain) fundamentally open to agile methods. After all, you don't have to adapt everything immediately if it seems too daring. Just using a stopwatch, which is used for timeboxing in design thinking, can work wonders to give certain agenda items the timeframe they need. So perhaps cherry-pick for now. A little agile goes a long way, too. Especially when implementing complex enterprise software solutions, such as SAP S/4HANA or

SAP ERP ECC, an "agile waterfall" is a good idea, because here it is not always possible to reach the goal with a purely agile approach. Agile methods usually rely on small solutions that directly generate value for the company or users upon completion. But integrated enterprise software probably can't really be rolled out in increments. Imagine you start with inventory management, but you haven't yet implemented financial accounting: that doesn't work because every movement of goods always entails a flow of value, which is then mapped in the financial module and in real time. Software manufacturers have recognized this and now offer project methods that include as many agile aspects as possible, but also traditional project management methods.

Another argument for dealing with agile methods is your junior staff in the company. At universities of applied sciences and other universities, the cohorts that are interesting for training and entry-level jobs are more and more involved with agile methods. If you recruit your people internationally, this is even more true. International professionals are almost certainly familiar with one or the other method from their home working environment, and German startups certainly are too. So if your company is interested in project-based collaborations or strategic partnerships with founders and young companies, which we'll get to in a moment, it also pays to understand each other's company culture and way of working for a successful collaboration. In addition, the agile project method is also suitable for quickly evaluating whether a collaboration with another company makes sense at all, since you can implement a small, very delimited project scope together and quickly assess the success.

If you use agile methods—selectively or intensively—it makes sense to book external experts for the corresponding workshops and seminars. They have to pay less attention to sensitivities and proven processes. I myself once led a workshop in which my own manager participated—and it didn't go smoothly. In the meantime, I had to remind him in a (successful) one-on-one meeting that he himself had commissioned me with the moderation. If you have the feeling that you should avoid such situations in your company, this would be a good reason to call in external support. An external coach for Scrum or design thinking should usually also help you get there faster. If your company has been stewing in its own juices for a long time, this may also be due to ingrained routines, the understanding of roles, and the team and leadership culture in your company. A breath of fresh air from outside can act as a turbo boost once the brakes are off. When acting as a Scrum master or design thinking coach, I myself follow the credo of giving companies the first and essential impulses but then leaving the companies again promptly. I don't have to plant myself somewhere; after all, I see myself as an independent entrepreneur.

The sooner your workforce understands and can implement the corresponding agile method, the sooner they can do without the external coach or Scrum master. It is not always absolutely necessary but certainly an advantage if the external professionals are familiar with the industry. I myself am at home in logistics and IT due to my studies, my SAP career, software and logistics projects, my startups, as they say. It's good to be able to draw on a certain wealth of experience to give the group dynamics new momentum at crucial moments. If you know what makes a company's competitors and customers tick, you can simply provide more concrete impetus and better assess ideas. Another option is to build up expertise within your own ranks. There are now good courses for design thinking coaches, and it is just as feasible and not particularly expensive to become a Scrum master or a Kanban king.

8.1.1 Scrum

The implementation of the Scrum method is based on the assumption that companies do not have the time to develop products or services quietly over several years before presenting them to customers. Instead, developments should be offered promptly in good, if not optimal, quality. Speed is more important than perfection.

The Scrum method was developed as a form of agile project management in the 1990s by the Americans Jeff Sutherland and Ken Schwaber. The approach was designed for use in software development and first gained notoriety through a software modernization project at the FBI. The US law enforcement agency had made a mess of digitizing investigative processes and frittered away hundreds of millions of dollars. Sutherland and his Scrum method came into play as a fire department, but not everyone really believed that they could save much. The project managers in the American Senate were all the more surprised that the promised results were achieved 100%—and with a fraction of the budget. After only 2 years, the software was actually up and running. Even though these are the early days: you don't have to be a software developer to implement Scrum. You can also tackle process topics or optimization projects in logistics or production with Scrum. Founder Sutherland, for example, also built aircraft turbines and his own house with Scrum. In beverage logistics, if the idea is to transport empties using a truck as a shuttle device equipped with IoT devices, it would be the Scrum team's job to test this system over a defined period of time. So the team would have to figure out in advance how much effort it would take to establish such an empties shuttle system. What costs are unavoidable? Which processes make sense? Can sales or productivity be increased somewhere?

You can read about how this works in detail, for example, in the Scrum Guide. This guide, compiled by Sutherland and Schwaber and updated in the meantime, provides 19 pages of instructions for carrying out projects according to specific patterns, processes, and rituals. You can certainly find the latest version of the Scrum Guide online for free, but be a bit careful what kind of website you end up on (unfortunately, there are also dubious providers mixed in with the recommended ones).

Even if a project seems gigantic at first glance, with Scrum, the project team breaks it down neatly into small components that are implemented within a set time: the sprints. These sprints usually last 30 days, but this can be shortened or extended. According to the Scrum system, the essential requirements are first worked out: What should be implemented first or delivered first? These requirements are recorded in a list and prioritized. The item with the greatest benefit, which can be implemented/delivered within a month or within the defined sprint period, is implemented first by the development team.

Most likely, only the most important requirements will be implemented in this way for the time being. This may include only 20% of the overall planning, while the lion's share of 80% has to wait for fine-tuning. It is also possible that this lion's share will not be implemented at all, should it become apparent during the course of the project that effort and benefit are in a poor relationship to each other, which is also a priceless insight. Many German companies are (still) struggling with this flexibility and the courage to take a step back.

The Scrum method provides for a specific distribution of roles:

- The *product owner* formulates the requirements.
- All those who have the prerequisites and skills to put the product owner's wishes into practice are called the *developer team*.
- The *Scrum master*, perhaps comparable to a trainer or a master craftsman, is responsible for ensuring that everyone understands the Scrum method and is aware of their own roles. He has to make sure that predefined times are adhered to in meetings.

A short meeting is held every morning. Usually 15 min are scheduled for this as a stand-up meeting, phone call, or video conference. In this meeting, the team keeps up to date on the status quo, the goals for the day, and the potential hurdles they need to overcome. The morning updates create commitment, making nasty surprises less likely. Different departments within a company inform each other in this way and coordinate. One goal of the first Scrum deployments at your company should be that the cross-departmental updates become routine.

The project team does not have to be particularly large, with at least three members, but it should not exceed a certain size: a maximum of nine team members is recommended, otherwise things quickly become confusing. If the team is relatively small, everyone has the chance to understand what the others are working on. Interfaces can then be coordinated along the way.

Even though Scrum focuses on flexibility and dynamics, the work is not just done on demand and certainly not without a set of rules (see Fig. 8.1). First, the requirements are recorded in writing. Then they are implemented in a concentrated manner. For this purpose, the product owner creates a product backlog. Feel free to call it a "homework book" or a "big laundry list" if backlog sounds too much of a software to you. This document presents and describes all requirements: from the user stories, that is, the experiences a user will have in the future when using the offering, to identified errors and suggestions for improvement. While the product backlog is understood as a plan for the big picture, the sprint backlog is only an excerpt from this list. The tasks that are recorded in the sprint backlog form a concrete agenda that is to be implemented by the project group in the respective sprint. Before a sprint starts, the requirements and essential details are discussed in a planning meeting, which in the original terminology is called a sprint planning meeting.

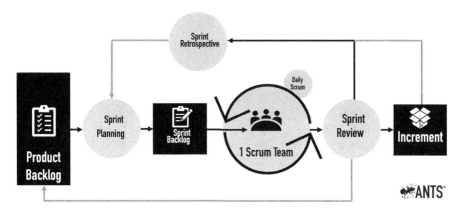

Fig. 8.1 Overview of the Scrum model (source: digit-ANTS GmbH according to Scrum guide)

If the Scrum method is also to be used in your company, those responsible should first bring all the departments involved into the team. In the area of beverage logistics, you would get the sales unit, logistics, production, and management excited about your project. Team members need to assess what they think is realistically achievable within a month/sprint. It's not a problem if the goal needs to be readjusted. It is always helpful to set a goal that is as clear as possible. With such goals, the bar can be set high so that the team feels challenged and can show its potential.

One more word on the question of whether it is better to buy in someone from outside as a Scrum master or to try to make someone fit within your own ranks: for marketing reasons, I should of course now motivate you to book people like me. But training a Scrum master in your own company is just as feasible and not particularly expensive. On scrum.org you can find various coaches who also train. You can simply write to them there. They are all pretty good about it and are happy to help. I did my certification as a Scrum master at scrum.org and would definitely recommend the certification, because you are dealing with the original there and this certification is also internationally recognized. It is best to start with the "Professional Scrum Master I." There are various in-depth options that you get to know when you start with the training.

8.1.2 Kanban

The Scrum approach has certain intersections with another agile method for software development and IT projects: We are talking about Kanban. Sometimes both methods are used in combination. The term Scrumban is even already in use. A major difference is that Scrum works with clear priorities and hard deadlines, while Kanban is focused on continuous, smooth processes. This makes this method interesting for companies that have to manage a lot of requests, jobs, and tasks that are not easy to prioritize.

Perhaps you are already familiar with the term Kanban from another area. Originally Kanban was developed as a method for production control. At that time, it was about optimal inventory management between idle and overproduction in production. With the help of signal cards—the Kanban boards, as they are called in Japanese—the team of the respective upstream production step was signaled that replenishment was needed for a product because a defined number had not been reached. This process has now been digitized. Of course, the method cannot be transferred 1:1 from manufacturing and the assembly line to the more creative software sector and comparable work contexts today with more fluctuating working time frequencies. But in an adapted form, it also works there. It can be used to avoid bottlenecks, waiting times, and overloads and to make processes smoother and more predictable. That's why the method from the Toyota factories is not only interesting for companies dealing with what are called C-parts or for developers working according to the "Software Kanban" or "IT Kanban." Basically, you can adapt the Kanban idea to all areas in which you want to use a well-visualized, limited pull system for cross-functional collaboration. I'll get to what that means exactly in a moment. You can also see from the success of business services for planning and task management such as Trello, which would not exist without Kanban, how much demand there is for such approaches.

I will not explain the basic idea of Kanban myself. Instead, I would rather let Kanban pioneer David J. Anderson have his say. The interview, from which the following excerpt is taken, is already 10 years old, but it is still worth reading and up-to-date.

> "**Question:** Can you try to explain Kanban in two sentences?
>
> **Answer: The** very simple idea behind Kanban is that you limit the amount of parallel work (work in progress), that you visualize this limited work by using, for example, a whiteboard with sticky notes on it, and that you only start new tasks when you have previously completed existing tasks. In addition, there is a signaling system that makes it clear when a new task may be pulled [4]."

Much of what has been seen, heard, or read about Kanban in Germany in recent years ultimately goes back to books and articles by Anderson. At the beginning of the 2000s, he had dealt with lean management and feature-driven development, simply put, with the question: What can we revolutionize in your company so that everything works better? Through various experiences over the years, he arrived at the Kanban approach, which he considers more "evolutionary" than Scrum and other agile methods. In his estimation, you don't run over the workforce as hard with Kanban because you give less direction and fewer rules. Arne Roock, who translated one of the standard works on Kanban into German a good 10 years ago and is one of

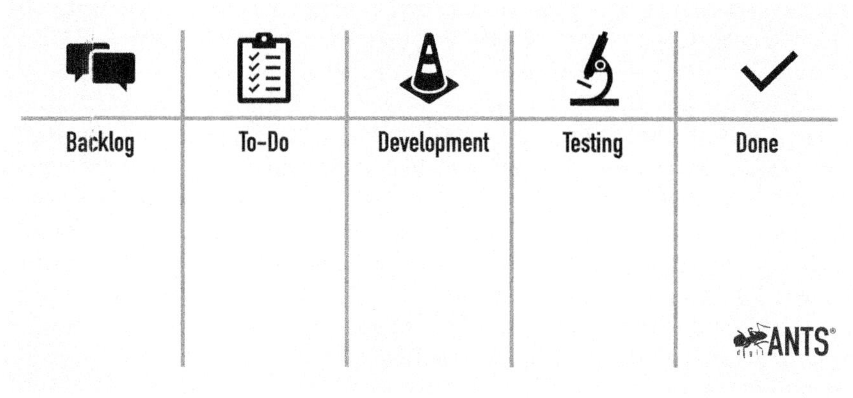

Backlog	To-Do	Development	Testing	Done
				ANTS

Fig. 8.2 Example of a Kanban table (source: digit-ANTS GmbH)

the Kanban experts in Germany, breaks down the Kanban philosophy into the following four instructions for action:

1. Visualize the actual state via Kanban board.
2. Limit the work to actual achievable capacities.
3. Introduce a pull system.
4. Think systemically: keep the customer in mind.

The visualization via Kanban board is shown as a model in Fig. 8.2. The board visualizes the status quo and the task distribution with sticky notes in the columns of a table: What is currently in development? What is in the test phase? What needs to be done? What is already running? What has been completed? Where are we stuck? The creation of such note tables on whiteboards or walls is typical of Kanban, but not a unique selling point, because you can also find it in a similar form in Scrum or design thinking. I would bet that you have already seen this or something similar in at least one German company. In any case, the purpose of Kanban boards is that they allow you to orient yourself quickly and they can be updated in real time at any time.

The example table shown in Fig. 8.2 starts with a column for the backlog and continues with columns for the statuses To-do, Development, and Testing up to Delivery (Done). Which column a topic/project (a backlog item) is currently sticking to reveals what status it is currently in. If the sticky notes are marked with the names of the responsible team colleagues, you can see at a glance which colleagues have idle time and which have too much to do. It also becomes clear which projects are stalled and where. Keeping things moving can be promoted by setting limits that you write on a board like that. For example, if a limit of five tasks has been defined for the development column, then no more than five notes should be stuck in this column.

The terms pull or push system, which appear in point 3 of the aforementioned action instructions of the Kanban philosophy, describe the way collaboration is organized. Pull system means that the team members give themselves independently new tasks, instead of getting them from above or from a preceding department on the table. For the Kanban board, this means in practice: you don't stick notes in the columns for which colleagues are responsible but only mark for the colleagues areas where they can take over something.

For Roock's fourth recommendation, systemic thinking, it is important to realize once again that Kanban fundamentally relies on self-organized teams that are sufficiently trusted by management. Nevertheless, a company wants and should keep the overall system in mind: The ideal state is not reached when everyone is working at full capacity. It is achieved when as many steps as possible that are relevant for the customer are completed in parallel with high quality and within a short time. This also reveals a risk of the Kanban method: sometimes parts of the workforce lack motivation if they are not guided by clear productivity goals and strict time targets.

8.1.3 Rapid Prototyping and Minimal Viable Products

The adjective "agile" contains meanings such as active, agile, flexible, and fast. Speed in particular is the focus of some approaches. While sprints are an important aspect in Scrum, but are also flanked by other elements, rapid prototyping and minimal viable product (MVP) or minimal viable service (MVS) methods are primarily concerned with speed. In times of dynamic markets and global real-time communication, one can perhaps summarize the basic assumption: it is desirable to approach projects in such a way that they produce results in the shortest possible time, are tested with the customers, and provide direct benefits. If, after a short period of time, it turns out that the project was a slow seller or a service that was probably not competitive after all, this chapter could be closed before much time and energy have been invested in the project.

Rapid prototyping serves as a collective term for different approaches that aim at a fast model which is uncomplicated in its creation. This is especially common for manufacturing technology, about which I have already written in Sect. 5.4 on 3D printing, and affects the aerospace industry relatively strongly, for example. In rapid prototyping, prototypes are produced by machines on an automated basis because the machines can easily take the dimensions and texture from the digital data world and reproduce them. For example, a rapid prototyping process could have the purpose of using 3D printing to create models of actual objects. This is a way to save time and produce visuals in a quick manner. Some use further differentiating related terms such as rapid tooling (for making tools) and rapid manufacturing (for making components and finished products). Occasionally, especially in software development, we also find the distinction between vertical and horizontal prototypes: vertical prototypes are samples for subsystems of an application. A certain functionality is worked out as completely as possible for test purposes, while the rest of the software is neglected very much. I borrowed the following example from computer scientist and nonfiction author Veikko Krypczyk:

A program for the administration of customer orders and bookings contains the administration of customer data as a subsystem. A vertical prototype is handed over to the customer for testing, which contains all aspects of administration, for example, entering, changing, canceling, deleting data. These functions are already fully implemented and can be extensively tested. The other functions of the software system are not yet present in this process [5].

Horizontal prototypes use only the top level of a software architecture. This includes app and website pre-stages to test the design and usability of software. Users can try out the interface as an overall design because the prototype already contains all or at least as many of the planned functions as possible. However, at this point, one does not yet go into depth or into the following levels.

The minimum viable product (MVP) approach is even more low threshold than the rapid prototyping method. The point of MVP and MVS is to offer products and services that contain only functions which are absolutely necessary. The product should be simple, but indispensable. On the other hand, it should not be cheap, but without customer value.

Think of a rudimentary online presence: before commissioning an extensive website or dealing with the conceptual superstructure for content and marketing, first create a landing page and get feedback on it, ideally directly from customers. Videos have also become a proven tool for MVP and MVS. There are companies that first generate test videos for promising ideas. In the age of YouTube, Facebook, Instagram, and TikTok, there is no shortage of channels to reach diverse target groups. Only in the event that such a video is well received does product development even begin. This form of development (and advertising) is something you first have to get involved with mentally. Who wants to be criticized for immature ideas or, even worse, appear to have no idea about the market and customer needs. But we can also turn the idea around, and then the advantages of the method shine through. Because which is actually worse: a total failure with MVP or a slow seller like the Ford Edsel, which bore the name of the only child of company founder Henry Ford, which was advertised with enormous effort and which in the end nevertheless became the flop of company history for the car company? We may assume that Ford learned from this story. Other companies that are now considered successful, such as Dropbox and Airbnb, have tested their business models at least in part using MVP methods.

For both approaches, MVP and rapid prototyping, it can make sense to look into the financing models of crowdsourcing and crowdinvesting. Crowdfunding allows developers and companies to address a broad mass of investors. The backers, in turn, can help a prototype reach series maturity or co-finance a product idea with small contributions. The spectrum of backers and supporters ranges from investors who have experience with advance investments to private consumers who simply like the idea. For example, Energieheld GmbH, founded in Hanover in 2012, successfully relied on the crowdfunding method when it needed money for a project related to energy-related home renovation. This project was financed in 2016 via the Companisto platform with over €220,000. According to the company, the website www.energieheld.de is now one of Germany's largest platforms in the field of energy-related renovation, with over 12 million visitors, 200,000 customers, and more than 1000 trade partners. The founders cited the relatively low support costs and the fact that crowdfunders do not legally become shareholders as advantages of such crowdfunding [6].

Of course, you can only use the agile methods presented here selectively and combine them with established approaches to create a kind of agile waterfall. In any case, I think it is important that you think about how the preparation and implementation of IoT projects are related to the business model, the company philosophy, and the innovation strategy at an early stage.

8.2   Building a Digital Business Model

Companies that have been on the market for 30 years or more have in particular learned to appreciate the traditional business model: services or products are offered, the bid price is calculated, and then the whole thing runs. In this way, construction companies build houses for their clients, engineering companies produce machines, and tour operators sell package tours. As a result, the companies listed as examples, like many other branches of industry, sometimes achieved high margins. Shortly after the business transaction, the respective sales could be booked. Business success is according to the following: Next customer please!

However, the rules of the game have changed as a result of the increasingly ubiquitous online supply and the ever more seamless networking. Markets and business models, production conditions, collaboration between companies, relationships between companies and customers, and the selling and billing of goods and services are subject to new influences and new opportunities are emerging. Instead of opening house and car doors ourselves, smartphone apps and the corresponding end devices can take over these tasks. Instead of whipping out a plastic card at the cash register, the modern phone transmits payment information. Many objects are literally disappearing into thin air: keys, means of payment, or remote controls. The entire production plants are now disappearing through the use of 3D printing.

Some of you may be familiar with the phrase: the customer doesn't want to buy a drill but asks for a hole in the wall. The new times make exactly that possible: borrowing from the concept of software as a service (SaaS) described earlier, innovative service providers offer—conveniently and quickly, as customers want—the end result. Seemingly irreversibly, technology companies are specializing in refraining from selling the tools and instead renting them out, thus placing increasing emphasis on customer benefits. Whether it's making a hole in the wall possible in the short term, rentable scooters, or a program like Photoshop that used to be sold differently, customers get on when they need a solution and off when the problem no longer exists. Streaming offers for movies and series are a good example of the dynamics that can be achieved when courting customers. On the other hand, the fact that tailored offers are catching on and that online ordering and shopping are so convenient means that customers naturally notice more when they are confronted with potentially superfluous processes on which they are wasting their precious time. The user experience (UX) can have to do with the usability and user-friendliness of programs, apps, and input screens. But it also describes the psychological aspect on a somewhat more general level. For example, many customers feel inconvenienced or not taken seriously if they don't receive exactly what they ordered, but something extra on top. Customer experience is not limited to the online world; it applies just as much to the physical world. In this physical world, it's no longer just people interacting with people but also all the things on the Internet of Things. As a consumer, I used to choose between Adidas or Puma, Rewe or Edeka, or Cinestar or Cinemaxx. Today, however, the decision as to where I watch TV online or order goods has more implications for us as customers. Among other things, we are literally connected to various devices, almost all of which produce data non-stop.

This data is the sine qua non for some new business models. Think of the success of Facebook and Google and the adjective "data-driven." But even pre-Internet business models are being impacted by connected devices and streaming data. In warehouse logistics, it is now possible for driverless forklifts located at sites on other continents to automatically report when there are technical defects. Depending on how the follow-up processes and network access are organized, the forklifts can also automatically call a service technician. The digital transformation is leading to far-reaching changes all over the world. They massively affect the question of which work can (and should) be done by humans and which by machines. Predictions concerning the behavior of this strange new generation of customers are also moving into the realm of the possible, because their behavior will in turn become more predictable as a result of the information and data generated by all these devices.

These changes in our digitized information society make it necessary to completely rethink and restructure some business models. For a machine maker, for example, this could mean that in the future he sells smart products and smart services in addition to his machines. The machine maker could charge for the use of his machines according to time or output. We can already find corresponding models in the catering industry, for example, in coffee machines or beer tapping systems. The major topic of the traffic revolution also has a lot to do with the changed production and sales conditions for cars, scooters, and bicycles and the triumph of mobile devices.

In the trend study "The Internet of Things in German SMEs. Significance, Fields of Application and Status of Implementation," the 161 companies surveyed were asked what their situation was with regard to implemented and planned services and business models based on IoT. If one equates the category "manufacturing" used here with industry and considers the study to be reasonably representative and still up to date, the results show that digitization projects in connection with IIoT often have strong startup difficulties. Most of the time, projects get stuck in the idea stage and don't make it beyond that.

This is very much in line with my personal experience. From the perspective of traditional providers, there are always understandable reservations about the changes described. After all, the cost and revenue structures are being turned completely upside down in some cases. Often, revenue can only be recognized much later today because upfront services play a significant role. In addition, the new business models and services demand a high degree of non-commitment, which clashes with entrepreneurial virtues such as reliability and commitment. However, there is a great willingness to innovate among many of the people I deal with, especially since German companies have already addressed digitization much earlier than many schools or government agencies, about which one had to shake one's head a bit during the COVID-19 pandemic. There is less a lack of courage in these companies than a lack of knowledge about the necessary steps.

Many companies that want to implement IoT projects also struggle with strategic aspects. The topics "benefit aspect and added value" and "transformation of the existing" were mentioned particularly frequently here. Two aspects that are important for strategically relevant added value and for building sustainable business models in the digitized world are the innovation strategy of the company itself and strategic collaboration with other companies and players. We deal with this in Sects. 8.3 and 8.4.

Since the industrial sector works somewhat differently in many areas than the business-to-customer (B2C) smart services and smart product business, there are a few points to keep in mind when building smart products and services in the industrial sector:

- In the B2C sector, it is usually easier to obtain information about what the end consumer benefits from and adds value to. Companies as customers, especially SMEs, are more cagey about their processes. So try to take a good look at the relevant value creation processes. After all, you want to generate actual benefits for your customer and partner in B2B through digital networking.
- If you want to start with new product and service offerings, it's best to do it in a small area. Test your offering early on using methods such as MVP to be able to test it extensively and gather feedback. When the change in the business model would be very large if successful and followed up, it is also better to have management backing already (change impact).
- Make sure that you involve all affected company units immediately at the start of the project. This will ensure that all colleagues are on board for necessary cross-departmental decisions in a later phase and that the implementation of the project is secured.

8.3   Strategic Partnerships for IoT

Almost all companies are in regular contact and exchange with suppliers and customers. Be aware, however, that such relationships do not yet constitute a strategic partnership or alliance. This is only true when larger goals are jointly pursued, agreed upon, and for which processes are then organized and the legal framework is defined. We have already looked at partnerships and external support when it came to preparing and implementing a single IoT project (see Chap. 6). In connection with the overall strategy of companies, partnerships can take on even more weight. They can take on strategic importance. Whether my partners are old companions or new contacts I make at trade shows, conferences, Future Talks, or on LinkedIn, they certainly won't approach and judge everything the same way I do. If two companies go part of the way together, conflicts can arise because completely different work cultures clash. How hierarchies and rules, traditions and innovations, and security and experimentation are handled can differ from one corporation to another or from one medium-sized company to another. If a startup and an established company join forces, real generational conflicts could break out. Okay, that's an exaggeration. But what is quite likely is that different experiences will clash on issues such as corporate culture, management style, or speed and that opinions will diverge accordingly.

To illustrate this, I have picked out two quotes for you that come from an exciting study on7 cooperation, which I will go into in more detail afterward. The first quote concerns the fundamental willingness to relinquish work and control:

> In the SME sector, there is a culture of wanting to do it yourself. You only work with consultants to a certain extent and in the end you prefer to hire the people and do it yourself. That takes longer, but it's rock solid. The question is whether the pattern of success in the past will continue.
> —Stephan Köhler (Brasseler Bros.)

The second quote is about money—which, as we all know, is where friendship ends. So where should a partnership begin and end?

> When I talk to corporates, they sometimes say they're investing ten million. It's different with SMEs. They say that there is no play money. Everything has to work best immediately. That's why they look more closely.
> —Mark Möbius (Berlin School of Digital Business).

You'd better not underestimate the possibility that partnerships can fail because of opposing corporate cultures. In the study [7] "Strategic alliances. Effective instrument or overrated hype? What medium-sized businesses say." from 2015, the team asked 500 decision-makers: What do you see as the hurdles in implementing strategic alliances? At the top of the list of answers were the contrasting corporate cultures. No wonder, I would say. I myself am always working with people who have different daily routines and different ideas about working hours and availability, although this is still not a major issue. By the way, this is not the study from which the quotes come. It's also well worth reading, but if you find personal assessments like the previous ones helpful in reflecting on your own viewpoint on collaborations and want to read more field reports, I'd like to recommend the aforementioned study "Collaborations between startups and SMEs. Learn. Match. Partner," from which the preceding quotes are taken. It was published in 2017 and is based on many conversations, interviews, and workshops with people from the startup scene and SMEs. The Alexander von Humboldt Institute for Internet and Society and Spielfeld Digital Hub GmbH are behind this study, which in turn is backed by the Visa credit card group and the management consultancy Roland Berger.

Before this comes across wrong, strategic partnerships with startups are not the only option, even if we are talking about the IoT market. For some, it seems to have become a kind of panacea. Those who need help with digital transformation look to startups. Those who want to modernize software turn to a startup. If you want to become more agile, you cooperate with a startup. There are certainly a few arguments for this: startups operate at the pulse of time. Their people think fast and work fast. They are more dynamic than Freddie Schulze's family business and more adaptable than large tankers from the public sector. Startups have already identified tomorrow's trends, and they are more likely to discover the trends of the day after tomorrow earlier than others. In the startup scene, they are better networked than any data collection operation. What's more, the employees seem to have boundless creativity and exuberant motivation, if you look at their photos and social media posts. As you can see, I'm intentionally exaggerating a bit. Of course, startups can bring in a breath of fresh air. Sometimes, initial collaborations also lead to long-term, strategic alliances. In some cases, startups are absorbed into companies, or at least a large proportion of the employees eventually find a safe haven with the larger partner. From the point of view of the young companies, this is just one of several advantages that such collaborations bring. Let's think first and foremost of the startup capital and market access. Of course, it helps a lot if a solvent company invests in my projects, backs me up financially, and provides me with security.

But we should not forget in all this that established technology providers also have good solutions for IoT, for software, and for hardware in their portfolio. It definitely doesn't hurt to do some research at Bosch, Siemens, ABB, or the sensor manufacturer SICK, for example, if you are looking for partners for prototypes or new projects. The old hands and big houses usually have reliable, scalable solutions up their sleeves. With a fledgling company, you may find that they factor in their investment and development pains when it comes to joint ventures and pricing of products and services. Customers, however, usually don't care about the back story behind the product range. Unless they've been involved in cleverly personalized crowdfunding campaigns to develop prototypes, they simply and unromantically want value at a reasonable price. And you, as a partner, also don't want to feed a money-grubber who may not have cared enough about financial self-sufficiency before their now nascent relationship. In any case, I myself always take a good look at where my potential partners are coming from. Sometimes I also conduct research for my clients to check what practical experience the founders in question have and what the references given on the phone actually have to say.

If two companies decide to collaborate in the long term, this can still look very different on paper and in practice: How long will the collaboration last? What is the goal? Which contracts will be concluded? Which areas remain autonomous, which parts are communitized? What happens to the employees? Do you have to deal with new colleagues, processes, and bosses? These are just a few questions that should be clarified.

The collaboration study from which the quotes are taken distinguishes seven collaboration models:

- Temporary activities
- Programs and assistance
- Shared infrastructure
- Incubators
- Internet innovations
- Partnerships
- Investments and acquisitions

The term "temporary activities" is intended for all measures that promote getting to know each other and help to acquire basic knowledge and skills in a rather casual setting. This includes workshops, conferences and meet-ups, startup safaris, hackathons, innovation camps, and similar formats that can perhaps be summed up with the formula "many things can, none must." Category or level 3 of collaboration would be shared infrastructure. This refers to physically shared spaces, for example, for co-working models or for creative centers and labs. Level 6 partnerships include joint ventures. At the bottom of the scale, the strongest, long-term form of collaboration in this 7-level model is long-term entrepreneurial funds, mergers, and acquisitions.

Unless the partnership is designed for a one-off collaboration or a short project, that is, if you want to work together in the long term and grow together strategically, it is of course the case that the companies involved—like people in a relationship—undergo some development. There are various models for such phases. They are often described with somewhat academic terms such as needs analysis and probing. More catchy is the five-phase model with the Ing-Ing-Ing rhyme, which you may have come across before. It talks about forming, storming, norming, high performing, and transforming. In this model, the beginning is the clarification of the roles of the two collaborating companies and at the end, if everything goes smoothly, a lasting transformation of both partners (for the better, of course). In between, there are conflicts about which lessons can be learned. Rules of the game are tested and established. The new partners become—like in a good marriage or relationship—a well-rehearsed team. If you want to simplify things a bit more, you can also use the three-phase model from the study mentioned above. In line with the subtitle, this is divided into learn, match, and partner phases. In the learn phase,

SMEs get to know as many startups as possible in a targeted manner. I already indicated how this can work in Chap. 6: in addition to startup fairs and scene events, you could also frequent the usual websites and online portals. The SMEs then enter into a more intensive relationship with the matches, that is, the favorites, and it becomes clear later with whom a truly lasting partnership can work.

Selection criteria in the (initial and in-depth) partner search could be, for example:

• Regional proximity
• Reputation and recommendations
• Experience with similar projects
• Safety concepts
• Scalability
• Prices

You should find out whether your potential partner meets the requirements for IT security, information security, data protection, and compliance if you rely on external help for software or hardware. For cloud solutions, there are certificates such as the STAR certificate. For software, automated updates and up-to-date authentication should be a matter of course. For hardware, there are security standards, such as Secure Boot for processors (for the requirements for the IoT reference architecture, see also Chap. 2). As far as scalability is concerned, realistic quantities and timescales would be important: if I need 200,000 sensors of a certain type within a few weeks of realizing the first prototype, my partner of choice should also be able to supply them without any problems. Does he have the production capacity and the necessary suppliers for this, or could that be tight? If I need new, IoT-capable devices, but I don't have an overview of the requirements for these devices for my entire international company network, it would be good to have an experienced partner who has the standards for IoT devices in different industries on their radar screen and knows delicate details such as the resistance of devices in the high-tech industry or the steel industry.

My final aspect in this digression on strategic partnerships is international collaboration. Depending on how big your company is and how many locations you have, you may want to serve markets and target groups on several continents. Cross-border alliances, in which two companies with headquarters inside and outside the EU join forces, will probably become even more important in the future. Although there is currently a tendency to replace US cloud and IT providers with European competitors in order to comply with all political requirements (GDPR, Privacy Shield, etc.), this will not be the end of transatlantic collaboration between Europe and the United States. There will probably be some changes in the framework conditions as well. Just think about the Brexit for a moment. In addition, the Internet of Things is, of course, a global thing per se: the data flows to all corners of the earth, the devices are available almost everywhere, and the 5G network continues to expand. You might find partners for robotics and automation in South Korea or Japan, or perhaps you'll be drawn to the Chinese market, which, as we all know, is going its own way with digitalization and setting quite a pace. In any case, my personal experience in my working life is that you can't and shouldn't do everything on your own. You can achieve more with the right partners.

8.4   Innovation and Transformation

Often, the disruptive can only be seen in retrospect. Some have compared the Internet to the introduction of electricity to illustrate the quality of change. In any case, I don't think anyone would deny that the world has changed a lot since the 1980s, when I was born. Do you remember when you started writing emails? How has your company's website changed in the past 3 years? Between my first personal computer, which I bought in the late 1990s, and my current notebook, I'm technically worlds apart. As a freelance editor at the Westdeutsche Allgemeine Zeitung in the Ruhr region, I still saw the inside of a darkroom to develop photos, and when I studied from 2004 to 2008, companies like Uber or Airbnb were still completely unknown in Germany. The education of tomorrow's professionals has to look different from the standard one or two generations before, no question about it. Even in everyday work and in the average company of 2021, we cannot avoid this change. The Internet of Things is here. COVID-19 aside, it will generate annual global revenues of around $500 billion by 2022 and save $400 billion in processes at the same time, at least that's how the auditing firm PricewaterhouseCoopers (PwC) calculates it.

If you consider Moore's Law, which says that processor performance and thus the complexity of integrated circuits double every one and a half years, it becomes foreseeable that there is still a lot to come in the future. How do you react to this? Again and again, I notice in projects that companies want to innovate by hook or by crook, but the whole thing seems somehow arbitrary. Sometimes it seems as if they just want to quickly check off an item on the checklist: AI? We have that now, too. Check! On my list of not-so-good answers to the why of innovation, two statements are at the top: "That's what the board of management said." "We saw something at a trade show with a market competitor. Now we want to apply it in our own company."

Innovations cannot be forced. You usually need suitable people in the company for this: specialized experts, technology-savvy employees, and co-thinkers. You also need good time management that allows you to act in a controlled manner instead of just reacting to customers, competitors, or industry developments. In addition, it's important to think outside the box by taking on additional perspectives, such as those of different customer groups. Moreover, innovations can also create new problems. Perhaps you cause stress in external relationships with customers, suppliers, and partners. They can also cause unrest within the company's own workforce, especially since the slogan "never change a winning team" also reflects the fact that well-functioning teams first have to find and develop each other. Finally, there is also a lot of fear involved in the digital transformation: the fear that technology will make people superfluous. The German Federal Ministry of Labor expects that around 1.6 million jobs could disappear by 2025 as a result of increasing automation and the greater use of technologies such as artificial intelligence. [8] In other market analyses, the forecasts are even more drastic. When you consider that repetitive tasks and workflows, routines, and rules characterize a great many professions and activities, the high number becomes more tangible. We don't just have this kind of thing with the simple work: lawyers, doctors, and scientific personnel are also familiar with it, if you honestly take stock.

Although innovations can cause and exacerbate problems, and although they create a lot of work, I still believe that innovations are indispensable. If a business model is so rigid that it doesn't allow for further development or any kind of reorientation, that business model pretty much has no future. Recognizing when to turn to new markets and understanding in which way to look left and right in order to notice relevant rearrangements in the industry environment as well as niche players that are preparing to do great things early enough is a challenge that has become even trickier in the IoT age. Another dilemma is that if you are always 100% customer-centric, you may overreact instead of being a pioneer yourself for once, which at the end of the day could bring in twice as many new customers. Henry Ford once said that if he had only listened to his customers, he might have had to develop faster and more resilient horses. The customers themselves didn't come up with ideas for how an automobile would satisfy their needs even better. A third challenge is how open you are about your own innovation plans. In this context, I would like to cite a passage from the aforementioned study "Cooperations between startups and SMEs. Learn. Match. Partner."

> In the past, it was customary to keep one's own innovations from the research and development department under wraps until the very end, if possible. However, this approach is hardly in keeping with the times today. [...] For very few companies, it still makes sense to rely on closed innovation approaches. Through isolation, there is a danger of missing out on exciting trends and ideas and being too slow, because new things are emerging everywhere and at all times. It is almost impossible in the current era to have all the necessary competencies on your own. The shorter innovation cycles are virtually forcing established companies to switch from closed to open innovation models. [9]

The authors distinguish between the inside-out and outside-in directions of open innovation models, referring to an established scientific model. The inside-out principle could also be called internal or in-house. Company-owned ideas are to be brought to the market. Here, for example, we are talking about intrapreneurship and business incubators. The outside-in principle describes attempts to integrate external knowledge into one's own innovation processes, for example, by looking for new technologies and innovations from others. Collaboration with startups would tend to fall under this heading.

It is certainly no easy task for a company to position itself sustainably while remaining permanently innovative and innovation-friendly. Innovations affect corporate management and the entire corporate culture. They are part of the company

DNA because they touch on the question: Where do we stand with our business model today, tomorrow, and the day after tomorrow? That's why they should not be thought of as isolated incidents in the sense of a new acquisition or a one-off repair. The innovation strategy is part of the corporate strategy. Its purpose is to align the development of innovations with future corporate goals. Innovation strategies specify which new products, services, and processes are to be developed within the next few years. With it, companies and organizations define the goals, the measures required to achieve them, and also the possible challenges: Will we need new products, new business areas, new processes, and new equipment in the future? What are the company's development goals? How quickly and with what steps can these goals be achieved?

Innovations don't happen automatically just because you press a start button. Innovation projects can come to nothing, either by switching to more promising irons in the fire or by discontinuing activities altogether. Future projects can fail because you miscalculate or are surprised by others. Is such a failure actually planned for in your company? Wouldn't it be conceivable as a worst-case scenario that you set up everything correctly from start to finish and the world still throws a spanner in the works? Strategic innovation considerations should take sufficient account of the fact that a company interacts with the world:

- Technology boosts open up new business models.
- Social trends shape customers and employees alike. This applies to matters of taste and fashions but also to more profound upheavals, such as our family and role models.
- Economic developments make it necessary to change course, for example, when important exchange rates vary significantly.
- Crises shake up the markets—be it a financial crisis, the COVID-19 pandemic, or climate change.
- New laws create new situations for companies—from lockdown to the GDPR.

As we have seen live during the COVID-19 pandemic, crises are both innovation drivers and innovation killers. You can, or you may even have to, freeze all future projects and innovation plans for the time being if you come under financial pressure because of work bans and lockdowns. On the other hand, companies were forced to change over and invest in online services and technical infrastructure so that they could still generate sufficient sales and continue to employ staff. While e-learning, videoconferencing, and other online applications have been added as innovations in many companies and jobs, the pandemic has also hit some founders and new openings badly, depending on their business model and coverage. Many economists and managers are watching with interest how the company Airbnb is coping with the COVID-19 period—a dynamic upstart with financial power, but one that can't change travel restrictions either. When hardly anyone wants to or is allowed to travel, a tourism company naturally loses revenue. The first thing the company did was to ensure that it remained liquid—with layoffs and by raising fresh capital. Of the innovation projects that are a permanent fixture at this still young company, it has completed some, but not quite all. Where the journey is headed is not yet clear. After the financial crisis of 2008, some markets and companies re-assorted themselves. Tool manufacturer Hilti, for example, was relatively successful in its transition from producer to service provider, while other business models (including some questionable ones) no longer worked. In the long term, we can observe time and again that healthy companies with flexible business models cannot be pushed away, while poorly managed competitors are forced into insolvency.

Innovation is often divided into two areas: exploit and explore. Exploit projects are designed to carry existing business models, products, and services into the future. The explore approach focuses on paradigm shifts and disruption. In critical times, the first thing executives have to do is make the core business leaner, better, and more efficient. Only in the second step would it be the explore part's turn. Which future projects should we maintain in order to continue to be able to act and compete on the market after the crisis has been overcome?

Personally, I am not any smarter than others about the future after COVID-19. I can only say this much: I have retained my optimism despite all the bad news. To conclude this book, I would like to join you in looking into the crystal ball with a smile. There is an interesting study [10] entitled "Work 2050: Three Scenarios." The authors have divided possible developments into three different paths, which can be seen in Figs. 8.3, 8.4, and 8.5. They are paths for the following questions: What will the economy and society look like in 2050? How will we work then? What technologies will we use for what? If you like, the variant "economic/political turbulence" (Fig. 8.4) is the pessimistic one, the path "it's complicated" describes the golden mean (Fig. 8.3), and the scenario "if people were free" (Fig. 8.5) is the optimistic vision.

I firmly believe in the potential of IoT. We can not only network devices; we can also bring people together through the Internet of Things and overcome various gaps. That's why we're leaving the pessimistic and the half-good scenario completely under the table with the necessary courage for the gap, especially since you are so sensitized to IT and IoT security, thanks to books like this one, that terrorist attacks via the Internet of Things could be ruled out anyway. No, let's look at the optimistic version instead: in it, the world of the future is full of possibilities, because the technology pushes and the reorganization of working life and political measures have cross-fertilized each other and led to more freedom for everyone.

"For the new generation of globals, the concept of unemployment no longer has any meaning. In 2050, there is finally a global economy that we consider sustainable, and which at the same time covers the basic needs of almost all people or provides an elevated standard of living for most. For some, New Technologies have been crucial to this success; others see the unfolding of human potential in the [. . .] economy as fundamental; still others see the respective political and economic strategies, including the various forms of Unconditional Basic Income. Important were all three of the mutually reinforcing areas and the synergies exploited accordingly" [10]. "In terms of work mentality, the new norm core in this future is personal responsibility and self-reliance, as well as a sense of responsibility, purpose and common good orientation. People have not approached the development of technologies with fear

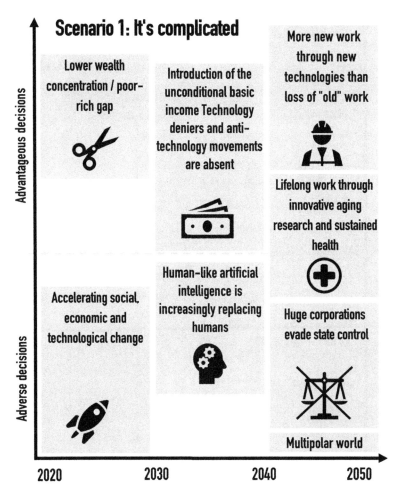

Fig. 8.3 Three possible developments until 2050: Scenario 1—It's complicated (source: Daheim, Cornelia/Wintermann, Ole: Work 2050: Three Scenarios. New results of an international Delphi study by the Millennium Project. 2019. published by Bertelsmann Stiftung, The Millennium Project and Future Impacts. S. 11)

and skepticism, but with openness and curiosity. Result: From the 2030s, moreover, synthetic biology and life-prolonging interventions were able to make people more 'robust' in advanced age and remove deposits from brain matter; seniors are now not so much 'financial burdens' as normal taxpayers. There is little difference between human consciousness and AI in all its manifestations. Humans are in such an intense and multi-layered exchange with AIs that it hardly matters which is which" [10]. "And more importantly for the more hands-on dreamers among you, In the last few decades, New Technologies have created more new kinds of work than they have destroyed old ones" [10]. This is not one hundred percent my dream vision, but it is an encouraging and refreshing variant. Whether or not I myself would be

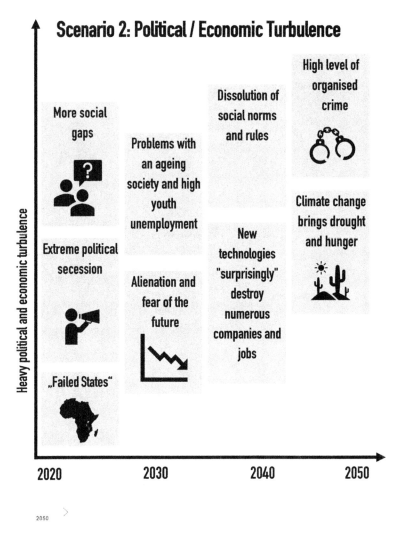

Fig. 8.4 Three possible developments until 2050: Scenario 2—Economic/political turbulence (Source: Daheim, Cornelia/Wintermann, Ole: Arbeit 2050: Drei Szenarien. New results of an international Delphi study by the Millennium Project. 2019. published by Bertelsmann Stiftung, The Millennium Project and Future Impacts. S. 11)

considered a senior citizen in this 2050 world with my then 65+ years doesn't really matter. Let's rather ask ourselves whether I could call an air cab in the Smart City of Ilvesheim with the blink of my bionic eye, which would then fly me to someone I could help with the digital transformation. I could certainly do that. But the cab AI would probably respond to me with something like, "Have you missed something, or what? This transformation is complete. Please enter a valid destination!"

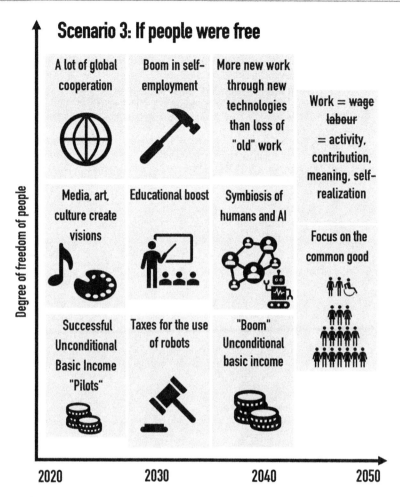

Fig. 8.5 Three possible developments until 2050: Scenario 3—If people were free (Source: Daheim, Cornelia/Wintermann, Ole: Arbeit 2050: Drei Szenarien. New results of an international Delphi study by the Millennium Project. 2019. published by Bertelsmann Stiftung, The Millennium Project and Future Impacts. S. 11)

References

1. Schasse, U., Gehrke, B., & Stenke, G. *Forschung und Entwicklung in Staat und Wirtschaft—Deutschland im internationalen Vergleich. Studies on the German Innovation System No. 2–2018* (p. S. 10). Center for Economic Policy Studies (CWS) of the Institute for Economic Policy, Leibniz Universität Hannover.
2. Schasse, U./Gehrke, B./Stenke, G. (2018). Forschung und Entwicklung in Staat und Wirtschaft—Deutschland im internationalen Vergleich. Studies on the German Innovation System No. 2 Chapter 1.1.2. Center for Economic Policy Studies (CWS) of the Institute for Economic Policy, Leibniz Universität Hannover.

3. Trend study *"The Internet of Things in German SMEs. Significance, fields of application and status of implementation"*. PAC Germany, April 2019. p. 7.
4. OBJECTSpektrum, Issue 02/10.
5. Krypczyk, V. *Rapid prototyping and low-code development.* https://www.dev-insider.de/rapid-prototyping-und-low-code-entwicklung-a-828294
6. https://www.crowdfunding.de/projekte/energieheld
7. https://www.ebnerstolz.de/de/forecast-studie-strategische-allianzen-88796.html
8. https://www.zeit.de/news/2019-09-23/digitalisierung-veraendert-nahezu-jeden-job
9. Wrobel, M./Schildhauer, T./Preiß, K. (2017). *Kooperationen zwischen Startups und Mittelstand. Learn. Match. Partner. A study by the Alexander von Humboldt Institute for Internet and Society.* p. 14 f. https://www.impactdistillery.com/graphite/hiig-sum
10. Daheim, C., & Wintermann, O. (2019). *Work 2050: Three scenarios. New results of an international Delphi study by the millennium project.* Bertelsmann Stiftung, The Millennium Project and Future Impacts.

Printed in Great Britain
by Amazon